AF739126

**Müşerref Yetim** is Clinical Assistant Professor, Program in International Relations at the Graduate School of Arts and Science, New York University. She was raised in Istanbul, and her research interests include natural resource conflict, international relations, international political economy, environmental conflict, and the political economies of the Middle East and Latin America.

'As the world population increases, access to dwindling natural resources will continue to be of utmost importance. Müşerref Yetim's *Negotiating International Water Rights* describes the complexity of international water resources and explains why countries succeed and fail at building institutions to govern these common pool resources. Using international relations theory as well as political economy arguments, Yetim has produced an enlightening account of international water rights that explores the international and domestic interests of watercourse states and their role in facilitating collective action and building international cooperation.

Based on her detailed knowledge of the Middle East, Yetim uses her theoretical framework to understand why Iraq, Syria and Turkey have failed to create institutions to govern the Euphrates and the Tigris. In a lesson that can be applied to other international watercourses in Asia or Latin America, Yetim argues that lack of trust and reciprocity in the region remain an obstacle to the creation of a community and the formation of institutions that govern these watercourses.

As natural resources are depleted and polluted at increasing rates, Yetim's excellent discussion and analysis of their governance comes at just the right time.'

*Alejandro Quiroz Flores, Department of Government, University of Essex*

# NEGOTIATING INTERNATIONAL WATER RIGHTS

## Resource Conflict in Turkey, Syria and Iraq

Müşerref Yetim

I.B. TAURIS
LONDON · NEW YORK

Published in 2016 by
I.B.Tauris & Co. Ltd
London • New York
www.ibtauris.com

Copyright © 2016 Müşerref Yetim

The right of Müşerref Yetim to be identified as the author of this work has been asserted by the author in accordance with the Copyright, Designs and Patents Act 1988.

All rights reserved. Except for brief quotations in a review, this book, or any part thereof, may not be reproduced, stored in or introduced into a retrieval system, or transmitted, in any form or by any means, electronic, mechanical, photocopying, recording or otherwise, without the prior written permission of the publisher.

References to websites were correct at the time of writing.

International Library of Human Geography 38

ISBN: 978 1 78453 552 0
eISBN: 978 0 85772 953 8
ePDF: 978 0 85772 750 3

A full CIP record for this book is available from the British Library
A full CIP record is available from the Library of Congress

Library of Congress Catalog Card Number: available

Typeset in Garamond Three by OKS Prepress Services, Chennai, India

*To my family*

# CONTENTS

# LIST OF TABLES AND FIGURES

**Tables**



**Figures**

# ACKNOWLEDGEMENTS

This book is the product of many years' work. As the adage goes, it takes a village to raise a child, and I could not have written this without the many people around me who have helped to raise this from a rough idea to the book in hand. I have incurred a substantial debt to a number of people in the process and I cannot think of a better place than this first book to thank my teachers, colleagues, friends, and family dispersed across two continents. Among them is Gun Kut, who first interested me in the topic. My dissertation co-chairs, Clement M. Henry and R. Harrison Wagner, and committee members, Brian E. Roberts, Gary P. Freeman, and Simon Hug, have my sincerest gratitude as the research for this project began as my PhD thesis.

I would like to express my deep appreciation for the support provided first by the Government Department at the University of Texas at Austin, and later at New York University, by the Department of Politics, the International Relations Program, the Hagop Kevorkian Center, and the Humanities Initiative. For their editorial guidance I thank my editors David Stonestreet and David Campbell at I.B.Tauris. I am also grateful to the anonymous readers for their comments. Rohan Boltan deserves thanks for preparing the index. I am grateful as well to Shinasi Rama and Michael J. Williams, the past and present directors of the International Relations Program, and our administrator Tina Lam for their support and good cheer over the years.

I am, however, most indebted to my parents who understood the value of education for attaining self-fulfillment and independence and who against many odds raised their three daughters to pursue higher education and their own professions. Fatma and Ahmet Yetim instilled in us the core values of diligence and what it means to be family. I am ever thankful for my sisters, Cigdem and Funda, for being my refuge and buttress, no matter the oceans between Istanbul and New York that too often separate us.

In America, I have been fortunate to find still more family. How to thank Peter van Alfen, my best friend, colleague and husband, I simply do not know: he read every word countless times and offered matchless commentary and moral support at critical junctures. While this book is dedicated to all my family in the New World and the Old for their unfailing love, support, and understanding, it is dedicated especially to Alara, who brought the greatest joy to my life four years ago today.

# INTRODUCTION

Over the last several decades, natural resource conflicts have increasingly become a focus of scholarly debate as the broadening concept of security now includes issues such as environmental change, natural resource abundance, scarcity, degradation, depletion, and their impact on international order and stability. In 1972, the Stockholm Declaration of the United Nations Conference on the Human Environment first laid out the groundwork for this new concept of security and for the principles of environmental sustainability. The challenges at the end of the Cold War presented an important impetus for expanding the classical concept of security to tackle these new challenges in the form of global collective action problems. Scholars and policy makers subsequently started to view security not so much as a zero sum game but as a positive sum game, making the transition to a more comprehensive view of security easier. The 1994 UNDP Human Development Report, for example, defined human security as 'freedom from such chronic threats as hunger, disease, and repression and protection from sudden and hurtful disruptions in the patterns of daily life'.[1]

This represents an important shift from *the security of the state* to *the security of individuals* and a new high for the development of a human rights agenda that now includes political and civil rights, social, economic, and cultural rights, solidarity and environmental sustainability. The broader definition of human security rests on the premise that international security problems following the end of the Cold War are best handled by insuring 'freedom from want' and 'freedom from fear' for all individuals. It also reflects the change in the sources of threat to humanity. Violent conflicts and even civil wars in Asia, Africa, Europe, and the Middle East has become commonplace, while threats from terrorism, organized crime, and weapons of mass destruction (WMDs) continue to grow. In the midst of these threats from both state and non-state actors, the rights of individuals, especially women, minorities, and refugees, have become our major concern. At the same time, global collective action problems relating to infectious diseases, environmental degradation, and climate change have started to dominate the international agenda. Global security now is contingent upon not only political and economic security, but also personal security, community security, food security, health security, and environmental security.

Indeed, at the turn of the century, UN Secretary General Kofi Annan highlighted the critical relationship between environmental problems and security: 'we can see real risks that resource depletion, especially freshwater scarcities, as well as severe forms of environmental degradation, may increase social and political tensions in unpredictable but potentially dangerous ways.'[2] Population growth and environmental problems in the meantime have also gained a place in the analyses of various US government circles. The Clinton administration's 1996 National Security Strategy report, for example, identified large-scale environmental degradation exacerbated by rapid population growth as a threat to political stability in many countries.[3] Even after the shift insecurity focus in the US to terrorism and WMDs, environmental factors continued to be on the US agenda. The 2006 US National Security Strategy report included environmental destruction 'whether caused by human behavior or cataclysmic mega-disasters such as floods, hurricanes, earthquakes, or tsunamis,' as one of its concerns as it could 'overwhelm the capacity of local authorities to respond, and may even overtax national militaries, requiring a larger international response.'[4] US Secretary of State Colin Powell also made clear connections between sustainable development and security in 2002: 'Poverty, environmental degradation and despair are destroyers – of people, of societies, of nations. This unholy trinity can destabilize countries, even entire regions.'[5] In more recent years, environmental security has been one of the critical missions of the US military in arid and semi-arid regions like Iraq and Afghanistan. In Iraq, for example, freshwater supply has increasingly become undrinkable and scarce due mostly to high levels of salinity, pollution, inefficient usage and management, and upstream water development projects.[6] As we look to a future in which our natural environment will continue to be ravaged and threatened by ourselves, in which air pollution and global warming increases while access to clean water decreases, we can presumably expect more crises and wars over dwindling resources. It is no wonder then that the loss of environmental sustainability, which is the loss of earth's capacity to carry us, has become a pressing concern among policy makers and their observers.

Underscored in the debates over environmental sustainability, especially those concerning fresh water supply, is the fact that international cooperation is hard to achieve in the face of seemingly quixotic efforts among states sharing common resources to overcome collective action problems on the rules, regulations, and institutions of effective and environmentally sound governance. Furthermore, the likelihood of a conflict over how to share and manage international water resources is exacerbated by the absence of previously agreed upon legal frameworks to determine the property rights of natural resources. Indeed, because of this it is often stated that water induced crises and conflicts are likely to dominate the international stage in the twenty-first century. Resource scarcity as a cause of war is not, of course, a new idea; the relationship between war and resources has long been a focus of war studies since many wars throughout history have been about territory and the resources they contain. Recent empirical studies on this issue have concluded that territorial disputes continue to be one of the most enduring features of international relations; over the last 300 years they have been the main cause of major power armed conflicts.[7] A similar trend is also seen in internal conflicts over territory.[8] Furthermore, the territories subject to dispute have gradually been expanded, as, for example, with the introduction of a 200 nautical mile exclusive economic zones on the continental shelves as part of the UN Convention on the Law of the Sea. Such exclusive economic zones effectively extend states' sovereign territories and add to their economic power as new natural resources, such as fisheries and oil, natural gas, and mineral resources developed through deep-sea drilling, are brought under their control. As history shows, strategic raw materials, sources of energy, shared water resources and even fisheries[9] have all traditionally been deemed worthy of fighting for by states. Even so, it is far from certain that water-related crises will in fact lead to an eruption of violent conflicts and even war in the coming years.

## The Central Problem

Recent studies on the state of the world's fresh water resources draw a dreadfully dim picture of the future by underlining the importance of growing water demand, the unequal distribution of water geographically, the degradation water quality, and salt-water intrusion from the sea.[10] The gravity of acute water scarcity has stimulated studies on managing and sharing water resources across the disciplines including political science, economics, environmental sciences, geography, hydrology, and international law. One constant theme in these studies is that as the world grows more populous and global warming looms, and so greater and more serious pressure is put on limited natural resources, the indeterminate status of water rights in many international watercourses presents a problem of growing importance, particularly since there have been many unsuccessful attempts to resolve water rights. In almost all water scare regions, international water resources are subject to intense unilateral exploitation in a highly competitive fashion.[11] If predictions of the twenty-first century being a stage for violent conflicts over limited natural resources are correct, then revealing where negotiations fail becomes imperative for facilitating the peaceful resolution of these conflicts before the outbreak of war.

This book sets out to explain failures in international water negotiations and challenges the conventional view that water scarcity inevitably leads to the outbreak of violent conflicts. My central question is this: how do states design property rights institutions to govern shared international water resources? My aim is to illustrate a path to the peaceful resolution of natural resource-based conflicts by attempting to clarify both the collective action dilemmas confronting Middle Eastern watercourse states, many of which are of vital security interest to the world at large, and also the bargaining bottlenecks where negotiations fail. Based on a political economy analysis of the Euphrates and Tigris water conflict, this book presents a novel framework that explains bargaining failures and proposes conditions for creating a new property rights regime among watercourse states to govern their shared water resources in politically, economically, and environmentally sound and effective ways.

The framework presented here consists of two general analytical steps. The first one focuses on the specification of state interests. The analysis of states' interests and how they are formed present clues to the varying incentives watercourse states have to settle water rights. It also underlines the importance of the character of governing institutions as societal interests are mediated through such institutions and inform state interests on international water rights. The second step is the specification of the strategic setting in which the bargaining takes places. The parameters of watercourse states' choices are crucial for understanding international water rights conflicts. Here the nature of the prevalent governing institutions plays an important role in facilitating the credibility of their commitments towards the solution of collective action problems. In addition, concerns about state capabilities and their resolve to finding a solution become an impediment to collective action in the face of the continuously shifting context in which states operate. Such volatility in the context of inter-state bargaining adversely affects the outcomes by increasing uncertainty, which in turn leads to conflicting expectations among watercourse states.

The framework offered in this study is based on the analysis of several factors. These include: the determinants of states' national interests on water rights; the political and economic incentive structure of the domestic and international context; the process through which property rights are instituted; and collective action problems that are both generic and specific to the type of the natural resource. This comprehensive approach allows a delineation of the causes of bargaining failures in designing property rights institutions in international watercourses. It also illuminates potential solutions to overcoming bargaining failures and institutional design problems, which include property rights regimes that are sensitive to the political, economic, and social realities of watercourse states. Such regimes constitute the most effective and efficient solutions to sharing scarce international water resources in arid and semi-arid regions. As noted earlier, the twenty-first century will likely be dominated by the challenges of building property regimes centered on shared, but increasingly scarce natural resources.

To expand upon the factors analyzed in constructing this new framework: first, the analysis of the preferences of each riparian state and of the bargaining determinants are necessary for understanding why particular property rights institutions, whether formal or informal, have emerged despite alternatives that would appear to be more cost effective and rational. Indeed, determining how economic and political incentives interact to create constraints and opportunities for rulers and stakeholders is critically important, particularly in addressing policy issues concerning water, something that affects daily lives in the most intimate way. Understanding this interaction is key to designing institutions, especially property rights for water resources, that are sensitive to political, economic, and social realities, and that also provide effective and efficient solutions to contemporary natural resource problems.

Secondly, any study of the process by which property rights are established in international water resources needs to take into account the full range of possible property-based solutions to the tragedy of unilateral exploitation of international watercourses, recognizing that, in this second-best world, no single regime is likely to be the first-best solution. The analysis here of property-based solutions to collective action problems in international watercourses underscores the choice between alternative institutional arrangements facing states sharing resources. The appropriate institutions for water rights are the ones that take into account the context-specific circumstances of the contested resource. This requires watercourse states to reach a voluntary contract that specify property rights institutions protecting their long-term benefits and ensuring the sustainability of common water resources. Any such endeavor always involves a costly and long bargaining process.

Thirdly, the analysis here of empirical evidence from international water rights conflicts delineates the causes and the processes of bargaining failures. The dynamic nature of the bargaining framework allows the analysis to move beyond a single, static dimension to mirror the continuum in which states adjust their goals and strategies to the shifting political environment of the domestic and international realms. Here bargaining is defined as a process through which states try to find each other's minimum terms of settlement; it consists not only of negotiations but also the use of force. There are significant advantages to this processual approach: it enables a non-static analysis of the problem; it allows the deliberation of the causes, processes, and consequences of emergence of water rights in international watercourses under one theoretically consistent process; and it seamlessly incorporates contextual variables into the analysis. Furthermore, it is better equipped to handle the intersection of water conflicts with other conflicts, such as ethnic or oil conflicts. In addition, this framework illuminates the intricacies surrounding states' policies. The emergence of water rights depends on the terms of settlement acceptable to all watercourse states. For this to happen, the expected utility of an agreement should be greater than the current status quo. Uncertainty surrounding a state's decision making environment generates conflicting expectations among states, not only on the terms of the settlement on water rights, but also about the consequences of a settlement on the domestic and international political realms. Water rights conflicts intermingle with the existing and the potential relative power capabilities of states, ongoing ethnic and religious problems within and among states, and the general nature of relationship among watercourse states. In light of the wealth-acquiring and generating capacity of natural resources, achieving a Pareto efficient allocation of water rights present a daunting task for watercourse states involved in protracted conflicts with each other.

Finally, the analysis of collective action problems highlights the problems of credibility and commitment, as well as the transaction costs of gathering information and of negotiating and executing the terms of agreement. Transactions costs are, of course, intensified by the uncertainty and the anarchic nature of the international system, but also by the institutional features of watercourse states. Informational asymmetries and incentives for states to misrepresent crucial information about their capabilities, goals, and means, as well as domestic and international political concerns, cause common interests to be superseded by conflicting interests.

## Competing Solutions

A review of the existing literature on international watercourse conflicts reveals that there is multidisciplinary scholarly interest on the issue, but interdisciplinary studies have yet to appear. A large part of the literature on international watercourse conflicts suffers from two general drawbacks that prevent the articulation of well-defined testable theories. One is the parochial focus on specific aspects of the conflict determined by a scholar's field, such as international strategy, economy, engineering or the environment. This often leads to narrow analyses of the problem that are oblivious to the importance of crucial variables. Economic approaches, for example, disregard the inherent political characteristics of the conflict, which in turn often pushes the economic efficiency concerns aside. Indeed in water scarce regions, international water resources generate interdependencies, vulnerabilities, and distributional tensions, and in the process also become a national security issue. Leaving aside the defining characteristics of watercourse conflicts depreciates the value of this scholarship and undermines its explanatory power as to why states are unable to locate agreements. The second category of drawbacks concerns the idealism found in some approaches, especially technocratic approaches, which leads them to dangerously unrealistic expectations and policy proposals.

In addition to the existing literature on international watercourse conflicts, international relations, as a field, provides extensive discussions of international cooperation and conflict as well as useful insights into how states reach an agreement on water rights in international watercourses. Based on the potentially dangerous combinations of limited water resources, population growth, and a subsequent food gap of Malthusian proportions, the realist explanations of international water rights conflicts predict an outbreak of wars over scarce water resources, if not a tragedy of commons, in which the rational pursuit of self-interest by individuals who share common resources leads to the overexploitation and destruction of the shared resources in many international watercourses.[12] Thus, a watercourse state's strategic concerns regarding domestic, regional, and international politics take precedence in determining states' choices on water rights issues. Liberal perspectives, on the other hand, based on a state's democratic processes and institutions, which are seen as less conducive to the (threat of) use of force predict a peaceful resolution of water rights conflicts among watercourse states. Indeed the possibility of a conflict over how to share and manage international water resources intensifies in the absence of a legal framework determining the property rights over water resources.

In international relations literature, the major challenges facing watercourse states vary. The realist approaches concentrates on the distributional problems of relative gains,[13] while the liberal approaches are concerned with the collective action problems of commitment and the enforcements of agreement.[14] Both the realist and liberal strands of international relations literature fall short of explaining how some states have managed to overcome these problems and have established cooperative arrangements while others have failed to do so. The collective action theories that are inspired by realist approaches explain international cooperation as depending upon the existence of a hegemonic state, while the ones inspired by liberal approaches present international institutions in lieu of the hegemonic state. Spelling out the conditions that favor cooperation is not always very helpful because of the fact that even in the existence of favorable conditions and gains, states can still fail to cooperate. The success or failure of hegemonic states and international institutions depends mostly on the context. Furthermore, the lack of consensus over the definition of the problem leads to different conceptualizations of the problem by these various approaches and thus again to unrealistic and implausible policy proposals leaving observers at best perplexed.

Another component of existing approaches derives from literature on the tragedy of the commons, which is normally thought of as a tragedy for all, whereas in a sequential use scenario, as with international rivers, there is a completely different relationship dictated by one's geographic position as an upper or lower watercourse state. An upper watercourse state's abuse of a river – e.g., through pollution, irrigation draw, etc. – does not have a symmetrical effect on the future use of that resource nor does it, from their perspective, deplete the resource. Therefore, powerful upper watercourse states may have little incentive to cooperate since any agreement will reduce their benefits and limit their future policy options in dealing with future water scarcities in their country. This focus on different aspects of the international water resources problem is crucial for understanding different conceptualizations of the problem, since these various approaches generate a variety of policy proposals, some of which are more than likely to fail *vis-à-vis* the resolution of international water conflicts.

Sharing and managing international waters creates some of the most intricate collective action problems of free riding, coordination, commitment, and compliance. Theories dealing with collective action problems provide invaluable insights for explaining the dominance of unilateralism in international watercourses. Similar forces that lead to the tragedy of commons, in which the rational pursuit of self-interest by individuals who share common resources leads to the overexploitation and destruction of these resources, also seem to be at work in international watercourses. In the chapters that follow, I discuss to what extent this reflects the reality of the situation concerning international watercourses.

## The Central Argument

How best to govern shared water resources requires an in-depth study of the strategic setting in which the structure or nature of the resource determines the available strategies available to the various users and the rules adopted by them to achieve an outcome that is efficient and ensures the long-term sustainability of the resource in question.[15] Resource depletion and capacity depletion (due mostly to pollution) will persist as the two primary problems in international watercourses until watercourse states agree on water rights specifying their rights and duties with respect to the common resources. Designing a new set of international institutions involves an often costly and long bargaining process. Economic, institutional, technological, social, and more importantly political factors determine the cost and duration of defining and imposing property rights regimes in international watercourses.

Reaching an agreement on the water rights of international watercourses and then implementing it relies heavily upon inter-state bargaining. Understanding the bargaining process among watercourse states is important for at least four reasons. First, the crucial yet often-overlooked fact in the literature dealing with natural resource conflicts, and more specifically international watercourse conflicts, is that states, before reaching any kind of agreement, have to agree on the terms of settlement. At a minimum, states should agree on the object of the conflict and the purpose of the negotiations. Second, states act in their dealings with each other under premises of strategic interaction.[16] The choice of one strategy over others in dealing with the depletion or degradation of water resources is influenced by the watercourse states' expectations about their adversaries' actions. Third, the outcome of most negotiations is puzzling in the sense that even in the existence of favorable conditions and gains, states may still fail to reach an agreement. Therefore, an understanding of the process through which states try to reconcile conflicting and common interests over the distribution of water rights can contribute to the peaceful resolution of water conflicts. This will not only help us to predict what type of agreement could come out of the bargaining between states but also to understand under what conditions failure in negotiations might lead to breakdown. Fourth, in the absence of a supra-national authority, the monitoring and enforcement of agreements often becomes a major problem and impedes cooperation among states.[17] The way and conditions through which states reach an agreement determines the credibility of states' commitments and the possibility of water rights agreement.

Drawing primarily upon evidence from the Euphrates/Tigris watercourse, I argue that the distribution of states' relative power capabilities and geographic position – upstream, midstream, and downstream – determine the nature and outcome of the bargaining process by creating asymmetric costs, benefits, and bargaining leverage for states. Exacerbated by uncertainty and the anarchic nature of the international system and institutional features of the watercourse states, high transaction costs lead to informational asymmetries about domestic and international political concerns, constraints, and the consequences of a water rights agreement. This strategic setting creates incentives for states to misrepresent crucial information about their capabilities, goals, and means. In addition, I argue that informational asymmetries, along with the continuously shifting context, contribute to watercourse states' conflicting expectations about the terms of settlement, and thus explain the common occurrence of bargaining failures in specifying international water rights in the region.

## The Case Study

Three major watercourse states have had legal claims to the waters of the Euphrates and Tigris basin since the formation modern nation states in the region in the early twentieth century. The main empirical conundrum of the Euphrates and Tigris is why Iraq, Syria, and Turkey have so far failed to locate an agreement, and what it will take for them to determine water rights in the watercourse. I focus specifically on the Euphrates and Tigris watercourse primarily because throughout its history this watercourse has suffered from the same pattern of conflict over the competitive exploitation of water resources among its inhabiting societies, and has suffered from the same pattern of environmental destruction, deriving from irrigation and the subsequent salinization of soil.[18] More importantly, the watercourse sits at the heart of the political fault lines of the Middle East, in territories of vital security interest to the world at large, not to mention the US specifically, which has spent an estimated US$ 2.2 trillion since 2003 – about US$ 70 billion annually – to secure the lower watercourse state, Iraq.[19]

In the years since the 2003 US invasion of Iraq, all three water course states, Turkey, Syria, and Iraq, have witnessed important, if not dramatically fundamental changes in their governance and societies that will seriously affect any watercourse negotiations. Of the three, the upper watercourse state, Turkey, has enjoyed the most stability, but has become increasingly contentious with both its neighbors and its allies, like the US, due mostly to shifts in the current strategic context. Meanwhile, the lower watercourse state, Iraq, which remains mired in sectarian conflict, continues to be plagued by instability and violence that has spread beyond its borders to Syria and neighboring countries. The billions of dollars spent on reconstruction have gone mostly to the security apparatus leaving the country's infrastructure, including roads, water systems, and heath care devastated. But it is the middle watercourse state, Syria, that presents the greatest problems. Since 2011, the Syrian civil war, for which currently (2016) there is no end in sight, has plunged the region into far worse chaos and conflict. Already long considered a rogue failed state, Syria's civil war has bred an entity still more rogue, un-state-like, and intractable: the Islamic State of Iraq and the Levant (ISIL), which now has captured large swaths of territory from Syria and Iraq with their unspeakable atrocities and violence. Since September 2014, the US-led coalition has launched almost daily airstrikes against ISIL and al-Nusra front, which has weakened ISIL's hold but not enough to deter it. The dramatic and sudden changes in the strategic context is such that while the US considered removing Syria's ruling Assad regime by force in 2013, with the rise of ISIL as a more dangerous threat, the Assad regime appears now to be an undesirable but necessary ally needed to contain ISIL. The same can also be said of Iran, a watercourse state on the Tigris, and also a state that has had few regional and international supporters, which is also now conducting airstrikes against ISIL. As a reflection of the common interest in defeating ISIL, there has been a shift in US attitudes not to the full extent that it considers Iran as an ally, but as a co-belligerent that could potentially help stabilize the region. Nevertheless, the history of the US' relationship with Iran and Syria caution us not to read too much into this convergence of interests on the ISIL issue. As we shall see in more detail in Chapter 5 both Syria and Iran had a hand in the current rise of ISIL and have either directly or indirectly fueled the sectarian divisions in the region.

ISIL, however, is not the only sub-state actor to emerge from the Syrian civil war and the failure of the peace talks in 2014. In addition to ISIL and the Kurdish autonomous regions, it is reported that over 1,000 additional groups and an estimated 100,000 fighters are participants in the civil war. While each of these groups has individually or in alliance carved out some territory for themselves, there are currently only four major players who have a shot at emerging successfully from the conflict: the Assad regime, the Kurds (YPG and its allies), ISIL, and the more nebulous 'Syrian rebels' who belong to various Islamic factions including Jabhat al-Nusra and more moderate ones like the Free Syrian Army, the Islamic Front, the Mujahedeen Army, and the Asala wa al-Tanmiya, together some of these formed on 26 December 2014 the Levant Front or al-jabha al-Shamiya in northern Syria. Of these, only the Kurds seem to have US coalition support, but the feasibility of a Syrian Kurdish state remains to be seen. There appears to be tacit cooperation between the Assad regime and the Kurds, perhaps because the YPG has been fighting other rebel groups over the control of various border towns and parts of Aleppo. But of all of these combatants, it is ISIL that currently (2016) controls the territory where the Euphrates flows on through to Iraq.

Regardless of what victors eventually emerge from the chaos in Syria, and which sect controls Iraq, the fundamental problems of negotiating water use among upper, middle, and lower watercourse states or state-like entities will remain. In order to provide for their populations, those in charge will need at some point to negotiate with their neighbors, or face the political, social, and economic consequences. Already the Euphrates/Tigris watercourse, famed for its abundant supply of water in a water-scarce region, has been central to many failed negotiations and disagreement outcomes among the watercourse states, Turkey, Syria and Iraq, whereas Israel and Jordan, on the other hand, have managed to find solutions for sharing the Jordan River despite seemingly more daunting problems. In the following pages, the focus will be on what determines the incentives for watercourse states to reach an agreement and the mechanisms that are available to the downstream states to compel a reluctant upper watercourse state, like Turkey, to cooperate. Turkey, it seems, has the least interest in watercourse-wide cooperation; its position as an upper watercourse state provides some advantages both geographically and hydro-strategically. The specific effect of a geographic position on watercourse states' strategic settings, preferences, choices, and actions is what makes the problem over the distribution of water rights a bargaining problem rather than a common pool resources problem.[20] Lower watercourse states often need to secure upper watercourse concessions and agreement on the nature of the problem, which is a common pool resource problem for all. Conversely, I argue that the nature of the problem in international watercourses is not a common pool resource problem for all watercourse states. Rather, it is a bargaining problem and a state's relative power capabilities and institutional features combined with strategically advantageous geographic position in the watercourse play a crucial role in determining the outcome.

The conceptualization of the conflict over the international water resources as a bargaining problem is one of the important contributions of this study. This study also serves as useful testing ground for several hypotheses that are drawn from the literature on water conflicts. All international watercourses states face similar challenges due to sequential use and the problems that go along with it, varying degrees of interests in reaching an agreement on water rights shaped by a state's geographic location and economic and political development levels. Accordingly, the study of the history of the dispute and the negotiation process of the Euphrates and Tigris watercourse conflict will contribute to our comprehension of international water conflicts, and should allow us to make generalizations about similar conflicts. The significance of this study lies in its attempt to clarify the generic dilemmas confronting watercourse states and to enhance our understanding of the nature of international watercourse conflicts, especially the Euphrates and Tigris conflict.

## The Structure of the Book

The book consists of two main parts. The first part presents the theoretical foundations of the bargaining framework for the emergence of water rights in international watercourses. To develop this framework I rely heavily on the literature of collective action problems, international conflict and cooperation, and bargaining.[21] I start with an analysis of the nature of collective action problems in international watercourses. This enables the isolation and articulation of the issues specific to sharing and governing international watercourses. Then I present the realist and liberal accounts of water rights conflicts. From the realist perspectives, I derive the importance of relative gains and from the liberal perspectives the importance of the information revealing capacities of a state's institutional structures and its participation in international institutions. In the final part, I develop the bargaining framework based on the conceptual and theoretical analyses presented in the previous chapters catering specifically to the nature of water rights conflicts in international watercourses. The second part of the book is the case study. The function of this part is to reveal the causal mechanisms through which key variables unfold and affect negotiations using an in-depth study of the Euphrates and Tigris conflict over the last half century as an example.

More specifically, Chapter 1 discusses the defining characteristics of international watercourse conflicts. It introduces the key terms, concepts, and issues underlying the impact of the collective action dilemmas, the tragedy of the commons, and transaction costs behind the conflict over water rights and defines the characteristics of the nature of the problem of international waters. The analysis of collective action problems highlights the problems of credibility and commitment, as well as the transaction costs of gathering information and of negotiating and executing the terms of agreement. Transactions costs are, of course, exacerbated by the uncertainty and the anarchic nature of the international system, but also by the institutional features of states, and play a crucial role in the emergence of a property rights regime.

Chapters 2 and 3 focus on the main theoretical arguments and the debate in international relations literature on conflict and cooperation and on their strengths and failures, drawing inferences for explaining the outcomes of international watercourse conflicts. Thematically, these chapters discuss the role of a state's relative power capabilities, geographic position as upstream, midstream, and downstream, relative gains concerns, democratic and authoritarian political institutions, international institutions, and the hegemonic state in overcoming collective action problems in the pursuit of achieving cooperation *vis-à-vis* the emergence of water rights. Chapter 2 presents the realist take on international water rights conflicts, which predicts violent conflicts, if not a tragedy of commons, over scarce water resources, while Chapter 3 explores the role of democratic institutions in the peaceful determination of international water rights.

Chapter 4 introduces the bargaining framework. It begins by introducing the main concepts, assumptions, and explanatory variables of the bargaining framework and then discusses the main complexities hampering successful collective action among watercourse states and the potential solutions leading to the emergence of water rights in international watercourses. Chapter 5 presents the modern history of the conflict over water rights in the Euphrates and Tigris through the lens of the bargaining framework. This historical overview provides greater depth to the context within which bargaining has occurred in the Euphrates and Tigris watercourse. Finally, the Conclusion discusses the theoretical and empirical findings of the book as a whole.

# PART I

# THEORETICAL FOUNDATIONS

# CHAPTER 1

# THE NATURE OF THE PROBLEM

> Two neighbours may agree to drain a meadow, which they possess in common; because it is easy for them to know each other's mind; and each must perceive, that the immediate consequence of his failing in his part, is, the abandoning the whole project. But it is very difficult, and indeed impossible, that a thousand persons should agree in any such action; it being difficult for them to concert so complicated a design, and still more difficult for them to execute it; while each seeks a pretext to free himself of the trouble and expense, and would lay the whole burden on others. Political society easily remedies both these inconveniences. Magistrates find an immediate interest in the interest of any considerable part of their subjects. They need consult nobody but themselves to form any scheme for the promoting of that interest. And as the failure of any one piece in the execution is connected, though not immediately, with the failure of the whole, they prevent that failure, because they find no interest in it, either immediate or remote. Thus bridges are built; harbours opened; ramparts raised; canals formed; fleets equipped; and armies disciplined everywhere, by the care of government, which, though composed of men subject to all human infirmities, becomes, by one of the finest and most subtle inventions imaginable, a composition, which is, in some measure, exempted from all these infirmities.
>
> David Hume, *A Treatise of Human Nature*,[1] Book 3 Part II.8

As it was in Hume's day, collective action continues to be one of the most bewildering challenges of the twenty-first century. Often at the eleventh hour states that are bargaining fail to reach a negotiated settlement despite the existence of very compelling conditions to do so, and so leave the international community perplexed. At other times the conundrum springs from the fact that despite the existence of all-encompassing political conflicts, a negotiated settlement nevertheless occurs. At its core, the empirical puzzle this book addresses is a generic collection action problem: How do international watercourse states that share water resources develop new sets of rules or institutions to govern their shared resources? In this respect, the Euphrates/Tigris watercourse is no different than any other international watercourse in water scarce regions. But unlike some others, it has yet to see voluntary cooperation forming among its affected states to govern the entire watercourse and to address the overarching concerns over sustainable development. Indeed, the Euphrates/Tigris watercourse states have yet to even agree on a definition of their shared resource. In this and in any other case, the sustainable and efficient use of international watercourses requires collective action among the watercourse states to achieve even a rudimentary level of integrated water resource management. But such collective action – or inaction – is not always in the best interests of all states involved. This ensures that socially optimal outcomes are something that cannot be achieved either automatically or spontaneously.

To begin to understand the nature of this problem, we must first define its characteristics. In this chapter, I begin first by seeking a definition for 'international watercourse', a term that is at times contentious, before moving on to discuss the key concept of collective action problems, as well as the concepts of the tragedy of the commons, transaction costs, and property rights, all of which are essential for understanding conflicts over water use. The chapter ends with a summarizing parable of water rights conflicts.

## What is an International Watercourse?

One of the most contentious issues in international watercourse conflicts is the definition of 'international watercourse.' The topic itself provokes intense debate among watercourse states, academics, bureaucrats, diplomats, and lawyers. This was especially the case during the codification process of the law on Non-navigational Uses of International Watercourses. On 8 December 1970, the United Nations General Assembly adopted a resolution assigning the International Law Commission the task of codifying the customary principles of international law and procedural requirements for notification and consultation among watercourse states. It subsequently took 17 arduous years for the International Law Commission to draft the convention on Non-Navigational Uses of International Watercourses. The difficulty in reconciling competing watercourse interests could not have been more apparent, and was further revealed when the convention failed to gather first a unanimous vote of the states, and second a sufficient number of ratifications required for it to enter into force. The General Assembly adopted the convention by a vote of 103 states in favor, three states against, and 27 states abstaining (on 21 May 1997).[2] All the member states of the United Nations (UN) were invited to ratify the convention by 20 May 2000. To date the convention has still not entered into force due to an insufficient number of ratifications.

The sessions of the International Law Commission provided a stage for watercourse states to play out their prickly politics. In those sessions, finding a definition of 'international watercourse' proved to be one of the most challenging tasks, with some states arguing that a distinction be made between an international river that forms a boundary between states and a trans-boundary river that crosses the border. Others opposed the usage of the term 'trans-boundary river' and suggested its removal from all the legal documents. Behind this conflict lay the competing interests of states determined, in part, by their geographic position in a watercourse. Each definition entails different rights and obligations for states. If, for example, it is defined as an 'international watercourse' *limited territorial sovereignty* claims finds support and puts upper watercourse states under the obligation to share the resource and not to cause significant harm to lower watercourse states. If, on the other hand, it is a 'trans-boundary river,' the absolute sovereignty of the watercourse state over the resource within its territories takes precedence limiting upper watercourse states obligations to the lower watercourse states.

Indeed, the definition of 'international watercourse' has been one of the prime sources of contention among the Euphrates/Tigris watercourse states. Turkey, as the upper watercourse state of the Euphrates/Tigris, makes a distinction between an international river that forms a border and a trans-boundary river that crosses the border and perceives the Euphrates and Tigris as forming a single trans-boundary water system. Therefore any water rights negotiations should include both the Euphrates and the Tigris. On the other hand, Iraq prior to the US invasion in 2003, was against the usage of the term 'trans-boundary river,' and in its commendation to the Draft Articles on Non-Navigational Uses of International Watercourses, stated that this term wherever it occurs should not be adopted. Syria's position on this issue has been equivocal, since it is a middle watercourse state of the Euphrates, the Tigris, and the Orontes watercourses. However, Syria has argued that while the Euphrates and the Tigris are international watercourses, the Orontes, which originates in Lebanon and crosses Syrian territory before reaching the Mediterranean Sea in

Turkey, is not an international watercourse. The distinction is an important one and determines the legitimacy of some water rights claims.

In light of the significant debate and compromises that have informed the definition, here I use the definition of the 1997 Law of Non-Navigational Uses of International Watercourses. The law defines international rivers, or 'international watercourses,' in article 2, as follows:

> An international watercourse is a watercourse parts of which is situated in different states, and 'watercourse' here means a system of surface waters and ground waters constituting by virtue of their physical relationship a unitary whole and normally flowing into a common terminus.[3]

This definition relies on a single criterion, that is, a watercourse is an international watercourse if it has parts in different states.[4] The inclusion of ground waters in the definition is also notable and raises important questions about the classification of these resources. I shall return to this problem in the discussion of the differences in ground and surface water resources below.

## The Nature of International Watercourses

Another central issue that needs to be tackled in defining an international watercourse is the clarification of what category of goods an international watercourse falls into; this is not easily done. The goods-categorization of international watercourses has important connotations and implications for the determination of the property rights of water and for the nature and resolution of international watercourse problems (Table 1.1).

Economists identify four main categories of goods, namely public, private, club goods, and common pool resources. Rivalry/non-rivalry in consumption and excludability/non-excludability of benefits from potential users are the determining criteria by which goods are classified under one of the above-mentioned types. Accordingly, private goods are subject to rivalry in consumption and the benefits are easily excludable; public goods, on the other hand, are not subject to a similar rivalry in consumption and the benefits are non-excludable. Club goods refer to goods that are not subject to rivalry in consumption, but the benefits are excludable. Lastly, common pool resources, or commons, refer to goods for which there is a rivalry in consumption and the benefits are not excludable. These are ideal types and most goods fall somewhere on the two dimensional continuum with varying degrees of

Table 1.1. Classification of Goods.

| Consumption / Benefits | Rivalry in consumption | Non-rivalry in consumption |
|---|---|---|
| Benefits are excludable | Private goods | Club goods |
| Benefits are non-excludable | Common pool resources | Public goods |

excludability and rivalry. Among the common pool resources that have received significant scholarly attention are fisheries, forests, wildlife, ground and surface water resources, irrigation systems, land tenure and use, and global commons including climate change, air pollution, and international watercourses.

The literature dealing with water scarcity and conflicts variously classifies international watercourses under the categories of private goods, public goods, and common pool resources. This has important implications for the suggested solutions to our main problem. As result, the oppositions between the different classifications of international watercourses, for example, public goods versus private goods versus common pool resources, comes to the fore as an issue of contestation in the literature, which will be dealt with in the coming sections. Table 1.1 shows that the main distinguishing characteristics of public goods are non-excludability and non-rivalry in consumption. Water as a commodity does not carry both of these characteristics. Yet, it has long been treated as a public good and a free commodity. For now, suffice it to say that the tradition of treating water as a public good by both states and the public presents challenges to states, since the uninterrupted provision of water is expected to be provided by a state. The idea of treating water as a private good is unacceptable to many societies. Indeed, water is often provided by the state free of charge or with a minimum charge to the public.[5]

Common pool resources or commons, on the other hand, require more scrutiny here because international watercourses carry some of the same characteristics and are subject to the same perils as are the common resources. Common pool resources are defined as 'natural or man-made resource systems that are large enough to make the exclusion of potential users from obtaining benefits from its use prohibitively costly, and the benefits obtained from its consumption by one individual user are sub-tractable from those available to other potential users.'[6] Since benefits are not excludable and someone's consumption is another's loss in common pool resources situations, the over-exploitation of resources to the extent of a resource's devastation becomes likely. International watercourses have some of these specific characteristics. For instance, it is difficult for a watercourse state to deny legitimately the benefits that are obtained from the development of water resources to other watercourse states, whether they have contributed or not to projects like dams, which regulate a river's flow and prevent flooding. This is a classical example of positive externalities or spillovers. Alternatively, pollution affects all watercourse states, but not equally. Indeed, lower watercourse states could bear the costs of pollution disproportionately. The nature of international watercourses is such that upper watercourse states could rationally choose actions with negative spillover effects imposing costs on other users while fully benefiting from the resource and vice versa. The cost–benefit analysis for an individual state though rational could be the wrong for the entire watercourse. Though it is virtually impossible to cut river flow running into lower watercourse states, upper watercourse states could significantly alter the nature of the resource. Moreover, the rivalry in consumption of international waters is nowhere more apparent than in the arid and semi-arid regions. Due to sequential access, appropriation and usage in international watercourses have close resemblance to private goods. International watercourses then are impure common pool resources with strong private good characteristics.

This situation with international watercourses fairly represents the underlying tension between collective and individual rationality, between the interests of the entire watercourse and its parts divided among different states. It is better for the users, be it individuals or states, of common pool resources to take particular actions, but these actions are not always in the best interests of some users. So how do users coordinate their actions and design institutions specifying their rights and duties with respect to their common resources? Here then coordination over common resources becomes a collective action problem.

## Collective Action Problems

Political philosophers have long recognized the problem of collective action within the context of the subversive incentive structure of common resources. One of the earliest accounts of this problem, in fact, dates to the fourth century BC. In *Politics*, Aristotle observed that what is common to the greatest number has the least care bestowed upon it.[7] Indeed, few are surprised when we read about current overfishing, overexploitation of groundwater aquifers, or air pollution, for example. Often, the incentives created by an open-access or non-property regime are to blame and the suggested solutions range from regulation by governments to privatization, and include voluntary self-government by the users. We can categorize such proposed solutions into three groups: hierarchical, market-based, and community based solutions. In hierarchical solutions a pre-existing structure, such as the state or a group leader, imposes order; in market solutions a price mechanism enables collective action by reducing cost and increasing benefits; in community-based solutions common values and knowledge play an important role. In what follows, I briefly trace and discuss the intellectual origins of each of these solutions in order to illustrate the diversity of collective action problems. For our purposes, this illustration underscores the need for a multipronged, rather than simply an either-or approach to locating a solution to the collective action problem of international watercourses.

There has long been tension between hierarchical, market-based, and community based solutions. Earlier literature was frequently marked by the presumption that collective action solutions must be provided by the state. The intellectual origins of this disposition go back to at least the seventeenth century. Writing during the English Civil War (1648–51), Thomas Hobbes argued that a Leviathan, a commonwealth or state with an authority to restrict individuals' unrestricted pursuit of self interest, was needed in order for there to be social order.[8] He famously described the causes of disorder and the dire results of an absence of central authority:

> [S]o that in the nature of man, we find three principal causes of quarrel. First, competition; secondly, diffidence; thirdly, glory [. . .] Hereby it is manifest that during the time men live without a common power to keep them all in awe, they are in that condition which is called war; and such a war as is of every man against every man [. . .] In such condition there is no place for industry, because the fruit thereof is uncertain; and consequently no culture of the earth; no navigation, nor use of the commodities that may be imported by sea; no commodious building; no instruments of moving and removing such things as require much force; no knowledge of the face of the earth; no account of time; no arts; no letters; no society; and which is worst of all, continual fear, and danger of violent death; and the life of man, solitary, poor, nasty, brutish, and short.
>
> Hobbes, *Leviathan*, Ch. XIII

Though Hobbes captured the primal need for central authority, it was Jean-Jacques Rousseau (1712–78) who gave a more accurate presentation of collective action problems in his story of a group of stag hunters. If the hunters coordinate their actions and cooperate they could catch a stag, which could feed all of them and more.[9] If one of the hunters defects and goes after a hare, he could only feed himself and the rest will go hungry. The defector will receive a higher payoff regardless of what the others do, but all the hunters will be better off if they cooperate. This gives the hunters strong incentive to cooperate, unless they believe one of the other players will defect. More recent commentators on this type of situation have named it an 'assurance game,' a type of collective action strategic situation that requires high-levels of trust among actors. In the classic prisoner's dilemma, another game of this type, there is only one dominant strategy,[10] for both players to defect, as shown by the Nash equilibrium, which reflects a situation in which no actor has an incentive to deviate, for this game. One of the most important insights of the prisoner's dilemma is that even though both actors prefer to cooperate, a cooperation outcome is not feasible, because neither can make a credible commitment. Each has a dominant strategy to maximize his payoff regardless of what other actors do.[11] Nobody, in other words, wants to be a sucker. The social dilemma we face in Rousseau's stag hunt is that the Nash equilibrium leads to a Pareto inferior outcome.[12] The stag hunt has, in fact, two Nash equilibria: cooperation (higher payoff) and defection (less risky). But only one of them, cooperation, is Pareto optimal, that is, it makes everybody better off without making anybody worse off. Defection, on the other hand, is less risky especially in a low-trust environment. The role the state plays here is not to impose order from above in a Hobbesian fashion, but to assist with coordination in order to achieve the better of two Nash equilibria: cooperation.

In *Treatise of Human Nature*, David Hume (1711–76) also ascribed a similar coordination role to the state (as political society or magistrates) for solving the collective action problems of large groups. While he saw no issue with two neighbors agreeing to drain a meadow and maintain an irrigation system, such an endeavor would impossible for a thousand to agree upon:

> [I]t being difficult for them to concert so complicated a design, and still more difficult for them to execute it; while each seeks a pretext to free himself of the trouble and expense, and would lay the whole burden on others.

For Hume, the function of government is to help citizens who have a propensity to think in the present to restructure their behavior to take into account long-term interests:

> [M]en, it is true, are always much inclined to prefer present interest to distant and remote; nor is it easy for them to resist the temptation of any advantage, that they may immediately enjoy, in apprehension of an evil that lies at a distance from them [. . .].

Furthermore, Hume presupposes that there are embedded moral values in society that emanate from moral sensibilities and our inclination to avoid pain while seeking pleasure and approval. In small communities, shame or trust might therefore be effective in managing the commons, as is likely the case in Hume's example of two neighbors. In such instances, strong moral values operating in the background prescribe and proscribe behaviors within society.

Hierarchical solutions to social dilemmas therefore require more than just the imposition and enforcement of a collective action solution from above whether by a Leviathan or a central authority. Indeed, the state's role can go well beyond the enforcement of social order to include coordination in order to achieve a Pareto optimal Nash equilibrium; it does so by supplying incentives to rectify individuals' lack of trust or shortsightedness. Such a range of hierarchical solutions parallels the range of strategic structures collective action problems can take.[13]

In direct opposition to hierarchical solutions to social dilemmas are market-based solutions, which originate in Adam Smith's (1723–90) explanation of social order. The actions of self-interested individuals motivated by private profit, Smith argued, can lead to socially optimal outcomes. Smith's logic of collective action driven by self-love/self interest finds its fullest statement here:

> [E]very individual necessarily labours to render the annual revenue of the society as great as he can. He generally, indeed, neither intends to promote the public interest, nor knows how much he is promoting it. By preferring the support of domestic to that of foreign industry, he intends only his own security; and by directing that industry in such a manner as its produce may be of the greatest value, he intends only his own gain, and he is in this, as in many other cases, led by an invisible hand to promote an end which was no part of his intention [. . .] By pursuing his own interest he frequently promotes that of the society more effectually than when he really intends to promote it. I have never known much good done by those who affected to trade for the public good.[14]

> [M]an has almost constant occasion for the help of his brethren, and it is in vain for him to expect it from their benevolence only. He will be more likely to prevail if he can interest their self-love in his favour, and show them that it is for their own advantage to do for him what he requires of them [. . .] It is not from the benevolence of the butcher, the brewer, or the baker that we expect our dinner, but from their regard to their own interest. We address ourselves, not to their humanity but to their self-love.

There is no need then for an external authority to impose and regulate order from above. The butcher, the brewer, or the baker motivated by self-interest will provide the goods and services needed by society. Furthermore, Smith opposed regulation, primarily because he was skeptical of a central authority's capacity to know or have all the information necessary to interfere in markets in such a way to produce positive outcomes:

> No regulation of commerce can increase the quantity of industry in any society beyond what its capital can maintain. It can only divert a part of it into a direction into which it might not otherwise have gone; and it is by no means certain that this artificial direction is likely to be more advantageous to the society than that into which it would have gone of its own accord.[15]
>
> [I]t is the highest impertinence and presumption, therefore, in kings and ministers to pretend to watch over the economy of private people, and to restrain their expense [. . .] They are themselves always, and without exception, the greatest spendthrifts in the society.

With his skepticism of the role of the state, and more generally of any top down approach, Smith's work provided the initial arguments for market-based solutions to collective action problems, arguments that, in the twentieth century, were continued by Friedrich Hayek, particularly in his critique of centrally planned economies, which is replete with hierarchical solutions.[16] The problem of resource allocation when knowledge is dispersed and tacit among individuals in society inspired Hayek to offer one of the best rebuttals yet to top down approaches.[17] Questioning 'the experts knows best approach' underlying hierarchical solutions, Hayek not only showed that scientific knowledge is not the sum of all knowledge, but also that social dilemmas do not always have purely technical solutions that can be conjured up by experts. As we all know well enough, in some cases, a (technical) solution may reside within the wider knowledge of a community, but we still have the problem nevertheless.[18] This is often due to a number of reasons: individuals do not have the necessary incentives or motivations to offer their specialized knowledge; the authorities do not have the incentives to acquire their knowledge; the authorities might have the right incentives, but the nature of the knowledge, tacit and unorganized, renders it unavailable. Hayek drew our attention to this type of knowledge laying latent within society: the knowledge of the particular circumstances of a time and place. In finding a solution to a particular problem facing a society, Hayek minimized the role of scientific knowledge, in which expert opinion may be heavily weighed, in favor of the tacit, hard-to-transmit, and unorganized knowledge, held by individuals in society. Solutions offered by imperfectly informed central planners, for example, could be far worse than the ones designed by voluntarily organized individuals who have the local knowledge and motivation to solve local problems. The key is to get access to and make the best use of this type of knowledge, as Hayek noted:

> It [n]ever exists in concentrated or integrated form but solely as the dispersed bits of incomplete and frequently contradictory knowledge which all the separate individuals possess [...] Every individual has some advantage over all others because he possesses unique information of which beneficial use might be made, but of which use can be made only if the decisions depending on it are left to him or are made with his active cooperation.[19]

Given that this type of private information exists in society, decentralizing and delegating decision making authority to those who knows best is preferable to centralized decision making, which must then deal with the problem of how to take into account the special circumstances of each case. This also relates to the problem of creating institutions with an incentive structure that motivates individuals to act in a manner that produces socially desirable outcomes without ordering them to do so from above. Indeed, Hayek saw this as one of the main problems of society:

> [T]he problem is precisely how to extend the span of our utilization of resources beyond the span of the control of any one mind; and, therefore, how to dispense with the need of conscious control and how to provide

> inducements which will make the individuals do the desirable things without anyone having to tell them what to do.[20]

In this respect, creating a water market, for example, removes the necessity of knowing the value of water and its alternative uses. The price mechanism acts to coordinate individual actions solving both the problem of knowledge and the problem of incentives. The outcome based on an aggregation of individuals' self-interested acts is therefore optimal. This notion of spontaneous order offers one of the most challenging critiques of hierarchical approaches.[21]

Predominantly advocated by liberal economists, market-based solutions gained widespread support starting in the 1980s. A spontaneous order arising from uncoordinated exchange relations among individuals in the market by means of the invisible hand (i.e., the price mechanism) appears to be more democratic and therefore desirable than imposed solutions. Market based approaches to environmental problems have gained significant traction since the 1990s particularly with the success of the cap and trade policy in the US, which was designed to control emissions by creating a market for them.[22] In fact, the cap and trade policy epitomizes the market-based solution to collective action problems by providing economic incentives to reduce carbon emissions. The government decides on a tolerable level of carbon emissions and the market decides on the price. The alternative, a carbon tax, is considered more problematic and rigid, since it requires the state to set the price, but ultimately with the market deciding how much to emit at the set price. If the tax is to low it may not reduce emissions and firms will simply pay the tax; if it is too high, it affects profitability, jobs, consumers, and society overall society as well as the resource.

The problem is not just getting the price right, but also obtaining the flexibility needed to adapt to local conditions and to promote innovation without distorting markets either through taxation or subsidies. While there can be little question that environmental disasters like the Aral Sea and air pollution in China, both of which have occurred under central planning regimes, seriously weakens the argument for hierarchical solutions, market based solutions also have their pitfalls. The greatest danger, in fact, may lie in less obvious market distortions that are common in democratically advanced countries. These include environmentally harmful subsidies in power, water, agriculture, and fishing industries to name just a few that keep prices well below their fair market value and so encourage overconsumption and overexploitation. Existing market and policy distortions produce perverse incentives by underpricing the use of natural resources and thus contribute to environmental degradation. To counter this trend, it may be advisable to include environmental degradation in the calculation of the cost of goods and services, thus moving us one step closer to achieving sustainable economies worldwide. In the meantime, the success in cutting sulfur dioxide emissions in the US with the amendment to the 1990 Clean Air Act allowing the emission-trading system has demonstrated the feasibility of such a schema. The *invisible green hand* seems to have achieved its policy objectives quickly and efficiently at a fraction of the estimated cost.[23]

Although there seems to be strong support for the liberal economic position that market-based solutions to the collective action problems are cheaper and generate more benefits, caution is in order here. First of all, we cannot always expect socially optimal outcomes to appear spontaneously since many benefit from it. Secondly, we cannot simply assume that one can easily and quickly create emission-trading markets or water trading markets[24] all over the world.[25] Such a belief could lead to environmental disasters similar to the economic disasters that followed the privatization of central-command economies in former the Soviet bloc countries. As was learned the hard way, markets do not exist in a vacuum and need political and social institutions, including the rule of law and property rights, to be effective. The introduction of markets without the supporting political institutions led not to the market allocation of scarce resources to the best use on the basis of prices, as was expected, but rather to the allocation of those resources to the politically connected on the basis of clientelism/patronage, thus creating oligarchs in the process. Russia's experience exemplifies how the unequal distribution of power naturally led to the very unequal distribution of valuable scarce resources.[26] State capacity is then a critical component of market based solutions; the context in which markets are embedded is of the utmost importance. Thus outlining the conditions under which market-based solutions will work in solving collective action problems must be done ahead of time.

One often understated aspect of Smith's (and also Hume's) work, which is essential for the invisible hand to function, is the existence of strong moral values to guide individual behavior, something that neither market-based nor state-based solutions fully incorporate. Collective action problems can be quite complex and diverse, evolving over time and varying based on the characteristics of the natural resource, its users, and its context. Solutions thus require us to take into account the context specific characteristics of collective action problems to achieve an efficient and effective management of common resources over long periods of time. Among smaller, rather than larger groups it is obviously easier to manage the problems, as the example of Hume's irrigating neighbors suggest, where the actors are operating in a small setting in which communication is easy, behavior is prescribed/proscribed by common norms and moral values, and relations are continuous and based on reciprocity. In many Turkish villages and rural areas even today, for example, collective goods are provided through *imece*, the voluntary cooperation of the villagers. The socialization process paves the way for *imece* to work and strengthens the social fabric of the society.[27]

Even in the best socialized situations, however, the pursuit of self-interest in collective action problems still sometimes fail to ensure that a socially optimal outcome prevails. How then do individuals who pursue their own interests simultaneously pursue common interest? In *The Logic of Collective Action* (1965), Mancur Olson, Jr, challenged head-on the view that the possibility of a benefit for a group would be sufficient to produce collective action, providing an alternative logic for this failure. In most every collection action situation, there is one (or more) who cannot be excluded from obtaining the benefits of the collective good, once it is produced, and who has little incentive to contribute to the provision of that good; this person is a free rider. Therefore, unless the number of individuals is quite small or there is coercion or a similar mechanism in place to make individuals pursue the common interests, rational and self-interested individuals will not act to achieve the common interests (Olson 1965, 1–2). The free-riding problem is one of the toughest dilemmas that users of the commons must solve, since it is a rational action for an individual, but the cumulative result of these rational individual actions is socially irrational. If everybody chooses to free ride, no collective goods can be produced.

In a subsequent seminal article, Garrett Hardin tied the incompatibility of individual and collective rationality to 'the tragedy of the commons' coining the term in the process and creating one of the most enduring metaphors of our time.[28] With a striking illustration of how rational pursuits of self-interests on the part of individuals sharing common resources can lead to the destruction of common pool resources, he named the root cause of the tragedy as the pursuit of self-interest. This was a rebuttal of Smith's invisible hand, which joined the individual pursuit of self-interest to socially optimal outcomes. Hardin is worth quoting at length on this account:

> Picture a pasture open to all. It is to be expected that each herdsman will try to keep as many cattle as possible on the commons. Such an arrangement may work reasonably satisfactorily for centuries because tribal wars, poaching, and disease keep the numbers of both man and beast well below the carrying capacity of the land. Finally, however, comes the day of reckoning, that is, the day when the long-desired goal of social stability becomes a reality. At this point, the inherent logic of the commons remorselessly generates tragedy.
>
> As a rational being, each herdsman seeks to maximize his gain. Explicitly or implicitly, more or less consciously, he asks, 'What is the utility to me of adding one more animal to my herd?' This utility has one negative and one positive component.
>
> 1. The positive component is a function of the increment of one animal. Since the herdsman receives all the proceeds from the sale of the additional animal, the positive utility is nearly +1.
> 2. The negative component is a function of the additional overgrazing created by one more animal. Since, however, the effects of overgrazing are shared by all the herdsmen, the negative utility for any particular decision making of herdsman is only a fraction of −1.
>
> Adding together the component partial utilities, the rational herdsman concludes that the only sensible course for him to pursue is to add another animal to his herd. And another [. . .]. But this is the conclusion reached by each and every rational herdsman sharing a commons. Therein is the tragedy. *Each man is locked into a system that compels him to increase his/her without limits in a world that is limited. Ruin is the destination toward which all men rush, each pursuing his own best interest* [. . .].[29]

Hardin describes a process of how decisions regarding open access resources reached individually are not always the best decisions for society at large. In his example of an open access pasture, individually rational strategies lead to collectively irrational outcomes as rational users of the commons make demands on the resource until the expected benefits of their actions are equal to the expected costs. Each user ignores the costs imposed on others and maximizes their own benefits; the aggregation of such individual decisions leads to the tragic overuse and potential destruction of open-access commons. The externalities or spillover effects of individual actions are not part of the individuals' decision making process. The 'tragedy' then refers to these types of situations in which all users suffer equally as the result of rationally pursuing their own self-interests. The prisoner's dilemma is often used to model these types of social situations in which two players seek to maximize individual gains, and yet the choices that they make lead to sub-optimal outcomes for both (Rapoport 1974, 22). This paradox between individual and collective rationality would seem to lend support for Hobbesian hierarchical solutions, challenging at the same time Smithian market-based solutions.

The problem is not just about the rationality of the users of common pool resources, but more about the underlying conflict between individuals' short-term and long-term interests. If individual users maximize their long-term interests, Smithian solutions might have a chance to work with no need for an external authority to design and impose rules from above. In both Olson and Hardin's accounts of collective action dilemmas, individuals maximize short-term material benefits, which inevitably leads to suboptimal outcomes. Indeed, when presented with a social dilemma, where free riding is the dominant strategy, no one would cooperate to gain collective benefits. The differences in individual preferences and necessities are the main reasons why some collective goods are produced even with the existence of free riders (Olson 1965). An individual or few individuals who might benefit more than the others, could provide the public good regardless of others' contributions. The logic here is not so different than that suggested by hegemonic stability theory. In an anarchic international system, the hegemonic state that benefits the most from the stability of the system will provide global public goods (Krasner 1975).[30] The usual framework of collective action analysis assumes an underlying game in the form of a prisoner's dilemma with non-cooperation as its Nash equilibrium and an external actor is needed to intervene to avoid resource degradation either by conferring control to the central government or by privatization. In the case of many open access resources, the theoretical expectations driven by the tragedy of the commons, the logic of collective action, and the Prisoners' Dilemma are confirmed in so far as individual users who are trapped in the structure of the tragedy of the commons have no choice but to play their doomed dominant strategy.

In the early 1990s, in a Nobel Prize winning study *Governing the Commons: The Evolutions of Institutions for Collective Action*, Elinor Ostrom confronted uniform solutions involving external actors and criticized the conceptual foundations of policy analyses related to natural resources, or, more precisely, to common-pool resources. Like Hume, Smith and Hayek, Ostrom was skeptical of the suitability of top down approaches and of the ability of bureaucrats or experts to know better than the individual users the particular circumstances of the resource.[31] Her work challenged scholars and government officials who based their policy recommendations and policies on models wherein individual participants were trapped in the prevailing structures of the tragedy of the commons. She argued that contrary to the predictions of these models, individuals jointly using common pool resources overcome the tragedy of commons by communicating with one another and establishing agreed-upon rules and strategies to improve their joint outcomes and to develop suitable institutional frameworks. Indeed, history is replete with institutional arrangements that have been created, modified, and monitored by the users of renewable common-pool resources in order to secure the long-term sustainability of common-pool resources, like communal forests, fisheries, pastures, ground water systems, irrigation systems, and so on. Furthermore, empirical observations also reveal that communities have designed institutions that lay outside the bounds of the state and the market to govern their common resources sustainably over long periods. In sum, Ostrom presented a strong case for the voluntary self-government of common pools resources by the users.

In these community-based solutions, the best way to deal with collective action problems is to let the users design, organize and govern common-pool resources by establishing cooperative institutions. Each common-pool resource requires careful analysis of a large set of variables influencing the suitability of potential solutions. Ostrom favored evolutionary processes that allow learning, adjustment, trial and error, and feed-back as opposed to the imposition of an inflexible plan from above. Shortsighted individuals who maximize short-term benefits are replaced by adapting and norm-adopting individuals. Furthermore, in small communities, the externalities or spillover effects of individual actions become part of the individuals' decision making process not only because of the strong desire to avoid social sanctions, but also because of the socialization process emphasizing collectivist values, such as cooperation, trust, and camaraderie.

The institutions that a community requires to achieve optimal and sustainable management of common resources are best build following a small set of design principles. Since there was no theory providing a coherent account of such principles, which include ways of making credible commitments, and the problem of mutual monitoring and enforcing, Ostrom outlined eight design principles that were common to all the successful cases of institution building she studied, such as the Swiss grazing meadows, Japanese forests, and Spanish irrigation systems. These principles are: (1) clearly defined boundaries; (2) a congruence between appropriation and provision rules and local conditions; (3) democratic decision making; (4) monitoring is done by the users or people who are accountable to the users; (5) graduated sanctions against violators; (6) access to low-cost local arenas to resolve conflicts; (7) the recognition by external government authorities of the rights of the users to organize; and (8) nested enterprises for common resources that are parts of larger systems (Ostrom 1990, 90).

Ostrom made a Hayekian case then for voluntary solutions to be devised and implemented by local people since these users of the common resource are better equipped to solve their problems than experts from afar. Without localized information or the trust of local people, compatibility between prevalent informal institutions and proposed formal institutions is hard to achieve leading to unintended consequences. Markets, for example, depend on the organic emergence of complex institutions and social norms which are often difficult to understand and sometimes difficult to change. Similarly, community-based voluntary solutions are more likely to emerge in communities with high levels of trust and reciprocity. Effective institutional design emerges organically taking into account local conditions and enables participants to act on the basis of long-term interests and with an eye towards long-term sustainability.

As we have seen with Hume's meadow, Rousseau's stag hunt, and Hardin's tragedy, contrary to the established assumptions of *laissez faire* economics and of the resourcefulness of a community of commons-users, rational actors' self-interested behaviors often do not generate the optimal allocation of resources and do not serve to maximize national wealth. Granted that markets have worked remarkably well for improving the living standards of millions of people, nevertheless in the realm of common resources, Adam Smith's invisible hand does not always lead individuals to pursue their own best interests, or to promote the interests of society, and thus to achieve an optimal societal resource allocation. Once rational individuals realize that pursuing their own interests eventually leads to over-exploitation and the inevitable destruction of common pool resources, they should, it would seem, be able to come together and coordinate their actions to limit the exploitation of the resources to a level of sustainability. But this rarely happens. The wreckage of their failure to do so is ubiquitous, as seen, for example, in the collapse of the herring fisheries in the 1990s in Prince William Sound, Alaska. The potential for similar tragedies looms over international watercourses everywhere.

Free-riding, as noted earlier, is one contributing factor to the problem, but so is sanctioning free-riders. Monitoring and enforcement costs run high and makes sustaining voluntary cooperation difficult. In common pool resources, securing users' compliance with the agreed upon rules cannot be based on the benefits that each user will accrue, since individual users will try to avoid the costs of collective action. Furthermore, they can often do so without being subject to punishment or sanctions. Consequently, as long as an individual user can benefit from collective action without incurring any cost, an individual will choose to not contribute, thus free-ride, as it is rational for each user to seek to maximize the benefits and minimize the costs or transfer of them to others. On the other hand, there is a negative externality or spillover problem: an individual's cost–benefit structure does not reflect the negative effects of their actions on others. In other words, this is a situation where the costs are socialized and benefits (profits) are private and this creates an incentive structure that is susceptible to producing perverse outcomes and moral hazard. This could constitute a heightened problem especially in international common pool resources where there is in fact rivalry among the users, especially if conflicting interests overwhelm common interest, such as with the long-term sustainability of shared common pool resources. Open-access and a lack of clearly defined property rights appear to be the root causes and aggravating factors of the tragedy of the commons.

As we have seen in the discussion of three generic solutions, namely hierarchical, market and community-based solutions, there are three generic governance structures, the state, the market, and the community. A solution to collective action could therefore be a formal or informal contract monitored and enforced by the state, the market, or the community. To some degree all these explanations are not complete, since they rest on a prior solution of social dilemmas. In many cases, open access in common pool resources is often the result of high transaction and monitoring costs even in communities with high levels of trust, since even voluntary compliance requires monitoring and the imposition of sanctions in the event of a non-compliance. In successful cases, incentives are structured such that some collective goods are produced and individuals manage to overcome free riding problems. Neither the differences in individual preferences and necessities as suggested by Olson, nor the interventions by an external authority can fully account for this. There are ample examples of both flourishing and ruined common pool resources indicating that in some cases users have managed to overcome free riding problems and have determined property rights to avert the tragedy of the commons. One possible explanation for these contradicting phenomena could lie in transaction costs. Transaction costs have a profound effect on the determination of property rights in scarce resources, as we now shall see.

## Transaction Costs

There are numerous definitions of transactions costs. Mathews, for example, defines them as the 'costs consist[ing] of the cost of arranging a contact ex ante and monitoring an enforcing it ex post.'[32] Arrow defines them as 'the cost of running the economic system,' including both information and enforcement costs.[33] Williamson, who is a key figure in the development of transaction cost analysis, perceives them as 'the economic equivalent of friction in physical systems.'[34] Barzel sees transaction costs as 'the costs associated with the transfer, capture, and protection of rights.'[35] Challen, on the other hand, broadens the definition to include the costs of discovering who is interested in the decision and who should be included in the decision making process, the costs of exchanging information between parties to a decision, the cost of negotiations leading to a decision, and the costs of uncertainty with respect to the outcome of the decision.[36] For Furubotn and Richter, transaction costs include:

> The costs of resources utilized for the creation, maintenance, use, change, and so on of institutions and organizations [...]. When considered in relation to existing property and contract rights, transaction costs consist of the costs of defining and measuring resources or claims, plus the costs of utilizing and enforcing the rights specified. Applied to the transfer of existing property rights and the establishment or transfer of contract rights between individuals (or legal entities), transaction costs include the costs of information, negotiation, and enforcement.[37]

As Eggertsson suggests, 'a clear-cut definition of transaction costs does not exist, but neither are the costs of production in the neoclassical model well defined.'[38] Eggertsson himself defines transaction costs as the costs that arise when individuals exchange ownership rights to economic assets and enforce their exclusive rights, and when information is costly, includes various activities related to the exchange of property rights between individuals as giving rise to transaction costs. He outlines these activities as follows: (1) The search for information about the distribution of price and quality of commodities and labor inputs, and the search for potential buyers and sellers and for relevant information about their behavior and circumstances; (2) the bargaining that is needed to find the true position of buyers and sellers when prices are endogenous; (3) the making of contracts; (4) the monitoring of contractual partners to see whether they abide by the forms of contract; (5) the enforcement of a contract and the collection of damages when partners fail to observe their contractual obligations; and (6) the protection of property rights against third-party encroachment; for example, protection against pirates or even against the government in the case of illegitimate trade.

The emergence of the study of transaction costs dates to Coase's two seminal articles, namely, 'The Nature of the Firm' and 'The Problem of Social Cost.'[39] In the first article, Coase tied the origins of the firm to the need to solve contractual problems in the market through vertical integration, or to put it differently, to lower transaction costs here defined as costs that are incurred in preparing, negotiating, and concluding agreements:

> [T]he main reason why it is profitable to establish a firm would seem to be that there is a cost of using the price mechanism. The most obvious cost of 'organizing' production through the price mechanism is that of discovering what the relevant prices are [. . .]. The cost of negotiating and concluding a separate contract for each exchange transaction which takes place on a market must also be taken into account.[40]

Market institutions, like firms, help reduce transaction costs by providing information, reducing uncertainty and allowing long-term commitments. The same logic is transferable to the emergence of non-market institutions, like legislative institutions (committees),[41] political parties, and also international institutions. The high transaction costs, such as costs of bargaining, monitoring, and enforcement, can prevent states from overcoming their collective action problem leaving all states worse off. International institutions can perform information-provisioning functions that allow states to overcome such collective-action problems even if they are considered to be weak in terms of their enforcement and regulatory powers.[42] In his second major article, Coase dealt with the problem of negative externalities, and since the publication of 'The Problem of Social Cost,' the absence of property rights, especially in common pool resources, has been attributed to the high costs of defining such rights.

Williamson further refined the concept of transaction costs[43] by introducing two important assumptions. First, people have bounded rationality, that is, they are limited in their ability to formulate or solve complex problems and to process information. Second, people are opportunistic, that is, they occasionally engage in behaviors such as lying, stealing, and cheating which also includes calculated efforts to mislead, distort and disguise. Behavioral attributes of bounded rationality and opportunism along with the environmental factors of uncertainty, and the number of bargainers, increase the transactions costs, which now include not only the usual information costs, but also bargaining costs, contract costs, bounded rationality and the costs of opportunism.[44] Williamson's study also underlined the similarity of logic behind market (economic) and other non-market forms of organization, clarifying the problem of credible commitments, especially in weakly institutionalized international setting[45] in which states have private information and strong incentives to act opportunistically:

> [T]ransactions that are subject to ex post opportunism will benefit if appropriate safeguards can be devised ex ante. Rather than reply to opportunism in kind, therefore, the wise is one who seeks both to give and receive credible commitments. Incentives may be realigned, and/or superior governance structures within which to organize transactions may be devised.[46]

Drawing an analogy to problems of market failure arising from, for example, time-inconsistent preferences, information asymmetries, externalities, principle–agent problems, Keohane argued that high transaction costs and asymmetrical uncertainty could lead, under conditions such as those modeled by Prisoners' Dilemma games, to suboptimal outcomes. By designing appropriate institutions, states could achieve Pareto optimal outcomes. Indeed, international institutions can structure the bargaining among states and states' strategies by changing the cost of alternatives and thus affect the outcomes. As Axelrod further demonstrated in his solution to Prisoners' Dilemma games, there is a possibility of changing the payoff matrix if games are iterated in so far as the costs of monitoring others' behavior, the cost of retaliating and the discount rate of the future were sufficiently low. Institutions also make this possible through their influence over possible bargains, monitoring, durability and enforcement of agreements.[47] An important caveat is in order here, however, especially with international collective action problems, such as those concerning international watercourses. As Krasner noted, distributional conflicts rather than market failures or concerns about relative gains could be the central concern for the states. This makes the location of the equilibrium generating bargain a main concern that is determined by bargaining among states. So far the concern has been achieving Pareto optimal resource allocation.

Here, in order to be as comprehensive as possible, I adopt a broad definition of 'transaction costs' as the costs of defining and measuring resources and claims, and also the costs of utilizing and enforcing specified rights. Transaction costs therefore refer to the costs of preparing (information), negotiating (bargaining), concluding (contracting), and enforcing agreements (monitoring and enforcement) in international watercourses. Listed below are the possible transactions costs that then arise from negotiating, assigning, monitoring and enforcing water rights in international watercourses:

1. The bargaining that is needed to find the true negotiating position of watercourse states.
2. The making of contracts or treaties.
3. The monitoring of the agreements to see whether other watercourse states abide by the contract or treaty.
4. The enforcement of a contract and the protection of the watercourse rights.

At the international level, transaction costs, broken down as bargaining, monitoring, and enforcing contracts, are higher and impede states from reaching an agreement on water rights. In general, the large number of states, private information, communication problems, bounded rationality, opportunistic behavior, the absence of a powerful third party that helps to enforce contracts, and uncertainty are all contributing factors in making reaching an agreement prohibitively costly. The degree of heterogeneity among states in conflict also contributes to language problems, misunderstandings, and disagreements, and therefore exacerbates the need for translation, arbitration, and costly coordination, which in turn increases transactions costs greatly.[48] The number of states involved in a conflict further amplifies the difficulty in preparing, negotiating, and concluding agreements.[49] The probability of reaching an agreement between two states is therefore greater with the difficulty of finding a contract agreeable to all parties increasing in a linear fashion as the number of states goes up.

This brief account suggests the centrality of transaction costs on the outcome of the bargaining on water rights. The lack of clearly specified property rights agreements on the overwhelming majority of international watercourses indicates how high the costs of determining water rights are in the international context.[50] Why then is it so difficult to determine property rights in international watercourses? The world painted by the Coase theorem is one of complete information and zero transaction costs, underlying the fundamental role played by transaction costs in the emergence of institutions. In this counterfactual world, property rights are either well defined or there is no need for their delineation.[51] When property rights are well defined and there are no transaction costs, resources will be used efficiently where they are valued most (Coase 1960). Rights and liabilities in such a case are clear. Information is costless and freely available which also makes monitoring unnecessary. This is the first-best world in which we do not need institutions. In this world of no transactions costs even defining property rights is unnecessary in order to ensure the efficient and optimal allocation of water resources and so preserving long-term sustainability. States will also easily overcome collective action problems and devise self-reinforcing contracts to allocate water rights achieving optimal efficiency and sustainability in resource use. In the second-best world, or our world, we need institutions to help reduce transaction costs and we need to define property rights in international watercourses to bring us closer to achieving efficient optimal outcomes.[52] Reducing transaction costs among states sharing common resources is particularly important in the weakly institutionalized international system. Since property rights cannot be fully delineated without cost, a study of the institutional setting, or the context, in which the states settle their conflicting preferences on various property rights arrangements with respect to their shared water resources is needed. This then brings us to the determinants of the emergence of property rights in international watercourses and the examination of the impact of states' incentives, strategies, and choices in the weakly institutionalized, high transaction costs, international context.

## Property Rights

What do we mean then by determining water rights in international watercourses? Property rights in general refer to the authority of individuals over goods to choose any use from an un-prohibited class of uses. An un-prohibited class of uses sets the limits on freedom of action and determines where one's freedom ends and another's starts. If one is to define freedom as the ability to do anything one wants without causing harm to others, then it also establishes liability in case of the breach of rights. Marx attributed the existence of property rights to social problems rooted in scarcity.[53] It is widely accepted that Marx was the first scholar to develop a theory of property rights based on scarcity.

The political philosophers of the seventeenth and eighteenth centuries, Hobbes, Locke, Hume, and Rousseau had also addressed the origins of property rights. However, their primary concern was to explain the origin of the state. Among them, Hobbes' analysis of property rights is seemingly the most interesting and relevant one for our purposes, since he essentially says that property rights do not exist in the absence of a sovereign power that can enforce them, and that therefore property ultimately is owned only at the discretion of that sovereign power.[54] At first glance, this implies grim prospects for international water rights. In the Hobbesian state of nature, which is a war of every man against every man, individuals use all the available resources to ensure their survival including frequent uses of violence. Each individual would be better off if all agreed to exercise self-restraint in his or her pursuit of self-interest and establish the rules of the game. It is, therefore, possible that for purely selfish reasons, individuals can devise the means of enforcement and can monitor the observance of the rules. The social contract theories developed by Hobbes, Locke, and Rousseau suggests that individuals who live in a state of the nature, whether it is riddled by violence or happy in peace, have solved the initial collective action problem and have made contingent commitments to create a commonwealth – a state – in the process. Ostrom also argued, consistent with her support for voluntary community-based solutions, that individuals will be willing to make the following type contingent commitment: 'I will commit myself to follow the set of rules we have devised in all instances except dire emergencies if the rest of those affected make a similar commitment and act accordingly.'[55] Thus, similarly to individuals who live in a state of nature, there is a possibility for watercourse states, which exist in state of nature like conditions, to enter into a contract with each other by surrendering some of their rights to protect their long-term benefits and ensure the sustainability of common pool resources.

In the absence of an external authority above states, the *self-enforcing* nature of these voluntary institutional arrangements becomes important. States will agree on property rights institutions only when they have a mechanism to enforce such agreements. This might take place a number of different ways: by the creation of an external authority, such as a supra-national institution with an authority to govern the water resources of the entire watercourse; by agreeing to abide by the authority of the International Court of Justice or a similar third party institution to adjudicate the conflicts arising from the implementation of the agreed upon water rights; or by a self regulation mechanism that ensures the enforcement of property rights when those rights are infringed upon. One primary task then for resolving international watercourse issues is to design a suitable property regime, or more specifically, to delineate the rights and duties of each watercourse state with respect to both consumptive and non-consumptive uses of the water, and with respect to its maintenance and long-term sustainability. The property regime could be a combination of different ownership categories as there is no such thing as absolute or allodial ownership.[56] It would be fitting to describe such property rights regime as a common property regime.[57] In international watercourses, the choice is likely going to be between a less desirable but relatively easier to achieve private property regime[58] and a more desirable common property regime.

In line with the presuppositions of scarcity-based property rights theory, in international watercourses, water scarcity is the primary driving force behind the attempts to develop an international legal framework as well as the attempts by the watercourse states in arid or semi-arid regions to determine water rights at bilateral and multi-lateral levels. There are only two multilateral treaties currently in force, one of which regulates water supply of the Rhine (1966) and the other in the Mekong (1995), and not surprisingly neither of these multilateral treaties is in water scarce/stressed regions. As per Hobbes, this begs the question of whether external institutions or hegemony are really needed to resolve water conflicts. An existing or projected scarcity of water forces states to clarify water rights in shared resources, but it does not necessarily lead to the emergence of water rights. Currently, all Middle Eastern and African international water resources are subject to unilateral exploitation in a competitive fashion with no common property regime.[59]

The unilateral exploitation of international watercourses regardless of their long-term sustainability has already caused or soon will cause a tragedy of commons in many of the shared water resources in water-scarce regions. The lack of coordination among the watercourse states causes undue stress on the limited water resources and endangers the natural resource's long-term existence. Understanding the process through which states determine water rights requires taking into consideration the natural distinction between surface and ground water resources. As we have seen, the International Law Commission's definition of international watercourses includes ground water resources along with the surface waters due to the complex nature of water systems in any given watercourse. Indeed, underground aquifers are more often than not linked to the surface waters and excessive water withdrawal from aquifers will likely have an effect on the surface waters. The fact that watercourse states face different degrees of threats and have different priorities due to the differences in the natural characteristics of ground and surface water resources also plays a crucial role and therefore must be accounted for in determining the likelihood of emergence/non-emergence of water rights in any given water conflict. The most important distinction between surface and ground water resources lies in their differing degrees of liability to the tragedy of commons.

The tragedy of commons is more detrimental to international ground water resources than international rivers because groundwater resources carry more of the characteristics of common pool resources than international rivers. The unilateral exploitation of underground water resources beyond their replenishment rate is likely to result in a tragedy for all. Regardless of their geographic position in the basin all users will suffer from the decrease and contamination of the resource; none of the users will be able to enjoy the benefits of the resource any longer. Thus, this joint/simultaneous use scenario of groundwater aquifers suggests different implications for the possibility of cooperation and the emergence of water rights. This more or less symmetrical distribution of detrimental effects can be a blessing, since it might be instrumental in bringing basin states together to avoid a tragedy for all.

On the other hand, 'a tragedy for all' is not exactly the situation in international rivers, as was briefly mentioned in the Introduction. By nature, rivers flow through different national territories sequentially, which enhances the importance of one's position in the watercourse. In this sequential use scenario, the nature of the (power) relationship among users is determined by one's geographic position as an upper, middle, or lower watercourse state. The asymmetrical distribution of the detrimental effects as well as upper watercourse states' capabilities to decrease the quantity and quality of water available for downstream use without being subject to the harmful effects of its own and downstream states' water projects separate international rivers from other common pool resources. This lack of a full-fledged tragedy of commons situation in which all users suffer from unconstrained unilateral actions and a subsequent deterioration of a resource requires the inclusion of different considerations into the analysis in international river conflicts, and it also drastically alters the conditions for cooperation in sharing and managing international rivers.

However, international watercourses share some of the specific characteristics of common pool resources. Often the relative costs of exclusion and coordination are quite high. For example, it is sometimes prohibitively costly for a watercourse state to legitimately deny the benefits that are obtained from the development of water resources to other watercourse states.

International funding agencies often require the prior consent of lower watercourse states to upper watercourse states' water development projects. At times, lower watercourse states block the funding to upper watercourse states' water development projects; in which case upper watercourse states finance the project by its own means causing delays in the implementation of the projects. In more severe cases, the lower watercourse states might use military force/or the threat of use of military force to halt the upper watercourse developments.[60] In other cases, lower watercourse states may benefit from upper watercourse states' water development projects like dams, for example, which regulate a river's flow and prevent flooding, thus create externalities, such as flood prevention. Furthermore, it is virtually impossible to halt a river's flow from entering lower watercourse states. This rivalry in the consumption of the international waters between upper and lower watercourse states is nowhere more apparent than in the arid and semi-arid regions of the world where freshwater resources are very limited. Thus, in many ways, international watercourses are subject to ailments similar to those for open access common pool resources. Recognizing this enables us to compensate for the inadequacy of the International Law Commission's definition of an international watercourse and to pay attention to the fine details in analyzing conflicts over property rights in international watercourses.

## Conclusion

To summarize with respect to international watercourses, property rights refer to any rules, formal or informal, which determine rights and duties among watercourse state with respect to the allocation and usage of water resources; they originate in the prevalent scarcity conditions. Institutions are defined as sets of formal or informal rules that govern relations among states. The inclusion of informal rules in the definition of institutions is needed because the absence of formal institutions or agreements does not necessarily mean that either pure chaos or a Hobbesian state of nature exists in international watercourses. It is a well-known fact that conflicts are likely to occur when the rules are not clear.[61] Property rights can be perceived as the rules of a game that determine ownership, corresponding duties, and liabilities when the rules are infringed upon. Though international law cannot be applied to states without a state's consent, it can still fulfill one of the most important functions in the international system, that is, to provide a clear legal framework for establishing property rights.[62] The definition of property rights can provide a basis for discussion and can bring conceptual clarity. The existence of a clear legal framework is also crucial for the resolution of conflicts over the distribution of water rights in international watercourses, mainly because it narrows the number of possible outcomes, which in turn reduces transactions costs for legitimate bargains and increases them for illegitimate ones.

The process through which water rights emerge is essentially a political one. The fact that water as a natural resource has been treated for such a long time as a common good, and in some cases as a public good, is only the beginning of the story.[63] Water is valued for its potential contribution to the well-being of nations. It has not only a capacity to generate income, but also a capacity to generate interdependencies, vulnerabilities, and distributional tensions. Furthermore, at the domestic level, water is often treated as a public good, the provision of which is considered to be a duty of the state.[64] In this context, the most important question is how to ascribe a monetary value to a natural resource, like water, which prior to becoming a commodity, was treated as a public good domestically and a common good internationally.[65]

Natural resources are valued because of their potential to contribute to economic development. In many less-developed and developing countries the provision of these resources are the main task of states. Failure in this task will determine a state's failure, which is a common phenomenon in many developing countries.[66] States are considered to be failed if they are unable to provide basic goods, which include not only internal/external security and order, but also material well-being for its population. Furthermore, if the regime type of a state is democratic, it is very likely that economic policies aimed at the well-being of the society are going to determine the longevity of a ruling political party's hold on power. Even if the regime type is more authoritarian, the legitimacy of the rulers still depends on popular will, which is predominantly determined by economic well-being.

The definitional issues surrounding international watercourses indicate that the conflicting interests of states in international watercourses are hard to reconcile and often lead to difficult conundrums, especially in arid and semi-arid regions. States, as rational actors with goals, try to serve their interests by engaging in strategic interactions, or interdependent decision making, with other states. A state's choice of a strategy depends on its expectation about what its counterparts will likely do. Thus, in order to understand states' actions in international watercourses, one needs to look not only at the states' preferences and their relative power capabilities, which is in part determined by their position in power hierarchies of international system, but also at their relations with other states and the information that is available to states about others states' preferences, goals, and capabilities during the policy making process.

## A Parable of Water Rights Conflict in International Watercourses

The latter half of the twentieth century was marked by a phenomenon of dwindling freshwater resources in arid and semi-arid developing regions of the world. Water has become increasingly a scarce resource due to both population growth and the requirements of economic development. Indeed, population growth pushes states to undertake massive irrigation projects, such as building dams and irrigation canals in order to open up more land for irrigated agriculture in areas that traditionally practiced rain-fed agriculture. This is done to increase productivity and to break frequent dry spells; the potential to increase food production with rain-fed agriculture is limited. The predominant subsistence level of agriculture worldwide, which is characterized by low productivity rates and also by significant fluctuations in production due to the inconsistency of precipitation and the lack of supplementary irrigation, is the main culprit of limited growth possibilities in food production.

Frequent droughts are unfortunately common in arid and semi-arid regions. Long dry seasons make it impossible to grow a second or third crop without irrigation, which ordinarily requires the existence of dams and canals along the major rivers. All watercourse states are aware of this potential of a regular water supply. The provision of a regular water supply by harnessing a river is costly and entails building dams to store water during high water seasons as well as building complex canal systems to distribute water when needed. However, costly irrigation projects per se do not magically solve all the problems and are also susceptible to generating new ones, such as water-logging and salinization.

Water-logging and salinization are common features of the soil in arid and semi-arid zones. Water-logging occurs when water is introduced to the soil faster than its drainage capacity. Likewise, salinization, which is also related to water-logging, occurs as an inevitable consequence of intensive irrigation. In arid regions, the soil is un-leached and the irrigation brings the salt content to the surface; as soon as the water evaporates the saline residue remains on the surface, thus causing salinization. Furthermore, the irrigation water which drains into rivers carries a large amount of salt and chemicals polluting the water flowing downstream. As a result, there is a positive correlation between aridity, water-logging, and salinization problems. Further compounding the problem is that as rivers follow their course from the highlands of upper watercourse states, the contribution to the water level decreases. Thus as rivers flow further away from their origin, the aridity of the ecological environment heightens, and, after a certain point no augmentation of water is possible. Indeed, in most cases in semi-arid to arid climates, more than 90 percent of river waters are generated in upper watercourse states.

Despite the existence of these problems, water is without a doubt a critical and highly strategic resource. It is critical because having no water means literally no life; one must have water in order first to survive, then to prosper, and finally to advance. Water has a substantial strategic importance as well, since it is the most crucial factor of economic production, the substitution of which is possible neither in agriculture nor in industry.

For the sake of simplicity, let us assume a linear economic development model, as proposed by Rostow, for our upper, middle, and lower watercourse states and the same level of economic development for all three.[67] In other words, they are traditional societies that are dominated by subsistence level economic activity, that is, output is consumed by the producers rather than traded. At this stage of economic development, agriculture constitutes the most important industry and production is labor-intensive with little or no capital investment.

In linear models of economic development, agriculture is typically the first sector to be developed and is expected to generate enough surpluses to provide the basis for the development of agro-industries and eventually heavy industries. In this context, the quantity and the quality of those resources available to the states will matter in determining a state's fate. States with a better natural resource endowment will likely develop faster and increase their economic power.[68] Clearly, economic strength, which also generates political and military strength, depends on the availability of natural resources. If a state is fortunate, it is already endowed with strategic resources that are crucial for its economic development. If not, it is likely that states will try to gain access to those resources, mainly land and water, and if denied they will to try to capture these resources by force.

The upper watercourse state is situated where most of the water originates. The watercourse then enters the middle watercourse state before eventually reaching to the sea following its course through the lower watercourse state. There is no agreement among these three states on how to share the common water resources. Thus, each state pursues its own interests and tries to extract as much water as possible from the watercourse. Here geography gives the advantage to the upper watercourse states, and inevitably the middle and lower watercourse states feel the impact of water development projects in the upper watercourse state. Among these three states, the lower watercourse state is naturally the one that suffers the most because it is subject to the negative effects of both the upper and middle watercourse states' water policies. All three are developing states more or less at the same economic level wherein agriculture is the main sector. They aim to prosper and thus have planned to undertake major water development projects in their portion of the watercourse. In this context what will these watercourse states likely do?

# CHAPTER 2

# REALIST PERSPECTIVES

> The most frequent reason why men desire to hurt each other is not security or glory but rather that many men at the same time have an appetite to the same thing; which yet very often they can neither enjoy in common, nor yet divide it; whence it follows that the strongest must have it, and who is strongest must be decided by the sword.
>
> Hobbes, *De Cive: Liberty*[1]

From the city-states of ancient times to the sovereign nation states of modern times, nearly every political organization has engaged in war over scarce resources. In the realist view, this is mostly due to the Hobbesian state of nature of the international system, which is characterized by all-out war of each against all. Wars thus appear to be an inevitable feature of the international system. This is so even if political organizations, like the Greek poleis, early empires, states, and super powers merely sought to ensure their own survival.[2] The distinction between survival-seeking states and ones seeking domination is blurry, since the drive for wealth ensures both survival and domination in the world system, and it is often hard to differentiate at which point states' drive for wealth no longer aims to ensure their survival but rather their domination. Considering the overriding importance of natural resource endowment in determining the likelihood of a state's survival and its prospect for becoming a hegemonic power in an anarchic international system, it is not surprising that the struggle over natural resources has become a prominent feature of the international system.[3] As a result, from early times on, the struggle to secure access and control over natural resources has been a driving force behind conflict among states.[4]

Land and water resources played a crucial role in the emergence of early empires as the only available means to achieve economic growth in pre-industrial societies. As Gilpin succinctly notes:

> A fundamental feature of the era of empires was the relatively static nature of wealth. In the absence of significant technological advances, agricultural productivity remained at a low level, and the primary determinant of economic growth and wealth was the availability of land and the man/land ratio. For this reason, the growth of land and power of the state was primarily a function of its control over territory that could generate an economic surplus. With only limited and intermittent periods of real economic growth, the dynamics of international relations were provided by the continuous division and re-division of territory and the conquest of slaves (or a docile peasantry) to till the land. Thus, when agriculture was the basin of wealth and power, growth in power and wealth was nearly synonymous with conquest of territory.[5]

As a result, early empires arose either by a merger of small states under the threat of external forces or by an actual conquest, and often the stimulus came from the requirements of economic and population growth.

Entwined economic and population growth intensify the pressure on natural resources. Eventually, territorial expansion becomes unavoidable for states even if they are primarily concerned with ensuring their survival. There is also a close link between a state's survival and its welfare. It is expected for states to redefine their interests as they reach to higher levels of economic development, which increases their economic, military, and political capabilities. After examining the historical record, Kennedy suggests the existence of 'a very clear connection between an individual great power's economic rise and fall and its growth and decline as an important military power.'[6] Zakaria also makes a similar observation adding that:

> Over the course of history, states that have experienced significant growth in their material resources have relatively soon redefined and expanded their political interests abroad, measured by their increases in military spending, initiation of wars, acquisition of territory, posting of soldiers and diplomats, and participation in great-power decision-making.[7]

In the process of transforming an economic power into a political and military one, wars function as a medium of change; Tilly's observation that 'War made the state and the state made war,' seems therefore to be valid.[8] According to Tilly, much like the process of natural selection, weak states are eliminated and give way to the rise of strong states. The drastic reduction in the number of political organizations from almost 500 in Europe and several thousand in the rest of the world during the Medieval Period to 40 independent states at the beginning of the twentieth century substantiates the process of natural selection through which weak states have disappeared.

Disparity in economic growth rates among states has been underlined by many scholars ranging from Carr to Gilpin as an unsettling fundamental problem of the international system that leads to the outbreak of wars.[9] As Keynes noted, 'The great events of history are often due to secular changes in the growth of population and other fundamental economic causes, which escaping by their gradual character the notice of contemporary observers, are attributed to the follies of statesmen or the fanaticism of atheists.'[10] Economic development and population growth force states to increase their demands on international resources, and thus create pressure on the international system. Consequently, the strained international system fosters the use of military force and the outbreak of wars.

In *Nations in Conflict: National Growth and International Violence*, Choucri and North showed that states facing high resource demands and limited resource availability within their territories seek needed resources through trade or conquest beyond their boundaries. Based on the findings of their study, Choucri and North advanced the lateral pressure theory. Here, the pressure created by scarcity conditions on states is necessary, but not a sufficient condition for a state to seek territorial expansion. States will opt for territorial expansion if they have the capabilities to do so. As Thucydides pointed out centuries ago '[...] right, as the world goes, is only in question between equals in power, while the strong do what they can and the weak suffer what they must.'[11] There is no doubt that economic wealth creates opportunities for states to expand their control beyond their borders.

Not only does economic wealth provides states with the means to achieve their goals, but it also gives states many kinds of leverage, such as economic, political, military, and cultural, over other states, and so it gives them an opportunity to exercise control externally. Also, in compliance with the predictions of Snyder's domino theory, the expansion also strengthens the state's power and further boosts its capabilities, since with the acquired territory comes new resources.[12] Gilpin observes that:

> Throughout history a principle objective of states has been the conquest of territory in order to advance economic, security, and other interests. Whether by means of imperialist subjugation of one people by another or by annexation of contiguous territory, states in all ages have sought to enlarge their control over territory and, by implication, their control over the international system [...]. In international society the distribution of power among coalitions of coalitions (states) determines who governs international system and whose interests are principally promoted by the functioning of the system.[13]

Thus, under scarcity conditions if states are strong enough they will seek a modification of the international system in such a way that it gives them the most control over territory and other states' behavior. In this context, the lateral pressure theory, forwarded by Choucri and North, predicts that wars occur when the growth and changes in population, technology, resources, markets and national expansion creates scarcity. A straightforward version of the merger of the lateral pressure theory with realist studies *vis-à-vis* water rights in international watercourses finds its expression in the hydraulic imperative theory.

Hydraulic imperative theory predicts that states will meet their water needs through the forceful acquisition and retention of neighboring territory and/or through restricting the free flow of rivers before they cross national borders.[14] Since water is a critical and a highly strategic resource in arid and semi-arid regions, states are ready to go to war in order to ensure a regular supply of water for their present and future needs. Realists argue that if human history is an account of resource wars and the relationship between the resource scarcity and conflict is positive, then fresh water resources will certainly be a source of future contention and conflict due to the fact that it is gradually becoming scarcer. As a result, the focus of analysis must be when and where resource related conflicts are most likely to arise, not whether environmental concerns can contribute to instability and conflict. Water as a source of economic and political power, as Gleick argues, justifies the use of force to ensure access to water resources.[15] The contexts the realists take on international water rights can be summarized as a limited water resources/ population growth/food gap of Malthusian proportions that eventually will lead to the outbreak of wars in water-scarce regions.

Homer-Dixon refines the scarcity analysis further and identifies three types of scarcity: (1) supply-induced scarcity which is caused by the degradation and depletion of resources; (2) demand-induced scarcity which is caused by population growth and/or increase in the per capita resource consumption; and (3) structural scarcity which arises from an unequal social distribution of resources in such a way that relatively few people have access to a resource while the majority suffers from resource shortages.[16] Thus the causality flows as follows: population growth and high resource consumption per capita causes deterioration of environmental conditions and produces supply-induced scarcity which in turn deepens resource scarcity and heightens the competition over the scarce resource. The combination of demand, supply induced scarcity, and structural scarcity generates a potentially explosive situation and suitable ground for the emergence of violent conflicts within states as well as among states.

However, serious methodological problems call for caution in any conclusions drawn from these studies that link environmental degradation to violent conflicts. Homer-Dixon, for example, only studied cases where there is armed conflict and environmental degradation and thus his work suffers from a problem of selection on the dependent variable and from generalizing from a few cases.[17] He does not consider cases where environmental degradation did not lead to armed conflicts. This limits the conclusions one can draw from his analysis and also raises serious questions about the causality. One of the most extensively cited large-N studies, one by Hauge and Ellingsen,[18] found only moderate support for a link between soil erosion, deforestation, lack of clean freshwater and conflict, but the conflicts in this case were rather small. Their study, which has nonetheless been used to support the position that environmental degradation leads to inter-state and intra-state conflicts, that is, large, not small scale conflicts,[19] also suffers from serious methodological problems related to the operationalization of its key variables[20] and the replication of the study.[21] For example, they operationalized supply-induced scarcity as annual change in forest coverage and in the quality of soil without taking into account available stock; fresh water scarcity is also measured for only a single year. Still more telling, the overwhelming majority of other quantitative studies,[22] found no link between environmental degradation or resource scarcity and conflict.[23] This seriously undermines environmental degradation as a suitable independent variable since environmental degradation itself could be explained by other variables, such as state weakness/failure or lack of proper institutions due to the level of both political and economic development.[24] The causal relationship then between environmental degradation and violent conflicts appears to be spurious. Topics like inadequate institutional development, or the exclusionary nature of institutions in resource rich countries where the state has become a rentier state and has had minimal or no incentives to develop institutions for taxation and infrastructure, have received a lot of attention in the resource course literature. But significantly these topics do appear in environmental security literature.

Leaving aside these methodological problems, let's continue with our analysis and explore the logical implications of this line of thinking for international watercourses. A combined supply and demand induced scarcity in an international watercourse makes the conflict over water rights a zero-sum game, that is, a gain for one state that means a corresponding loss for the other state/s. This inevitably exacerbates the security dilemma facing watercourse states. Under scarcity conditions, water becomes a strategic resource and therefore giving up even the smallest degree of control over it runs against the interests of states.[25] The upper watercourse state in accordance with the predictions of realist theory will expand its territory at the expense of the relatively weaker lower watercourse states and will emerge as a hegemonic state that will not hesitate to use the threat of use of force, or the use of force in order to further its interests and expand its spheres of influence. It is generally argued that the importance of territory, which varies from state to state, has two dimensions, namely material and symbolic. For the upper watercourse state, assuming that there are no prior territorial conflicts, the conquered territory initially has only a material value, that is, the value generated by the economic uses of resources such as land and water. But for the lower watercourse states the lost territory can have both material and symbolic values. The juxtaposition of water conflict with territorial conflict has important implications for the nature of the conflict.[26] Most importantly, this suggests the possibility of the issue of indivisibility. In accordance with the predictions of realist theory, the upper watercourse state will conquer the watercourse, and once the lower watercourse states cease to exist, the issue of indivisibility will solve itself. However, this brings to the fore the question of options that are available to lower watercourse states. More specifically, should lower watercourse states enter into an alliance or bandwagon?

The issue of whether states balance or bandwagon is highly disputed and brings two schools of realist thought into open theoretical conflict.[27] There seems, on the one hand, to be close ties between defensive realism and Waltz's systemic balance of power theory. Waltz's theory assumes that in an anarchic environment states seek security before anything else.[28] However, it should be noted that Waltzian Neorealist theory is categorically different from both defensive and offensive realism as being strictly a theory of international relations, whereas both defensive and offensive realism present a theory of foreign policy and brings unit level variables into account.[29] Balance of power theories, as set forth by prominent defensive realists, suggest that states are primarily concerned with security in an anarchic international system, as a result balancing is the policy they adopt.[30] Defensive realists argue that states' response to the rise of an hegemonic state will be to balance against rising states, since states primarily seek security and will resist the attempts of domination by other states. Furthermore, according to defensive realists, states will likely feel more secure if they make an alliance with weaker states due partly to the possibility of a greater exertion of influence on weak states, and also partly to the low probability of being dominated by a weaker state.

In an attempt to respond to defensive realist arguments, offensive realists underline the importance of the structure of the international system. Offensive realists contend that states seek security as well as wealth. Since power is essential for security, and wealth is the primary mean to acquire power, powerful states cannot help but seek to structure the international system in such a way that generates wealth and power for themselves. If only the most powerful states can guarantee their survival, then a state will naturally be drawn to wealth and to wealth maximizing behavior. Offensive realists argue that hegemony provides guaranties of the survival of the strongest. Mearsheimer, for example, argues that the security dilemma will prevail as long as states operate in anarchy.[31] Legro and Moravcsik, on the other hand, emphasize the importance of the distribution of material capabilities in international relations. They argue that, 'Interstate bargaining outcomes reflect the relative cost of threats and inducements, which is directly proportional to the distribution of material resources.'[32] Schweller further underlines the triviality of the security dilemma in the absence of predatory states and writes:

> If states are assumed to seek no more than their own survival, why would they feel threatened? [...]. Anarchy and self-preservation alone are not sufficient [...] Predatory states are motivated by expansion and absolute gains, not security and the fear of relative losses, are the primary movers of neo-realist theory. Without some possibility of their existence, the security dilemma melts away, as do most concepts associated with contemporary realism.[33]

The main conclusion of realists since Thucydides repeats itself: the strong do what they can and the weak suffer what they must. Material capabilities predominantly determine the outcome of conflicts.

Bandwagoning also changes its meaning for offensive realists. It is no longer just the opposite of balancing or Walt's alignment with the source of danger. For Schweller, bandwagoning is not a response to threat but an opportunity to secure profit and easy gains.[34] He notes:

> My argument is straightforward: Unthreatened revisionist states (those overlooked by Walt and Waltzian neorealists) often bandwagon with the stronger revisionist states or coalition for opportunistic reasons. My use of the term conforms to the standard definition of bandwagoning as joining the stronger side; and I show that this behavior is quite prevalent throughout the history among a certain class of states.[35]

Aside from these definitional differences, the important point in the discussion of whether states balance or bandwagon is that states do both depending on the conditions.[36] What matters is the conditions under which states are compelled to choose one over the other. Furthermore, as Schweller argues, alignments are likely to be determined by the compatibility of goals rather than imbalances of power or threat.[37]

## An Assessment of Realist Approaches

The realist approaches to international watercourse conflicts predict competitive unilateral exploitation of the watercourse in accordance with the distribution of relative power capabilities. The upper watercourse will first try to complete as many of its water projects as possible, including dams, irrigation canals and so on. Its goals are twofold: the first is to store water during high seasons in order to break dry spells in areas practicing rain-fed agriculture; the second is to expand irrigated areas, which were previously limited only to the areas in the vicinity of water, in order to increase agricultural output. Also, the upper watercourse state does not currently have any proximate interest in either limiting its water consumption at present or giving up its future water projects; therefore, the upper watercourse state is not eager to reach an agreement on the distribution of water rights. Nor is there any apparent incentive for the upper watercourse state to do so. Contrarily, everything indicates that the upper watercourse state will be better off if it takes full advantage of its natural resources, which implies an extensive utilization of water resources within its territory. An upper watercourse state can reach the level of full utilization of its water resources to some extent without the acquiescence of the lower watercourse states.

However, when an upper watercourse state reaches that level, there is nothing that would necessarily prevent the upper watercourse state from expanding its political sphere of influence once it acquires the necessary political and military capabilities from its economic wealth. It is likely that as soon as an upper watercourse state announces and starts to implement its plans concerning the utilization of water resources, the lower watercourse states, foreseeing the adverse effects of the upper watercourse state's consumptive water usage in water quantity and quality and also the possibility of upper watercourse state's territorial expansion, would try to prevent the upper watercourse state from implementing its projects and would try to reach an agreement with an upper watercourse state on the distribution of water rights. Their success will likely depend upon their relative power capabilities and also their ability to reconcile their conflicting interests in order to establish a united front against the upper watercourse state.

Against the unilateralist tendencies of the upper watercourse state, the lower watercourse states have two options: to acquiesce to the upper watercourse state's unilateral policies or to oppose them, which might inevitably bring military action upon themselves. Negotiations would not likely result in an agreement on water rights concerning the common waters, since not only does the upper watercourse state not have any interest in reaching an agreement on water rights, which likely would require limiting its current or future consumption, but also the lower watercourse states bring different concerns to the negotiating table. Like the upper watercourse state, they need water to offset growth in population and economy. Indeed, the most common rationale for demanding more water is projected population growth. Frequent droughts also caution states against the dangers of water shortages across the watercourse. For the lower watercourse states, a decrease in the flow would hurt agriculture, limit the viability of existing and planned water projects, and impede economic growth. In addition to this, the concerns of the lower watercourse states often entail the quality of water reaching them. Unfortunately, for upper watercourse states, neither releasing enough water for navigational and downstream use nor taking necessary precautions to prevent water contamination constitute significant priority. As a result, the decreases in water flow as well as the quality of the flow are detrimentally high for lower watercourse states and to some extent for middle watercourse states. In the face of these incompatible interests and varying degrees of concerns on common issues, the likelihood of successful tripartite negotiations is almost zero.

Given the low probability of reaching a multilateral agreement on water rights, middle and lower watercourse states thus have only two options: capitulate or resist. If they choose to resist, the question of a possibility of an alliance between the middle and lower watercourse state comes to the fore. This model predicts that the possibility of an alliance between the middle and lower watercourse states is very limited and inherently unstable. The main reason behind the limited possibility of a successful alliance is the conflict of interests between the middle and lower watercourse states, not to mention the intrinsic instability of triadic conflicts. There is always a possibility that states will shift their alliance from one state to another in the hopes of securing better terms of settlement. Therefore, the costs of entering an alliance for states are very high. The greater the cost of an alliance between the middle and lower watercourse states, or any combination of an alliance between the upper, middle, and lower watercourse states, the less likely it will occur. An alliance between middle and lower watercourse states, or any other combination, would likely be weak and temporary. Furthermore, at the first sign of an alliance between middle and lower watercourse states, an upper watercourse state will likely try to forestall the emergence of such an alliance by offering either one or the other better terms of settlement.

The realist take on water rights in the literature is more in accordance with the classical and offensive variants of the realist school. The distinguishing characteristic of the realist school from other competing schools of thought, such as the liberal, institutional, constructivist, and critical schools, is the primacy of the material capabilities assumption. The other two core assumptions, that rational unitary states are the major actors, and, that state preferences are fixed and conflicting, are more problematic in their ability to differentiate the realist school from the others. Anarchy is a constant feature of the international system and as a result it cannot explain variation in international politics. Furthermore, all theoretical approaches to international relations agree on this assumption to the extent that consensus is almost unanimous. Most scholars in the field would also agree that states are self-interested and a harmony of interests among states is non-existent, especially on security matters. In this regard, Carr's seminal work *The Twenty Years Crisis* practically demolished the idealist-liberal belief of the existence of 'harmony of interest' among states.

In the final analysis, only the primacy of power, which is mostly defined in terms of material capabilities, including economic, political, and military capabilities, is what makes a theory realist. International water rights issues on international rivers are considered to some extent to be a part of security issues. Water data have been kept confidential to date in some countries and governments have tried to tie water rights issues to national security, insisting on a political solution to the problem. The existence of only a small number of multilateral agreements on water rights in international watercourses strengthen the belief that it is hard to get powerful states to agree on the distribution of water rights if it is not consistent with their interests. Again note that none of these existing multi-lateral agreements are in water stressed/ scarce regions. As a result, the literature on water rights is dominated by mostly conflict-driven realist approaches – almost all of which would predict outbreaks of war over international watercourses in arid and semi-arid regions – and their critiques.[38]

The realist model of international watercourse conflicts and the general theory behind it, leads then to two strong policy recommendations: (1) increase power and indirectly increase military spending because military power will determine the resolution of the conflict; (2) build dams unilaterally and/or to try to capture the whole watercourse. It is, in other words, a world of perpetual competition among states over the control of scarce resources.

The capacity of any state to act upon these recommendations, however, is determined by its domestic political situation. Domestic determinants are critical in states' choices of strategy to achieve foreign and domestic policy goals, which underscores the fact that regime type and its probable effects on any outcome are of central importance. There is little question that a state's choice of strategy in dealing with international problems is influenced by its regime type, and this takes us into the center of state-society relationships and into the issues, such as those relating to state autonomy, legitimacy, and accountability all of which have strong connotations on states' capabilities to use its relative power capabilities effectively. Watercourse states' capabilities, especially in dealing with resource depletion and degradation in their portion of the watercourse, have a significant effect on the strategies that states adopt during water negotiations. It is likely that at the heart of the decision to preserve the status quo lies the nature of the domestic institutions and the priority given by national leaders to economic considerations relative to political ones.

Watercourse states have clearly conflicting interests, which are tied to their economic, political, and security interests. Any approach which takes into account, among other things, domestic political structures, the effect of economic interdependence, ethnic and religious divisions, the socio-economic and political distribution of goods, the role of international institutions, and so on, are inherently non-realist and so likely fall into the category of liberal theories. Of these, the most significant are democratic peace theories, which look to the domestic political processes to find the origins of state preferences, and the neo-liberal institutionalist strand of common pool resources studies, which look to collective actions problems of international cooperation and commitment.

Regime types and their impact on foreign policy has been the subject of many quantitative studies over the last couple decades. Democratic regimes are defined here following Dahl's criteria as having:

> effective participation, equality in voting, gaining enlightened understanding, exercising final control over the agenda, and inclusion of all adults and see the following institutions as necessary for the functioning of a democracy: elected officials, free, fair and frequent elections, freedom of expression, alternative sources of information, associational autonomy (which is basically the right to establish political parties and interest groups), and inclusive citizenship (which includes the right to vote in free, fair, frequent elections, the right to run for elected office, the right to have access to independent source of information, and the right to other liberties and opportunities.[39]

As inclusive as democratic regimes may be, authoritarian regimes are exclusionary, and are defined as the opposite of democratic regimes.

In studies on the effects of regime type on foreign policy decision making, democratic regimes tend to show restraint in their foreign policies and seek to settle their disputes, especially with other democracies, by means short of war.[40] Immature or transitioning democratic regimes, however, tend to be conflict prone and unstable.[41] This is likely because it takes longer for informal institutions to adapt to the changes in the formal institutional structures. Like immature democratic regimes, semi-repressive and semi-exclusionary regimes tend to refrain from lowering their demands, while repressive and exclusionary regimes tend to lower their demands and settle disputes due in part to their anticipation of severe punishment.[42] The difference between repressive and exclusionary and semi-repressive and semi-exclusionary regimes is a matter of the degree of repression and exclusion, which is related to a regime's ability to stifle domestic opposition and dissent and exclude parts of society from accessing political and economic power.

The more repressive the regime the higher the cost of an attempt to overthrow the regime and the less likely it is for domestic opposition to overcome coordination problems in their pursuit of change. The higher the proportion of the population that is excluded from power, the higher the cost of losing power for the existing repressive leaders who will likely suffer consequences beyond just losing political power. The degree of repression employed is also a function of the proportion of the excluded population: the greater the proportion of the population excluded from accessing political and economic power, the greater the degree of the repression employed to stifle domestic political opposition. What makes semi-repressive and semi-exclusionary regimes more dangerous is the higher likelihood of a successful attempt by the domestic opposition to overthrow those in power. In repressive and exclusionary regimes, severe repression and exclusion render the domestic political opposition weak and the cost of any attempt to overthrow the existing regime high. The regime's ability to repress domestic political opposition makes any attempt to undermine the regime dangerous. Iraqi Kurds paid a heavy price for their attempt to undermine Saddam Hussein's regime on at least three occasions, in 1975, 1988, and 1991. Similarly, in Syria, Hafez al-Assad did not hesitate to use unrestrained force during the Muslim Brotherhood rebellion in 1982 and ruthlessly suppressed the revolt by taking the lives of up to 25,000 civilians in Hamah.[43] Similarly, his son, Bashar al-Assad, who took power in 2000, violently repressed the Arab Spring protests in 2011, igniting the current civil war.

Domestically, however, the drought has been pinpointed as a causal factor leading to the outbreak of the Syrian civil war.[44] Even then the main cause of conflict is likely the existing incentive structure created by the organization of these societies resulting in exclusionary political and economic institutions. Societies with exclusionary political and economic institutions are much more limited in their ability to deal with change and negative shocks like economic crises or natural disasters. The institutional make up of such societies is not conducive to producing an adaptive and innovation oriented incentive structure and this seriously undermines their capacity to deal with their problems through peaceful means. How influential domestic institutions, norms of conflict resolution and political competition are in determining international politics is what we turn to next.

# CHAPTER 3

# LIBERAL PERSPECTIVES

At the end of the fifth century BC, Thucydides presented an account of the Peloponnesian War fought between the democratic Athenians and oligarchic Spartans and their respective allies in which, for the first time on record, the differences in national character and institutions came to the fore in the context of growing hostilities.[1] Thucydides drew attention to the importance of the differences in national character in explaining a state's foreign policies.[2] These differences, or to put it differently, the differences in behavioral patterns and attitudes, have attracted considerable scholarly attention in the centuries since. A link between national character and climate, for example, was argued by both Hippocrates in *Peri aeros* and by Aristotle in *Politics*.[3] Two millennia later, in the eighteenth century, Montesquieu made similar observations in *The Spirit of Laws*, drawing attention to the possible relationship between a nation's general spirit (i.e., culture), and climate and geography.[4] Montesquieu's observation that monarchies were more common where the soil was fertile, and republics where it was barren, preceded theories about the impact of the quality of soil on the form of government, such as Wittfogel's theory on the need for large-scale irrigation and its effects for the birth of despotic states.[5]

Montesquieu's contributions, however, are not limited to the effects of geography and climate on political culture. His thoughts on the positive effects of international trade on the peaceful relations among states are more important for being the early harbinger of theories of democratic peace, preceding Kant's *Perpetual Peace* in 1795. Apart from having no disadvantages of conquering or plundering a territory, according to Montesquieu, trade operates as 'a cure for the most destructive prejudices.'[6] Despite its variegated effects on different types of government, international trade represents an important mechanism through which international peace could become reality.[7] Overall, it helps the development of international markets, thus the development of an international finance, which compels states to create favorable conditions for the further development of trade. Economic interests, of course, play a driving role behind state's choices. These choices then underpinning peaceful relations are less dependent on a particular regime type, since the pacifying impact trade holds for all types of regime types.

The impact of international trade on states is thought to be twofold. On the one hand, it fosters the development of formal and informal relations among people from different countries, which might eliminate national prejudices. It also indirectly sows the seeds of peaceful relations among states by reducing uncertainty and by revealing information in all areas of interaction including political matters. The liberal-institutional proposition that a peaceful solution can be attained if the means are discovered for the contestant states to collaborate on technical and non-political matters finds its source in these eighteenth century idealist currents. On the other hand, trade obliges those in power to be credible and trustworthy in their dealings with others. The effectiveness of this proposition is further strengthened if the rulers come to power through elections. Like most of the philosophers of his time, Montesquieu thought of a republic, a government elected by people, as the best form of government, the one best able to deal with commitment problems, since a republic represented at the time the most inclusive form of governing institutions.

Although Kant has received much of the credit for this notion, republicanism as an ideology was widely sanctioned by scholars already in the eighteenth century. As the leading representative of republicanism, Kant envisioned a perpetual peace among democratically governed states. His emphasis on republican constitutions as a foundation of perpetual peace has become the focal point of more recent institutional variants of democratic peace theory. In *On Perpetual Peace*, which was published in 1795, Kant laid out his plan for achieving political stability and security. If statesmen would listen to philosophers, he argued, an international federation of independent republics could easily be achieved, which in turn could lead each republic to reduce its standing army, in order not to interfere in the internal affairs of other states, and to agree to be governed by the notion of universal hospitality. He foresaw a constructive role for an enlightened public in constraining policy makers by linking political legitimacy to the consent by the people. In a representative democracy, not only does the public have an opportunity to give its consent to the policy makers, but it also has an opportunity to hold those in power accountable for their policies.[8] Kant's emphasis on public opinion has become the keystone of later studies on public opinion and the transparency of government. Once multiple states share Kant's three critical features, namely, representative democracy, adherence to international law and organizations, and advanced commercial integration, peace is expected to materialize inevitably among them.[9]

The expectations following the expansion of international commerce and the development of market economies from the sixteenth to the eighteenth centuries led scholars to foresee a decline in the arbitrary actions and power displays of monarchs and a rise in levels of civilized behavior among states.[10] States that are tied to each other through a network of common institutions were thought to be the key to international peace. Consequently, democracy and war have often been seen as incompatible with each other.[11] Similarly, the observation that democratic states have not engaged in war with each other over the course of two centuries has led scholars to argue that democratic states do not fight with each other.[12] Doyle, for example, building on this literature, declared, '[. . .] the political bond of liberal rights and interests has proven a remarkably firm foundation for mutual nonaggression. A separate peace exists among liberal states.'[13] Differences in the forms of government, ideology, and institutional capacity are suggested as sources of conflict among states.[14] The surge of scholarly work on this topic, which has refined democratic peace theory, is more or less a by-product of the 1990s.[15]

During the last decade, several important studies have underlined the importance of domestic institutions in dealing with negative shocks, such as economic crises, droughts, natural disasters, climate change, and so on. Institutions have become the central foci of the scholarship on long-term economic development and by extension on sustainable development. The general conclusion is that the more inclusive the institutions, the better a society is able to deal with negative shocks, controlling violence and achieving sustainable long-term development.[16] In 2009, North, Wallis and Weingast, for example, concluded that poor countries are not poor because they grow more slowly. They are poor because they experience more years of negative income growth and more rapid declines during those years. The conceptual framework they developed for interpreting recorded human history identifies three types of social orders, two of which are relevant to the contemporary world,[17] the limited-access (or natural) state and open access orders. The limited access order emerged between five and ten thousand years ago. Personal relationships among the elite form the basis for political organization. A dominant coalition ruled these societies and people outside the coalition had limited access to organizations, privileges, rents, and valuable resources and activities, hence the name limited access indicating the exclusionary nature of economic and political institutions. Open access orders on the other hand emerged in the nineteenth century and are associated with the development of impersonal relationships and the lack of restrictions on the ability to form organizations by meeting a set of minimal and impersonal criteria. Both limited- and open-access social orders have public and private organizations, but natural states limit access to those organizations. The expansion of suffrage, the use of elections to select governments, constitutional arrangements to limit and define the powers of government, and unbiased application of the rule of law represents the transition from limited- to open-access societies. These two social orders have delivered different outcomes regarding economic and political development. Until about 1800, the long-run growth rate was close to zero meaning that for every period of increasing per capita income there was a corresponding period of decreasing income. Modern developed societies have become wealthier than any other in human history by reducing their episodes of negative growth by virtue of their transition to the open access order. North, Wallis, and Weingast argue that the difference between the economic performances of limited-access and open-access societies reflects the differential ability of the two social orders to deal with change, including a wide range of sudden changes or shocks. Open access orders are by nature more inclusive and this feature makes them better able to deal with change.

Acemoglu and Robinson have also made a strong case for how the nature of institutions weighs on the success of societies.[18] They argue that political institutions that concentrate power in the hands of a few without constraints, checks and balances or rule of law on the one hand, and economic institutions that lack law and order, have insecure property rights, and present entry barriers and regulations on the other, can simultaneously create an incentive structure inimical to development. The opposite holds true for societies that have political institutions that allow broad based participation and pluralism, and that have rule of law and constraints and checks on politicians, and that have economic institutions that ensure secure property rights, uphold contracts, offer state support in the form of public services and regulation for markets, and provide access to education and opportunity for the great majority of citizens. These inclusive economic and political institutions facilitate economic growth by encouraging investment, innovation, and the better allocation of resources in more or less competitive markets with low barriers to entry and broad-based participation. Overall, the most important implication of these studies is that institutional make-up has a strong correlation with the ability of societies to deal with both endogenous problems, such as rapid population growth, fast urbanization, and inequality, and also exogenous challenges, such as those induced by the international economic system, climate change, and so on. The more inclusive the governing institutions, the higher is the state's capacity to handle distributional and other types of conflicts without the outbreak of violence. Since no man is an island, conflict is an inevitable feature of societies; this makes the nature of institutions crucial for peace and stability.

Where population growth and environmental problems might lead to conflict and the outbreak of violence, Kahl identified the nature of institutions as one of the two key intervening variables, the other being the existence and the degree of societal cleavages or groupness.[19] Institutional inclusivity[20] and groupness[21] have a bearing on whether demographic and environmental stress, which is a composite variable of rapid population growth, environmental degradation, and unequal renewable resource distribution, will push a state toward failure or exploitation, the two causal pathways to conflict. In countries with high degrees of groupness and exclusive state institutions, the likelihood of conflict is greater, in Kahls's estimation, since it is easier to form conflict groups that overcome collective action problems. Also, exclusive institutions facilitate conflict by providing opportunities and incentives for state elites to engage in violence. Kahl avoids the problem of overestimating the occurrences of civil wars by taking into account the collective action potential of conflicts groups.[22] In an exclusive state, a narrow group of state elites makes decisions that advance their narrow interests; resource scarcities and societal divisions simply present an opportunity to further their narrow interests. Kahl draws our attention away from the dominant state failure hypothesis that sees weak state institutions as the main culprit behind the breakdown of order. His study suggests that state elites could exploit demographic and environmental pressures in order to engineer conflict in highly divisive societies characterized by exclusive state institutions (2006: 50–51).[23] The spread of democracy and the associated development of strong cross cutting civil society are inversely related with the risk of demographic and environmental stress induced violence. Inclusive institutions, again, hold the key to peace.

This brief historical overview of the liberal approaches maps out the most commonly held propositions found in current international politics, namely that democratic states are more peaceful in their relations with each other;[24] that states that are in highly interdependent economic relationship tend to refrain from resolving their disputes by using force; and that states that are part of international institutions tend to refrain from using force in the resolution of conflicts with the other member states. Each one of these propositions comes with policy prescriptions that shape international politics.

The first proposition has important implications for the understanding of international water rights problems. First, it forces us to look at the regime types of conflicting states and analyze what it is about democratic regimes that makes a peaceful resolution of international conflicts possible. The implications of this on the resolution of international water rights conflicts suggest that international watercourse states should be able to institutionalize water rights if they are democratically governed. This is because they have the institutional structure that enables them to make credible commitments and facilitate solutions to collective action problems. Secondly, it has implications on the role of hegemonic states for the viability of international institutions. Is it necessary to have an external enforcer, a hegemonic state, to enforce order and stability in the international system? As we have seen, one of the most important aspects of determining international water rights is about how to enforce international water rights. Monitoring and enforcement of agreements are costly in the international system. If there are no external enforcers, are there no property rights in international watercourses? Or as liberal institutional and normative approaches claim, there is no need for a hegemonic state since international institutions are viable alternatives to a hegemonic state in providing order to the international system. States are capable of creating international institutions and both the existence of strong economic ties and being part of the same international organization facilitate the peaceful resolution of conflicts among states. Indeed, states can solve the problem of violence by creating institutions to govern their affairs. The European Union presents a successful example in this regard. Under which conditions this happens is the question that needs to be answered.

## Domestic Institutions

The normative strand of democratic peace theory argues that democratic norms, culture, perceptions, and ensuing practices allow compromise and the peaceful resolution of conflicts. Liberalism is a shared ideology of democratic states and it strongly sustains the belief in the value of freedom, democratic ideals, and freedom from foreign intervention, while also creating high trust in society, which is better overall for solving collective action problems. Democratic states are assumed to follow similar peaceful methods of solving conflicts arising from the competitive exploitation of resources, including land, natural resources, and so on. To the extent that democracies facilitate the emergence of a culture of compromise and trust, which is also a characteristic of societies that have successfully managed their common pool resources, the higher their chances of reaching peaceful resolutions in domestic and international conflicts.

Furthermore the nature of prevailing institutions plays a key role in the resolution of conflicts. To the degree that domestic institutions are inclusive regardless of regime type,[25] conflicts are more likely be solved through peaceful means. The congruence between inclusive institutions and democracies often leads scholars to argue for the importance of regime type. Here I suggest that institutions, broadly defined to include both formal and informal types, play a critical role in how a society will deal with its current problems and face new challenges. Incentives matter and these are largely determined by the prevailing institutions. The nature of institutions of democracies contributes to the peaceful resolution of conflicts through at least four ways: (1) facilitating the solution of credible commitment problems; (2) reducing uncertainty through information revealing capabilities; (3) creating an incentive structure for elected officials so that they provide public goods to improve the quality of life for the majority of the people rather than adopting adventurous and harmful foreign policies; and (4) making these societies more resilient and immune to the exploitation of ethnic and religious divisions by other actors.

## Institutions Matter

In Chapter 1, I defined institutions as sets of formal or informal rules governing relations among states. Keeping this broad definition of institutions in mind, the democratic peace argument suggests the following: liberal norms and principles along with formal democratic institutions, such as free speech and regular competitive elections of decision makers, make democratic states peaceful in their dealings with each other. Like individuals everywhere, states pursue self-preservation and material well-being as fundamental goals for their survival. These goals are best achieved through peaceful means, because coercive and violent means are always by definition counter-productive and, more importantly, more costly. In fact, the cost of waging war over scarce water resources is likely to be higher than, for example, than generating potable water through the desalinization of seawater, assuming that states have seashores.[26]

Domestic political institutions and norms prevalent in democratic states condition decision makers to use peaceful means for the resolution of conflicts.[27] Electoral accountability, checks and balances, and the state's ability to extract resources from society have all been proposed as viable explanations of democratic peace. The general assumption is that in democracies, foreign policy decisions are debated openly due to the high-level importance attached to foreign policy. This increases public awareness. Both public and elected officials are certainly concerned with the cost of war – human and financial – and since the public will ultimately bear the burdens of any war, there would likely be an electoral backlash compelling decision makers to be more calculative and cautious, particularly if the cost is too high. In democratic states, elected officials are subject to both vertical and horizontal accountability and peaceful means of government turnover are available.[28] Consequently, not only do democratic states seem to be less prone to Lord Acton's well-known proposition that absolute power corrupts absolutely, but they also have strong incentives to address problems that society faces, like economic crises, rapid urbanization, environmental degradation, and so on. In these political systems both the incumbent parties and the opposition have strong incentives to find solutions to problems. Democratic institutional structures make commitments, both domestic and international, more credible and they have an inherent flexibility to address changes. The inbuilt system of checks and balances ensures that the government's commitments to protect property rights, for example, are credible.[29]

The practice of dealing with domestic political conflicts via peaceful means among competing elites strengthens the preference for peaceful means for international conflict resolution. Indeed, democratic conflict resolution mechanisms that rule out both the threat of the use of force and the use of force as viable means to resolve domestic political conflicts certainly have similar effects on the conflict resolution mechanisms of international conflicts. Therefore, it would not be inappropriate to expect democratic states to avoid aggressive military methods in conflict resolution with other states. Decision makers in democratic states are the products of their societies. They are cultivated in an environment where differences of opinion and conflicting interests are settled by negotiations and compromise, and the threat of the use of force and/or the actual use of force to get concessions from the opponents as legitimate options are rejected. Both political and economic institutions in these countries are inclusive and facilitate innovation, adaptation to changing circumstances, and investment, thus generating both political and economic development.[30] As Olson has argued, the conditions necessary for a lasting democracy are the same needed for the security of property and contracts that generate economic growth.[31] In addition, the greater respect for legal principles and the legal system in democratic states leads to a greater reliance and trust in the legal system to solve disputes.[32] Accordingly, democratic states would be more willing to submit their disputes to international arbitration and adjudication rather than use force. In the final analysis, the democratic governance system functions in such a way that it reduces the legitimate means of bargaining for states. Thus, if nothing else, it helps to reduce uncertainty about possible state actions.

Also, it has been noted that democratic states are primarily concerned with their citizens' interests, which are categorically defined as pacific, conciliatory, and compromising. This is the result of an incentive structure created by democratic institutions in line with the dictates of the logic of political survival.[33] Since the public is likely to suffer the most from the effects of any adventure by shouldering the burdens of war both in terms of manpower and finances, the use of force to resolve disputes becomes unappealing. Democratic states for much the reasons do not engage in wars of conquest and plunder. Another important point to note is that the public in democratic states is more likely to be resistant to strategic mythmaking by virtue of having access to information from multiple sources, meaning that it is not easy to incite the public to support an aggressive response to international crises. The existence of the free press, democratic freedoms, and the liberties that individuals enjoy create conditions in which the public are able to question the validity of strategic myths advanced by the decision makers and the opposition.

Democratic domestic political structures are instrumental in generating domestic audience costs and forcing decision makers to be selective and to engage only in the conflicts they are likely to win. The audience cost also makes their commitments more credible. But, whether democracies are pacifistic in general or only towards other democratic states is a contentious issue.[34] Democratic institutions, such as elections, legislatures, judiciary, independent commissions, and so on, constrain the executive branch's ability to embark on foreign policy adventures. These same institutions force the decision makers to be risk-averse. However, under certain circumstance, democratic institutions can push the governments to war, especially in their dealings with non-democracies.[35]

## Information Matters

Traditionally, foreign policy as an arena is insulated from the democratic decision making processes. For instance, in ancient Athens, the Athenian

Assembly delegated foreign policy decisions to the Council of Five Hundred – the executive and preparatory body for the Assembly.[36] This trend has continued in modern times. In most democracies, the executive branch still enjoys greater authority in security matters. The degree to which the war-making powers of the state are centralized in the executive branch likely has substantial effects on the outcomes of decisions.[37] Yet the incentive structure created by democratic institutions constrains the executive to adopt policies that are costly to the public. An attentive and informed public watching foreign policy is important to restrain democratic governments even though foreign policy seemingly insulated and is mostly left to the hands of a few foreign policy decision makers. There are several legitimate reasons behind this delegation of power. First of all, foreign policy historically is considered high politics and consequently governments always hold diplomatic negotiation behind the closed doors. Foreign policy has included national security matters that are deemed to be secret by governments. Information has been kept secret and manipulated by governments in order to strike better deals during negotiations. On the surface, asymmetrical information in this situation appears to work in favor of non-democratic states, since information is power and non-democratic states clearly have more access to it due to the information revealing features of democratic states. But, this also makes democratic states commitments more credible and eases monitoring and enforcement problems.

Secondly, the general public often does not have the necessary information to make informed decisions about foreign policy matters, or put simply in Owen's words 'they pay little attention to the everyday foreign policy.'[38] Most of the time the relations with other states generally do not have a clearly perceivable impact on their daily life and therefore it is not worth the time to invest in learning the details of the issues. This gives autonomy to foreign policy more so than any other policy arena. However, this autonomy is still constrained by inclusive institutions and having to win a majority of votes in elections to stay in office. In democratic societies, elites[39] and the interest groups they represent have different interests and opinions about foreign policies, whether it be a trade policy or a water rights agreements, especially if such policies have distributional consequences and their material well-being is threatened, and they will compete to shape foreign policy to ensure their interests are protected. The competition between the incumbents and the opposition to serve the interest of citizens acts as a constraint on adventurous foreign policies, regardless of the regime type of opposing states.[40] The same mechanisms that lead to peace among democracies should also lead to peace among democratic and non-democratic states. Democratic norms also should function more or less in a similar manner.

Another major contribution of democratic institutions in the peaceful resolution of international conflicts lies in their information revealing capacities. Democratic institutions bring transparency, which in international crises or negotiations helps states signal their intentions and true preferences clearly. Transparency helps by removing any informational asymmetries and thus it makes the breakdown of bargaining negotiations and recourse to methods other than diplomacy less likely. Schultz, using a simple model of crisis bargaining, tests the propositions about the informational properties of democratic states and the institutional constraints.[41] He finds that the informational properties of democratic states make them less likely to engage in bluffing and therefore more likely that the threats made by them are genuine and thus more credible. It is in fact the information revealing capacities of institutional constraints in democratic regimes that matters. These institutional constraints make it harder for states to convince their followers and domestic opponents that the threats are serious and thus bringing accountability and competition and increasing the risks associated with war. Secrecy, on the other hand, can also be a culprit and more of a liability for states in a crisis situation, because even if a state is innocent, official investigations and the subsequent official explanation could easily come too late. Syria has traditionally been a victim of this problem with regards to international terrorism, and consequently on various occasions it has acted inadvertently against its own interests. The official procedure is secretive and takes too long to respond to or comment on current events.

The informational properties of democratic institutions facilitate the conveyance of the decision makers' intentions, logic, and calculations behind policy choices, because they have to sell their policies not only to their followers, but also to their domestic opponents. Open discussion of alternative means to achieve goals or the different terms of settlement might also reduce uncertainty about the causal relationship between the policies adopted and outcomes. Sometimes uncertainty stems from the fact that states are unsure about the means to achieve their goals. Since wars are costly and risky, states have incentives to reach an agreement. Reaching mutually acceptable agreements are determined by the states' ability to overcome informational asymmetries about the preferences and also the best way to achieve goals. Democratic states are at an advantage in revealing information and conveying their true preferences and their willingness to fight better due to the requirements of democratic institutional structure, enabling free, fair, frequent elections and access to multiple sources of information. As Doyle further notes elaborating Kant's list of sources of pacification, the regular rotation of office in democratic states makes the decision makers extra cautious in their policies, particularly in very costly foreign policies.[42]

## Economic Relations Matter

As discussed earlier, the expansion of international commerce and the development of market economies from the sixteenth century on inspired theories about the pacifying role of trade in international relations. With the coming of the free trade era in the nineteenth century, which was characterized by a high level of internationalization and economic interdependence, ideas about the obsoleteness of war began to appear. The ensuing peace movements culminated in the 1928 Kellogg-Briand Pact on the Renunciation of War. World War I and the massive destruction of human lives and countries it engendered were the main impetus behind the Pact. In the Pact, the contracting states 'solemnly declare in the names of their respective peoples that they condemn recourse to war for the solution of international controversies, and renounce it as an instrument of national policy in their relations with one another.'[43]

For the early twentieth century peace movements, wars had become destructive and costly to such an unprecedented extent that it seemed irrational to engage in war. Economic interdependency was highlighted as the key to peaceful resolution of conflicts regardless of the fact that such interdependency is likely a result of a state's choice, with effects on both directions.[44] Economic interdependence as well as some forms of trade dependence sometimes increases conflicts among states.[45] Still, international trade creates strong incentives for states to solve their disagreements through peaceful means, because it generates gains for all states. A common understanding is that since wars disrupt, if not actually eliminate international trade, international trade prevents costly wars.[46] Most neo-liberals concur with these arguments concerning the relationship between trade and war.[47] Furthermore, even if the results were otherwise, wars are by definition costly and risky and losses from trade in comparison to the human losses and material destruction that wars cause, especially modern ones, does not seem to present compelling reasons to avoid war. After all, World War II occurred after the massive destruction of World War I, when classical liberals were pursuing the utopian dream of eradicating war from international relations.[48] Furthermore, the losses from trade disruptions are likely to be uneven among countries. During the years of both world wars, the terms of trade benefited primary goods producers – agricultural, metallurgical, etc. – therefore some states gained from the Wars, notably the US.

Classical liberals and their successors base their views of trade theory on David Ricardo's doctrine of comparative advantage: states should specialize in making what they are most efficient and good at and trade it.[49] From an economic perspective specializing is desirable since it encourages the efficient use of resources. Ricardo developed his theory in 1817 and assumed full employment, the immobility of factors of production, and perfect competition. The theory does not delve into the issue of the distribution of gains and the terms of trade that often favor industry at the expense of agriculture. Also, no economists today disagrees with the idea of trade benefiting states, yet we know more about its varied impact on the internal economies of states and the distribution of gains, which are certainly not distributed equally among and within states. Trade policy has distributional consequences and it creates domestic winners and losers, thus leading to political conflict.[50] In fact, most international agreements of an economic nature likely have domestic distributional consequences, thus identifying relevant stakeholders, who will objectively stand to win or lose from such agreements will help us understand the domestic political conflict and the bargaining position of states. Also, to the extent that the unequal distribution of gains from international trade has an impact on the distribution of the power capabilities of states, it may cause tension and conflict among states.

The international context in which states operate has important implications. The world economy vacillates between periods of openness and closure and likely corresponding business cycles.[51] Krasner correlates openness with the ascendancy of a hegemonic state and closure with its decline.[52] A hegemonic state under certain circumstances thus facilitates the exchange among states. Mansfield, by contrast, replaces the hegemonic state with a concentration of power in the international system and finds a U-shaped relationship between trade and the concentration of power: trade is higher when the concentration of power is very low or very high.[53] More central to our discussion is Gowa and Mansfield's finding that '[. . .] free trade is more likely within, rather than across, political-military alliances.'[54] This somewhat challenges the effectiveness of the trade argument – that is, international economic relations – in further lowering the probability of war among states since the probability of war among allies is already very low. But their finding may also be unique for the time period under consideration. It is important to note that democratic states do not restrict their choice of forming political-military alliances with other democratic states alone. Regardless of regime type, states seek alliances to advance their political, military, and economic interests, and in most cases alliances emerge between states with common interests. Consider, for example, the United States' alliance with the monarchies and the authoritarian states in the Middle East. Pericles' Imperial Athens did the same thing in the late fifth century BC by selectively intervening in some authoritarian city-states in order to create democratic regimes and simultaneously putting up with others, such as oligarchic Lesbos and Samos, in order to protect its interests.

In sum, there are three important consequences of economic relations among states. First, it fosters peace by increasing the wealth of states. International trade is beneficial for all the participants since each state can focus on producing to their comparative advantage and thus enriching themselves in the process. More importantly, wealthy states are often satisfied with the status quo and therefore are less likely to seek change. Furthermore, if all states, particularly those in a watercourse, were economically interdependent, the cost of war would be high enough for the states to refrain from any threat of the use of force, let alone the physical use of force. States are likely to pursue their interests through peaceful means under the conditions of economic interdependency. It can also potentially supply desperately needed issue linkages for settling the conflicts of interests in other areas among states. From this follows the second consequence, the impact of the liberal economic order on participating states is one of economic interdependency, which makes each state even more vulnerable to the breakdown of the relations and more likely to find issue linkages enabling agreements in difficult topics. Thus, by making the breakdown of economic relationships among (watercourse) states prohibitively costly and presenting opportunities for issue linkages, economic interdependence fosters peace in international relations.

Lastly, ever-increasing political and economic cooperation leads inevitably to the emergence of various international institutions. The development of international institutions bolster international peace, because institutions evolve into self-interested actors overtime and acquire some independence, and may eventually become strong enough to force states to act against their parochial interests. Also, if international institutions evolve and acquire a status of supra-national authority, the chances of peace and harmony among states dramatically increase. The existence of a supra-national authority solves one of the most important problems of collective action: the lack of central authority over states to enforce the rule of law and mediate the conflict as they arise through established institutions. Although this argument may be far-reaching, institutions do indeed reduce uncertainty and provide the most needed media for negotiations and conflict resolution. Most importantly, institutions reduce transactions cost when information asymmetries are high.[55]

## International Institutions

A network of institutions crossing national boundaries creates common ties among states. This has long been thought to be another key for international peace. As Keohane has suggested, international institutions are important in facilitating negotiations and in leading to mutually beneficial agreements.[56] Although it could be misleading to consider international institutions as exogenous actors, since institutions are created by states, which rarely allow international institutions to become autonomous actors with supranational authority over them, international institutions do have an impact on outcomes and once they are created they tend to perpetuate inertia making them quite sticky.[57] Indeed, grueling negotiations over institutions can be considered a perfect indication of this impact and the importance of international institutions. However, states form international institutions to further their own interests and their adherence to international institutions is pragmatic. As long as it benefits the states, institutions will endure. For example, the US approach to international institutions, most of which were championed and formed under the US' leadership after World War II, is undeniably pragmatic. There are several additional important ways that institutions facilitate the emergence of mutually beneficial agreements, which we will now consider.

The primary importance of international institutions lies in their capability to reduce uncertainty and therefore transaction costs by increasing transparency and the information available to states.[58] While some neo-liberal scholars, like Keohane, emphasize the importance of the functional/institutional aspect of international institutions, other scholars focus on their normative aspects. Ernst B. Haas' 'epistemic communities' is a prominent conceptualization of the normative-cognitive aspect in which shared beliefs are the central focal point.[59] Defining 'epistemic community' as 'a specific community of experts sharing a belief in a common set of cause-and-effect relationships as well as common values to which policies governing these relationships will be applied,'[60] Haas also sees the primary function of epistemic communities in their ability to reduce uncertainty. To the extent that these networks of experts or institutions are successful in locating common denominators in defining the problems and formulating general strategies to solve these problems in the fields of high complexity and uncertainty, they can facilitate the peaceful resolution of water rights conflicts.

Neo-liberal institutionalism makes a distinction between economic and security issues in international relations and predicts cooperation in economic and environmental issues. Lipson, for example, enunciates the need for 'significantly different institutional arrangements' for economic and security issues,[61] and a higher probability of cooperation in economic and environmental issues, such as water rights. Nevertheless, international water rights conflicts present daunting challenges even for neo-liberal institutionalist theories. The issue of water rights in international watercourses is linked to both economic and environmental issues. Yet, it also has a strong connection with security issues. The intermingling of economic, environmental, and security issues under one rubric presents vastly complex problems for states to overcome in order to achieve cooperative outcomes in international water rights conflicts.

Also, neo-liberal institutionalism presents the threat of cheating or, in other words, non-compliance as the primary obstacle to cooperation as epitomized in the prisoner's dilemma. Non-compliance is a consideration for states, but it is not crucial even in some economic issues. The anarchic international system does not have the guidance of Adam Smith's invisible hand, which involuntarily leads rational actors to achieve peaceful outcomes while pursuing their own best interests. In lieu of the invisible hand other mechanisms have been suggested as guides for international stability. International institutions and hegemonic states have become, from the analytical point of view, the most important and common of such mechanisms.

States have both common interests that create incentives and suitable conditions for cooperation, and conflicting interests that undermine all. At the crux of conflicting interests, there are often security concerns that are deeply entangled in concerns over relative gains. Grieco accused neo-liberal institutionalists for neglecting relative gains concerns and focusing instead on absolute gains.[62] As he observed, today's friends can be tomorrow's enemies by making relative gains a primary concern for state survival. Keohane also concedes the importance of relative gains and the central role of power.[63] As we saw earlier, a state's power capabilities is one of the most important determinants of a state's capabilities, goals, and available means to achieve these goals. States, therefore, are expected to be sensitive and cautious in committing to any type of cooperative arrangement with other states, especially considering the resilience of institutions once formed.

In fact, institutions are resilient, as Keohane observed, even after the needs that precipitated their formation disappear, as they tend not to dissolve. There are two important consequences of institutions' resiliency: (1) it makes it hard for states to create institutions; (2) once institutions emerge, it makes the existence of hegemonic power to enforce compliance redundant. International institutions are presented as means for dealing with collective action problems in the anarchic international system and are underlined as substitutes for a central authority in competition with the hegemonic state.[64] Keohane downsizes the importance of the hegemonic state as an enforcer for the continuation of cooperation.[65] It is possible for self-interested states to pursue common interests. As we saw in Chapter 1, due to the free-riding problem, the possibility of a benefit for a group is not sufficient to produce collective action. In other words, the possibility of avoiding suboptimal outcomes is not always sufficient to force states to cooperate and achieve mutually beneficial outcomes. In cases where a state can get the benefits of cooperation regardless of its participation, free riding is a rational strategy for the state. On the other hand, the collective goods are not going to appear out of thin air if everybody chooses to free ride. At both the domestic and international level, collective goods are produced, and individuals, groups, or states find ways to overcome free riding problems. In most of these cases, success seems to depend on the differences in individual preferences and necessities, as Hardin predicts.[66]

A different explanation comes from neo-institutional studies of common pool resources. Though burdened by collective action problems, in some cases, the users of common pool resources manage to get together and agree on how to share, manage, and secure the long-term sustainability of common pool resources, such as communal forests, fisheries, pastures, ground water systems, irrigation systems, and so on.[67] As one of the leading scholars of common pool resources, Ostrom has argued that the best way to deal with the collective action problems of free riding, commitment, modifying, monitoring, and enforcement of agreements is to let the users design, organize and govern common pool resources by establishing cooperative institutions.[68]

No doubt, the self-government of common pool resources is a more desirable solution to the common pool resources problems than external authority interventions. It may even work, as some existing examples in domestic commons situations indicate. However, there is a good reason why many scholars, including Hardin, believe that cooperation in most cases is not a viable solution. The greatest challenge is to secure the commitments of the users, especially at the international level. Cooperation is supposedly possible if individuals/states think that it will generate higher benefits and effectively prevent/punish defection. Ostrom's examples of successful commons-management regimes share an important feature, which is that they operate within village communities in societies that have fairly strong communal village institutions. In strategic terms, there is a very strong issue linkage, because cooperation in the use of the common pool resource is tied to being part of a village community, which affects one's life and livelihood in many other ways. There are a lot of ways a village community can enforce cooperation by making a non-cooperator's life difficult.

Furthermore, there is a striking resemblance between the contingent commitment of the common pool resources users and the social contact theories developed by Hobbes, Locke, and Rousseau. Ostrom supposes that individuals will be willing to make the following type of contingent commitment: 'I will commit myself to follow the set of rules we have devised in all instances except dire emergencies if the rest of those affected make a similar commitment and act accordingly'[69] As a result, individuals who live in a state of nature with respect to common pool resources, were supposed to enter into a contract with each other by surrendering some of their rights in return for protection and guarantee of the sustainability of common pool resources. The international system has long been acknowledged to exemplify the Hobbesian state of nature, and therefore, this analogy is appropriate and the resemblance is important.

Hobbes established that in the state of nature each individual would be better off if all agreed to exercise self-restraint in his/her pursuit of self-interest and to establish the rules of the game. It is, therefore, quite possible that for purely selfish reasons, individuals can devise the means of enforcement and can ensure the observance of the rules. Although, there is a possibility of gains for each user if he/she cooperates, as long as gains from cheating are higher, the possibility of cheating remains high. In *Leviathan*, Hobbes revealed his solution to this problem: an external authority, which can be public agencies, government, hegemonic states, or international authorities, is required to detect and punish cheaters. Hardin, Olson, and other mostly realists also go along with Hobbes in their prescription to deal with collective action problems.

In *Governing the Commons*, Ostrom challenged this view by highlighting the dangers of formulating policies based on overly generalized collective action theories and by underlining the inadequacies of the tragedy of the commons, the prisoner's dilemma, and the logic of collective action reflected in the real world common pool resources situations. Indeed, the users of common pool resources in those models are assumed to have high discount rates, almost no trust, and, especially in the prisoner's dilemma, no capacity to communicate or enter into binding agreements.[70] In cases of international common pool resources, no external/central authority exists to intervene and restrict state sovereignty. The absence of such an authority to intervene and enforce agreements among sovereign states increases the importance of self-government and self-enforcement mechanisms, in other words institutions,[71] to share and govern international common pool resource, such as international watercourses.[72]

One of the most significant contributions of Ostrom's analysis is that the watercourse states would be willing to make commitments to each other given the possibility of effectual agreements. In real life situations there are many factors facilitating the emergence of agreements among states by diminishing the predicaments of the tragedy of commons or the prisoner's dilemma. The interactions among the watercourse states are continuous; instead of the one-shot prisoner's dilemma games in which states choose their strategies simultaneously and independently of each other, watercourse states play iterated games. Nevertheless, these facilitating factors do not always work and leave us with a need to explain either the disagreement outcome in water negotiations or the existence of partial settlements among some of the international watercourse states.

The contributions, which realist and common pool resources studies offer to our understanding of the conflict in international watercourses, are very illuminating. The tragedy of the commons, the logic of collective action, and the prisoner's dilemma have revealed the possibility that it might be rational for a watercourse state to choose not to cooperate. Individually rational actions do not always produce socially optimal outcomes. Likewise, non-cooperation in an international watercourse might serve the interests of upper watercourse states; their pursuit of self-interest might damage the interests of lower watercourse states and produce collectively sub-optimal outcomes.

Common pool resources studies indicate that it is possible for watercourse states to make contingent commitments and conclude that cooperation among self-interested actors is possible. Facilitating cooperation is the regime type of states. As we saw, democratic norms and negotiations as the preferred means of conflict resolution, which create transnational epistemic community, constitute one of the pillars of the democratic peace argument.[73] The second pillar is the information revealing capabilities of democratic states, which is influential in reducing uncertainty and revealing private information. These are the two firmly grounded important contributions of democratic peace theory to the peaceful resolution of conflicts among states and can be instrumental in the formation of international institutions.

International institutions are formed to reduce transactions costs, to provide both focal points of action and means for coordination among states in order to deal with collective action problems and achieve optimal outcomes in the anarchic international system.[74] The formation process of international institutions suffers from the same problems afflicting reasons behind international institutions. In this context, a hegemonic state appears to be superior. As one the main substitutes of a central authority in the international system, a hegemonic state is the central focus of Hegemonic Stability Theory.[75] The issues related to a hegemonic state's role in ensuring the smooth functioning of international institutions and facilitating the development of strong international institutions are inconclusive in the literature.[76] As for international watercourses, the role of hegemonic states can be instrumental in two different situations: the first is the existence of a hegemonic state within the watercourse, meaning that one of the watercourse states is a hegemonic state, and the second is the existence of a hegemonic state outside of the watercourse. In theory, if there is a hegemonic state in an international watercourse, it can impose the terms of agreement on other watercourse states, secure the compliance of other watercourse states, and punish them in case of violations. Indeed, in the Middle East, the most powerful state often imposes its will on the others or disregards the other states' demands.

In the Euphrates and Tigris watercourse, Turkey has the potential to be a hegemonic state. As an upper watercourse with a higher level of economic development, Turkey is in a very advantageous position with respect to Iraq and Syria. As a result, Turkey has avoided signing any agreement that it does not deem to be in its best interests, and has implemented as many water development projects as possible before any final settlement might be reached. Furthermore, in 1982, Turkey initiated the Joint Technical Committee in an attempt to mitigate the conflict which had intensified due to the unilateral exploitation of the Euphrates/Tigris waters by Turkey and Syria, and to advance its plan for the utilization of water and land resources of the Euphrates/Tigris watercourse. However, Turkey did not succeed in securing the lower watercourse states' compliance. The failure of the Joint Technical Committee and the rejection of its plan for the utilization of water and land resources of the Euphrates/Tigris watercourse indicate that Turkey is powerful enough to avoid settlement of water rights in the Euphrates/Tigris watercourse, yet is not powerful enough to impose its will on the lower watercourse states.

The second situation that we should consider is the existence of a hegemonic state, for example, the US, outside of the watercourse,[77] since the existence of a hegemonic power not only could help the adversaries to settle their disputes but also has the power to enforce the agreement. First, the regional or international hegemonic state should be willing to intervene, or at least should have an interest in the peaceful resolution of international water rights conflicts. Given the current context of the deteriorated political situation in the Middle East, it is not very likely that the US will play an active role in the establishment of a water regime in any of the international watercourses in the Middle East, except the Jordan watercourse.[78] In the case of the Euphrates, on the other hand, the US is likely to avoid further deterioration of the stability in the region following its intervention in Iraq in March 2003. The rebuilding and repairing of Iraq's existing water infrastructure destroyed by the war will take years even once the current insurgency ceases. The longstanding US-Turkish alliance in the region is also a factor that will likely affect the terms of settlement on water rights. Any role played by the US would likely meet with rejection from Syria, which has long been on the US' rogue state lists and is now facing international isolation headed by the US and therefore is suspicious of the US' intentions.[79]

Furthermore, the international and domestic distributional consequences of agreements affect states' choices to cooperate and reach an agreement. It is highly unlikely for a watercourse state to act against its interests and comply with a hegemonic state's plans. There is simply nothing to prevent states from walking away. Even if a hegemonic state's pressures leads watercourse states to establish an international institution to share and govern international water rights, the compliance problem persists. Once established, international institutions, as emphasized by Young, can perform their functions even in the absence of a central government. Nobody, however, can assure their effectiveness or endurance in dealing with problems. The failure of the Joint Technical Committee of the Euphrates/Tigris watercourse is a good example contradicting the argument that a peaceful solution could be attained, if the means were discovered for the contestant states to collaborate on technical and non-political matters. The conditions of political and ideological conflict among the watercourse states make even the achievement of technical cooperation difficult.[80] Aside from the political and ideological conflicts, exogenous challenges, like droughts, also affect the success and failure of international watercourse institutions.

## An Assessment of Liberal Approaches

In this chapter, I have mapped out both the theoretical roots of domestic and international institutional and normative structures and also their effects on the emergence of water rights in international rivers. Any approach or theory which takes into account regime types, in other words domestic political structures, economic interdependence, ethnic and religious divisions, socio-economic and political distribution of goods, domestic political squabbles over the provision and distribution of public goods, and so on, are inherently non-realist theories and likely fall into the category of neo-liberal theories. In general, neo-liberal theories take into account exogenous variations in state preferences and look to the domestic political process to find the origins of state preferences.

I have focused on regime types and their likely effects on the process of foreign policy formation, with particular emphasis on the contributions and weaknesses of democratic peace theory and its alternative explanations. The informational properties of democracies provide the most plausible explanation for democratic peace; having access to information is one of the key factors for explaining the emergence of water rights or the lack of them. Secrecy and its ailments are generally thought to be better cured in democratic than non-democratic regimes thus making them better candidates for successfully resolving water rights issues.

One popular, but still controversial expectation is that democratic watercourse states will not fight over water rights because of their shared democratic ideals, norms, or institutions. The structure and context in which foreign policy is formulated, it is thought, leads predominantly to the emergence of peaceful outcomes among democratic states. The foreign policy decision making processes of democratic states result in the peaceful resolutions of international conflicts either because of democratic political norms or democratic political institutions or the combination of these two. As a result, international water rights conflicts among democratically governed states are likely to be resolved through peaceful means. Democratic peace theory predicts that the more democratic a pair of states, the less likely it is that any international dispute will break out, and if it does break out, the less likely it will escalate to a war. Furthermore, studies on the effects of regime type on foreign policy decision making shows that semi-repressive and semi-exclusionary regimes tend to refrain from lowering their demands, while repressive and exclusionary regimes tend to lower their demands and settle disputes due in part to their anticipation of severe punishment.

Iraq and Syria have been, and to some extent still are ruled by repressive regimes and have refrained from escalating the water rights conflict to a military level with Turkey. The raison d'être behind the continuation of the current status quo, despite urgings on the part of Syria and Iraq to reach an agreement on water rights with Turkey, is their limited freedom of movement in respect to both domestic and international politics. Fearing their future hold on power and also being unable to resolve their differences due to their ideological and personal antagonisms as rival branches of the Ba'th party, leaders in Syria and Iraq before 2003 were not able come together to push Turkey to give concessions on water rights. Since 2003, the situation has been in flux, but will ultimately depend on the outcome of the formation of the government in Iraq, and the resolution of Syrian civil war. The political developments in Iraq and Syria could give rise to the establishment of a democratic state in the lower watercourse. However, as we saw earlier with Iraq, this may not necessarily create the conditions for peace. Quantitative studies indicate that immature democracies are conflict prone and belligerent in their relations with the outside world.[81] In any event, it would take considerable time for stable democratic institutions to take root in both Iraq and Syria.

If domestic political and economic structures have an effect on foreign policy decision making on water rights, two issues need to be addressed: the first one is to determine which domestic sectors have vested interests in the issue, and the second is to determine how their interests translate into foreign policy outcomes. A watercourse state's institutional capacity, especially in dealing with resource depletion and degradation in their portion of the watercourse, has a significant effect on the strategies that it might adopt during water negotiations. The competition over scarce resources has sometimes been fierce not only among states but also internally within states among different interest groups. Domestic sectors that have strong interests in the determination of water rights include not only agriculture and agro-industries, such as textile, food processing and packaging, but also those sectors that depend on hydropower production. Energy is one of the primary inputs determining the costs of products and the primary driving force behind large-scale water development projects. The situation is further complicated if we consider ethnic politics, and the implications for domestic and international politics when the primary beneficiaries, or some cases the target, of these development projects are minorities or ethnically sensitive populations. A state's capacity to deal with these daunting challenges is the direct result of the nature of its political and economic institutions. Inclusive governing institutions are crucial in not only containing violence and but also putting states on the sustainable long-term development path.

The asymmetrical distribution of power among states exacerbates the problems of how to distribute benefits and costs, thus increasing commitment and coordination problems. As we saw before, nature gives the upper watercourse state an advantageous position in negotiations. The cost of the lack of a water rights agreement in the watercourse is minimal to the upper watercourse state, or in relative terms, it is not as high for the upper watercourse states as it is for the lower watercourse states. For a threat to be credible requires the preexistence of strength in terms of both physical and psychological capabilities. Commanding the awe and respect of other states is important, but it is the military capability to inflict damage that really matters and produces the complacent response. It is expected that the terms of any agreement reached on water rights will reflect the relative power position of watercourse states. The powerful watercourse state has a de facto veto power, if not *de jure*, assuming the sovereign equality of states over the terms of settlement. Thus bargaining tends to converge toward the lowest common denominator of the powerful watercourse state's interests.

By limiting the available legitimate strategies to states and also providing information to states by making costly signals unnecessary, democratic institutions and norms may increase the probability of an agreement on water rights. Furthermore, the transparent political process of democratic states provides the required assurances that each state clearly understands the intentions and preferences of the other one and that they are rational and trustworthy. Nonetheless, democratic states still have to deal with the problems of commitment, coordination, enforcement, and reconciling conflicting interests. If the settlement has the power to change the distribution of power, cooperation will be unlikely even among democratic states in situations of conflicting interests. Compliance and enforcement problems become issues sooner or later if the initial agreement does not reflect the interests of agreeing states. Therefore, the question we try to answer is how states reach an agreement that reflects their interests, revealing in the process the secondary nature of compliance and enforcement of agreements problems. If the agreement reflects the distribution of power among states, the interests of the powerful states by definition are going to be protected along with some of the less powerful states' interests in order to eliminate the compliance and enforcement problems. No state would challenge the situation since it is not in their interests to do so.

International institutions and hegemonic states appear to address the problems of commitment and compliance in international relations. Yet, most policy proposals for dealing with collective action problems are not appropriate for international watercourses. On the one hand, the concerns about relative gains undermine a state's willingness to commit, whatever the nature of its regime. On the other hand, the anarchic nature of the international system and state sovereignty weaken an external/central authority's interventions. As Keohane notes, 'International regimes are by no means a substitute for bargaining; on the contrary, they authorize certain types of bargaining for certain purposes.'[82] Accordingly, any attempt to explain different bargaining outcomes within the bargaining framework, which we now turn to, can be very illuminating. The partial agreements governing the international watercourses in the Middle East, such as the 1994 Treaty between Jordan and Israel, the 1959 Treaty between Sudan and Egypt, and the 1989 Treaty between Syria and Iraq, require explanation. Obviously, it is easier to achieve a partial settlement rather than a comprehensive agreement for watercourses, but why is this so?[83] This is what we shall explore next.

# CHAPTER 4

# A BARGAINING FRAMEWORK FOR INTERNATIONAL WATER RIGHTS

> I could never make myself understood; I could never understand what he thought; and he could never understand what I thought.
>
> Mark Sykes' description of his dealings with Lord Kitchener[1]

The emergence of water rights institutions for governing international watercourses requires collective action among watercourse states. Achieving such collective action presents one of the most challenging bargaining problems of our time. As noted earlier, watercourse states have varying degrees of common and conflicting interests with respect to shared water resources and the consequences of non-cooperation, therefore the failure to form comprehensive water rights institutions does not have a uniform impact on them. In fact, though non-cooperation may present socially suboptimal watercourse-wide outcomes and may be more likely be Pareto inefficient, some watercourse states could accrue benefits from such non-cooperation and thus might have a strong preference for the continuation of the current status quo. Building on the collective action theories of common pool resources, as well as the realist and liberal perspectives of conflict and cooperation in explaining such conflicts, the bargaining framework presented below provides a complete model for understanding international water rights conflicts.

The bargaining framework has two general analytical steps. The first one focuses on the specification of state interests. The examination of the formation of states' interests present clues to the varying incentives among watercourse states to settle water rights. Indeed, the relative intensity of a state's preferences, that is the weight a watercourse state places on various outcomes, plays an important role in this. This intensity, in turn, is determined in large part by how the domestic stakeholders are organized and the size of their stakes in the status quo. For example, if powerfully concentrated and organized interests within the watercourse state benefit from the current status quo, that is, the continuation of a lack of clearly defined water rights, reaching an international agreement would be more difficult. Diffuse unorganized interests, on the other hand, would have the opposite impact due to the collective action problems discussed earlier. These societal interests are mediated through states' governing institutions. The nature of governing institutions, whether they are inclusive or exclusive, has an impact on the formation and intensity of watercourse states' interests. The more inclusive the governing institutions, the more incentives for the government to undertake infrastructure projects and provide public goods, such as access to safe drinking water and developing efficient irrigation networks serving the needs of unorganized diffuse interests like farmers. This also indirectly lessens the conflict over water rights, since these societies are more capable of finding solutions to challenges like long droughts, climate change and so on. In these institutional settings, governments are also more likely to take into account local conditions and to incorporate users into the decision making process, and by doing so adopting more appropriate bottom up approaches to problems. The more exclusive the governing institutions, on the other hand, the lower the incentives are to provide public goods, the greater the likelihood of top down approaches to water problems with minimal regard to local context, and the more likely those in power are to blame external forces for the problems and the plights of citizens.

The next step following the specification of watercourse states' interests is the specification of the strategic setting in which the bargaining takes places. The nature of the parameters of watercourse states' choices is crucial for understanding international water rights conflicts. Any concerns over state capabilities and their resolve, in addition to the collective action and commitment problems, could become increasingly disabling in the face of a continuously shifting context, especially if the majority of watercourse states do not have institutions, formal and informal, that facilitate the credibility of their commitments and the solution of collective action problems. The continuously shifting context could originate from foreign interventions as well as regional sources. Indeed the instability of the Middle Eastern subsystem relative to other regions is often the result of frequent foreign interventions. My main argument here relates to how the volatility of the context of inter-state bargaining adversely affects the outcomes by contributing to uncertainty. In general, two immediate types of uncertainty could imperil watercourse states in an attempt to reach an agreement: (1)

uncertainty about each other's preferences, goals, and capabilities, and (2) the causal relationship between the policies adopted and the desired outcomes. The best way to achieve a stated goal is not always obvious and some ways could be even counterproductive. Uncertainty is one of the prime reasons behind the conflicting expectations of watercourse states.

In the following sections, I bring together the theoretical findings of the preceding chapters identifying the main causal mechanisms and conditions leading to the emergence of comprehensive water rights institutions in international watercourses. It begins with the introduction of the main concepts, assumptions, and key variables of the bargaining framework. It then discusses the main complexities hampering successful collective action among watercourse states focusing on credibility and commitment problems and the role of international institutions and third parties in overcoming bargaining bottlenecks in the path leading to the emergence of water rights in international watercourses.

## The Foundations of the Bargaining Framework

As Young noted in *Bargaining Formal Theories of Negotiation* more than a quarter century ago, although the concept of bargaining has achieved an influential position in social science, there is little consensus among scholars about the content of the concept.[2] This is largely due to the complex nature of bargaining as a social science concept. For example, focus on different aspects of bargaining leads to the formulation of different theories and makes it impossible to talk about the 'Theory of Bargaining' per se. A focus on outcomes, for instance, has led scholars to formulate static theories, while a focus on the processes through which outcomes emerge has generated several dynamic theories of bargaining. Yet there are two crucial common themes tying all these conceptions and theories of bargaining together. In every case, as Young notes, 'bargaining is conceptualized as means (though not the only one) through which purposive actors can reach specific settlements or outcomes under conditions of strategic interaction or interdependent decision-making.'[3]

I define bargaining in a similar but broader fashion. Bargaining is a process through which states try to find the other's acceptable minimum terms of settlement; besides negotiations it also includes the threat of use of force and the use of force. Following Schelling, war is seen here as a continuation of the bargaining process,[4] 'in which threats and proposals, counterproposals and counter threats, offers and assurances, concessions and demonstrations, take the form of actions rather than words, or actions accompanied by word.'[5] The use of force and the threat of use of force here have a function similar to the role of strikes. Indeed, under certain circumstances, the use of force and the threat of use of force can allow states to signal their intentions credibly and can also cause an overlap in the bargaining range by revealing information.[6] Thus when negotiations fail, states continue bargaining but choose to do so by other means leading to different outcomes.

Both alternatives to a negotiated settlement, namely the continuation of the status quo or the escalation of the conflict, mean to varying degrees the continuation of the conflict. The escalation of the conflict does not necessarily lead to the actual use of force; in some cases the threat of the use of force, the risk of war, may be enough. The real source of bargaining power, as Schelling states, 'comes from the physical harm a nation can do to another nation, which is reflected in notions like deterrence, retaliation, terrorism, and wars of nerve, nuclear blackmail, armistice and surrender, as well as in reciprocal efforts to restrain that harm in the treatment of prisoners, in the limitations of war, and in the regulation of armaments.'[7] The escalation of the conflict to military levels thus could serve as one of the means by which states attempt to reach a negotiated settlement if states fail to convey their resolve on the issue and choose to change the current status quo.

Though available as an option, the escalation of a conflict to include the deployment of troops along a border and limited cross-border strikes, rarely leads to the outbreak of wars when the driving issue of an interstate conflict is solely water rights.[8] The empirical evidence from the Euphrates/Tigris watercourse suggests that the threat of use force and indirect interventions, in the form of covert support of insurgent movements, are more likely to be employed for the purpose of creating an overlap in the bargaining range or of strengthening a weaker bargaining position.[9] The existence of clear power asymmetries among watercourses states also acts as a direct deterrent to the escalation of a conflict to military levels.[10] Given the availability of alternative means, the inherent unpredictability and the costs of wars make the escalation of the conflict to military levels too risky.[11] In many international watercourses the clear power asymmetries dramatically increases the range of bargaining solutions that are preferable to violence. So, even though water wars are unlikely, the relative power capabilities that make the threat of use of force and the risk of war credible do matter in explaining outcomes in water rights conflicts.

Central to all bargaining situations is strategic interaction. Young defines strategic behavior as 'the behavior of any individual member of group involving a choice of action contingent upon that individual's estimates of the actions (or choices) of others in the group, where the actions of each of the relevant others are based upon a similar estimate of the behavior of group members other than himself.'[12] States' choices of a strategy to achieve desired outcomes are interdependent. As Jervis notes:

> if he is to decide intelligently how to act, a person must predict how others will behave. If he seeks to influence them, he needs to estimate how they will react to alternative policies he can adopt. Even if his actions do not affect theirs, he needs to know how they will act in order to tailor his actions accordingly.[13]

Snidal also emphasizes the pervasiveness of strategic interaction among states that

> [real international issues lead] directly to a strategic rationality which incorporates the realization that pursuit of egoistic interest requires consideration of interactions of one state's choices with other state's choices. No state can choose its best strategy or attain its best outcome independent of the choices made by others [. . .] [and] the distinguishing trait of strategic rationality is that actors choose courses of action based on preferences and expectations of how others will behave.[14]

Watercourse states engage in strategic interaction in an attempt to settle water rights.

The process of resource allocation through bargaining between two parties that have both common and conflicting interests is widespread in the modern world.[15] Operating under the conditions of uncertainty, watercourses states with both conflicting and common interests also seek to allocate water rights through bargaining. Their choices are interdependent: a choice of one strategy over others depends on what a watercourse state expects its counterparts are likely to do while assuming that the counterparts are doing the same thing. Furthermore, for watercourse states this also entails attempts to alter their own or their counterparts' situation, especially if they are in weak positions.

Generally speaking, reaching an agreement on water rights in international watercourses requires that states' minimum terms of settlement be compatible with each other. In other words, when no state is asking for more than the other one is willing to give up, the water rights issue should be settled easily unless there are strong incentives for avoiding the formalization of water rights.[16] The Euphrates/Tigris watercourse states have been unsuccessful in reaching a negotiated settlement that all prefer because each side expects to gain more than the acceptable terms of settlement that each state is willing to accept. When Iraq's minimum terms of settlement change to commensurate with what the middle and upper watercourse states, Syria and Turkey, are willing to give, and Syria changes its terms to commensurate with what the upper watercourse state, Turkey, is willing to give up for the usage of lower watercourse states, the water rights conflict would likely be resolved. In this framework, any change in a watercourse state's minimum terms of settlement is a function of new information about the possible outcomes of the conflict, namely the continuation of the status quo, the escalation of the conflict, and the negotiated settlement.

By generating conflicting expectations about the possible terms of the settlement, private information feeds into informational asymmetries heightening transactions costs. States have private information about their relative power capabilities, resolve, and the expected costs and consequences – both domestic and international – of various outcomes. They also have incentives to misrepresent this information. These incentives may include a desire to overstate a state's power capabilities and resolve and to understate the cost of outcomes short of a negotiated settlement in order to get better terms. If a state wants to reduce the probability of the escalation of a conflict to military levels, and limit their vulnerability, it would likely overstate the expected cost of war and its relative power capabilities and resolve. Alternatively, states might want to understate their relative power capabilities and resolve if, for example, there is a chance of balancing by other watercourse states. A combined effect of private information and incentives to misrepresent private information is the inconsistency of expectations about the cost of different outcomes and of what each watercourse state can secure. All this feeds into informational asymmetries preventing watercourse state from locating an acceptable bargain. The cure for conflicting expectations is the revelation of more information about states' relative power capabilities, resolve, and the cost of various outcomes. This presents one of the most compelling answers for how and when states change their minimum terms of settlement.

In addition to private information, uncertainty surrounding the international and domestic consequence of potential outcomes factor in watercourse states' conflicting expectations. Each outcome has a different cost-benefit structure that is also subject to change overtime. A preference of any other outcome over a negotiated settlement is determined by a comparison of domestic and international consequences of all outcomes at a given time period (Figure 4.1).

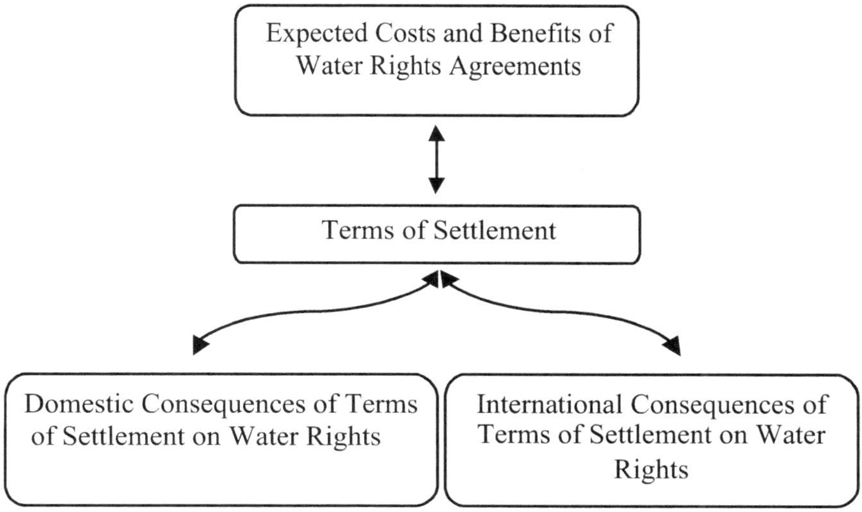


**Figure 4.1.** Determinants of the Expected Costs and Benefits of Agreements.

## Bargaining Framework for International Water Rights

Four general assumptions follow from the previous discussion:

### *1. States are purposeful agents*

States try to maximize their expected benefits. Each state will calculate the expected costs and benefits of each available course of action.

### *2. States are adaptive*

Through learning states change the minimum terms of settlement in accordance with new information about the outcome of a different course of action and about the probability of securing better/worse terms of settlement in the future. Any new information has an impact on the cost/benefit calculations of the continuation of the current status quo and other actions since states update their estimates and expectations as a result of what they learn.

### *3. States engage in strategic interaction*

Strategic interaction is the central feature of all bargaining situations. Watercourse states engage in strategic interaction in an attempt to adjudicate their common and conflicting interests on water rights in international watercourses. Their choices are interdependent: a choice of one strategy over others depends on what a watercourse state expects its counterparts are likely to do when assuming that their counterparts are doing the same thing.

### *4. States try to reconstruct choice situations in order to manipulate outcomes*

Heresthetic is the name given to the art of constructing choice situations so as to be able to manipulate outcomes. Rationally, states that are in weak positions try to change the current bargaining situation either by attempting to alter their own or their counterparts' situation. Preference intensity of watercourse states varies and status quo bias favors the watercourse state with the least interest in the determination of water rights. Again, this is consistent with the general assumption that states try to reconstruct choice situations in order to manipulate the outcome.

Throughout history, water has been claimed to be private, public, and common property. The tradition of treating water as a public good – a provision expected to be free of charge – presents challenges to states, especially in the developing world. Historically, states provided water to their population free of charge or at a very low nominal charge. The idea of treating water as a private good is therefore difficult to accept in many societies. Water resources, like all natural resources, are valued because of their potential contribution to economic development. In many less-developed and developing countries, an adequate provision of these resources is the main challenge for states. If a state fails to provide water for the needs of its people and agriculture – typically the main sector of the economy and often the main source of gross national product in developing countries – the consequences will be detrimental to those in power.

The institutional capabilities of states are important for determining the severity of water scarcity conditions for the domestic political system. Sound and effective management of water resources directly affects water availability and the severity of scarcity conditions. The success of economic policies aimed at improving the well-being of the society will determine the longevity of the party in power in democracies and the legitimacy of the rulers in authoritarian states. In this regard, states with inclusive political and economic institutions are better able to cope with conflicts arising from water scarcity as well as other economic or ethnic conflicts. The domestic political consequences of a failure to meet the water needs of the people can be costly and could contribute ultimately to the incompatibility of the terms of settlement among watercourse states.

Furthermore, under certain circumstances, domestic considerations could even create incentives for states, especially those with exclusive political and economic institutions, to initiate a limited international crisis in order to avoid internal culpability while offering a means for blaming external factors, that is, other watercourse states, for the scarcity conditions afflicting people. Certainly at times governments have incentives to escalate international conflicts in order to avoid dealing with domestic political issues or to distract public attention from domestic politics. This is often done to cover up political, economic, and institutional failures. Occasionally, governments may just need an excuse to crack down on opposition groups. For example, the 1975 water crisis provided the Syrian Ba'thists with a pretext for expelling regime dissidents and consolidating their hold on power.[17] In other cases, rulers could intentionally escalate the conflict if there is the likelihood of severe domestic political consequences for agreeing on the opponents' terms of settlement. If the terms of settlement on water rights are unacceptable to the general public because of reasons other than the terms of settlement, rulers will likely avoid agreeing on the terms settlement, not because the terms are unacceptable, but for the political consequences of the agreement. For instance, it may not be acceptable for Syrian leaders to sign a treaty over the Orontes River water rights if it means the official recognition of Alexandretta as Turkish territory. Syrian leaders may not feel secure enough in their position – domestic and international – to sign such a treaty even if they stand to benefit from a water rights agreement in economic terms. Severe domestic political consequences include a removal from power in democracies by elections, or undermining the legitimacy of those in power in semi-authoritarian or authoritarian regimes that can trigger *coups d'etat* or political upheaval and discontent. As this line of thinking alludes, the regime type of a state and its institutional features are instrumental for the choice of strategies that impinge upon the challenges of governance. Political actors are primarily concerned with their (political) survival and depending on the regime's institutional structure the available strategies for achieving their goals and the consequences of each vary.

The international consequences of water rights are no less important than the domestic political consequences. International water resources have a capacity to generate wealth, but they also have a capacity to generate interdependencies, vulnerabilities, and distributional tensions. In general, water rights refer to the delineation of rights and duties with respect to the allocation, usage, and regulation of water resources among all watercourse states. The water rights institutions might be both formal and informal. The absence of formal institutions does not necessarily mean chaos or the existence of Hobbes's state of nature in international watercourses. In most watercourses, a de facto regime, which is established often by bi-lateral treaties involving some of the watercourse states, is in place. The uncertainty over the final settlement of water rights could still create fertile ground for conflicts and a treacherous environment for the development of water resources.

Geopolitics creates asymmetric costs, benefits, control, and bargaining leverage for watercourse states. The issues related to international watercourses indicate that the conflicting interests of lower and upper watercourse states in international watercourses are hard to reconcile. In international watercourses, a combination of geographic position and relative power capabilities determines the relative strength of states' bargaining positions, for example, an upper watercourse position makes the ability to bear and impose costs high for upper watercourse states. In contrast, a lower watercourse position decreases the ability to endure costs for lower watercourse states even if they have comparatively strong power capabilities.

In combination with geographic position in the international watercourse, the distribution of power reinforces the asymmetric costs, benefits, control, and bargaining leverage for watercourse states. As discussed in Chapter 2, the Realist perspectives emphasize states' power capabilities as the most important variable in determining the outcome of international crises.[18] Accordingly, relations among states are often relations of power, and the behavior of states is expected to be a function of the distribution of power. Indeed, in international watercourses power capabilities determine states' preferences, goals, and strategies available to achieve these goals. Powerful states can afford to avoid a negotiated settlement if it runs against their interests, and can compel other states to change their terms and offer issue linkages and side payments to achieve their desired outcomes. Furthermore, the existence of power discrepancies among conflicting states likely deters the escalation of a conflict into a war due in part to the fact that weaker states are less likely to challenge the 'vital' water interests of other watercourse sates. A state's relative power capabilities are closely linked to the use of force or the threat of the use of force in international crises. States use (the threat of the use of) force as often as other bargaining strategies to achieve their goals. Indeed, coercive cooperation that manifests itself in imposed agreements, or even some negotiated settlements, contains (the threat of use of) force as one of its primary means. Weak states can also use force in order to prove their resolve or to prove that strong states underestimated their power capabilities. The use of force, in this context, functions as a way of revealing private information about relative power capabilities, thus it is a way for weak states to get better terms in a settlement.

To understand states' actions in international watercourses, consideration should be given to a state's geographic position in the watercourse, its relative power capabilities with regard to the other watercourse states, its international relations with other watercourse states, as well as the watercourse states institutional capabilities, though this is directly related to state power. Furthermore, informational asymmetries and prevailing (mis)perceptions about other watercourse states' preferences, goals, and capabilities during the policy making process is crucial in determining a watercourse state's course of action in international watercourses. Not only are states limited in their ability to process information, but states are also opportunistic, that is to say they have incentives to misrepresent private information in order to extract better terms of settlement.[19] Thus, elevated by the uncertainty inherent in the anarchic international system, the distortion of information about watercourse states' preferences, goals, relative power and institutional capabilities to achieve these goals commonly results in increased transactions costs. The cost of gathering information in the process of making informed decision in strategic situations gives rise to transactions costs. In this context, transactions costs include the costs of the search for information about other watercourse states' true positions, the costs of defining and measuring resources and the credibility of watercourse states' claims and threats. In short, transactions costs are the costs of preparing, negotiating, concluding, and enforcing agreements in international watercourses.

To summarize, the factors that play a crucial role in the (non-)emergence of water rights are:

1. The geographic position in the watercourse
2. The distribution of relative power capabilities in the watercourse
3. The states' institutional features
4. The transactions (information) costs
5. The context of international relations at all levels: a) bi-lateral; b) regional; c) system levels

The bargaining process through which water rights emerge is essentially a political one and the domestic and international consequences of water

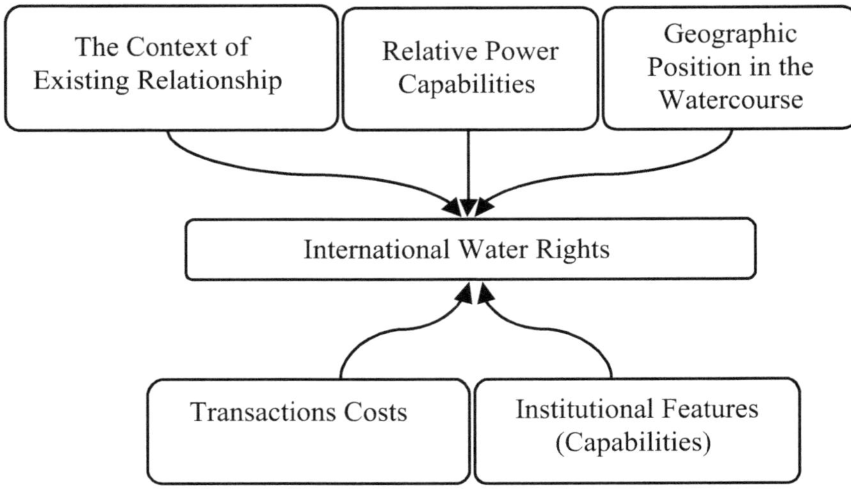


**Figure 4.2.** Explaining Water Rights Conflicts.

rights determine the terms of a negotiated settlement on water rights, but in turn they are affected by the final settlement making the task of locating an agreement rather complex. As we have seen, the geographic position in the watercourse creates real conflicts of interest over water rights. Lower watercourse states are likely to support a negotiated settlement often formalizing their historical rights, while major contributor states, especially if they are powerful and well positioned, are likely to oppose it.[20] In these situations, negotiated settlement is possible only if upper watercourse states concede to release more water or promise not to develop water resources in return for some sort of compensation. It is very likely that the factors contributing to the durability of negotiated settlement in the sharing and managing of international watercourses lead to inefficiencies in exploiting resources.

Often the negotiated settlements that are most likely to emerge and survive are those that contribute least to economic efficiency. This is because any agreement on water rights has distributional implications within and among the watercourse states. Any negotiated settlement that has a chance of changing the distribution of power capabilities among states triggers problems, such as the commitment problem. A watercourse state's expectations about its adversaries' actions determine the choice of one strategy over others in dealing with the degradation or depletion of water resources. Thus, they include in their expected cost/benefits calculations any future undesirable outcome of the negotiated settlement. Marginal benefits of any additional demands should be less than the marginal cost of securing them. Furthermore, by creating asymmetric costs, benefits, and bargaining advantage for conflicting states, upstream/downstream positions in international watercourses exacerbate the political intricacies surrounding international water rights conflicts.

The anticipated benefits of a continuation of the current status quo/de facto water regime and the anticipated benefits of an escalation of the conflict depend on the expectations about the future terms of settlement. A state may prefer a continuation of the current status quo, if the upper watercourse expects better terms of settlement in the future as it completes more water projects, for example. States also have expectations about their counterparts' actions and make decisions based on these expectations. Through a process of bargaining, states try to find each other's reservation values, in other words, the minimum terms of settlement. As long as a watercourse state asks more then what the others are willing to give up, a bargaining space will not open up. For this to happen, at least one state's reservation values/minimum terms of settlement should change. A reservation value depends on both the value of proposed negotiated settlement and the value of alternatives to negotiated settlement. If the values of alternative outcomes are higher than the value of a negotiated settlement for a state, it will not change its minimum terms of settlement. If the alternative outcomes become costly, a state will likely lower its minimum terms of settlement allowing a bargaining space to appear.

There are several conditions of a negotiated settlement in international watercourses. First, the terms of the agreement have to be acceptable to all sides. Secondly, at least in appearance, the benefits of reaching an agreement should exceed the use of force or the status quo. And third, all watercourse states should believe that securing better terms is unlikely. Agreements, of course, are also subject to revisions and transgressions are always a possibility. States often implicitly assume a certain amount of defection in an agreement and accept this because it is better than no agreement at all. Good institutional designs feature mechanisms to address transgressions and to allow modifications when the conditions call for it. What makes negotiated settlements self-enforcing is primarily the lack of incentives for states to renege on their commitments. A negotiated settlement by definition refers to a situation, an equilibrium, in which states have no desire to change the terms they agreed upon and there is no reason to expect other states to defect.

In other words, a negotiated settlement is an outcome of states being able to make credible commitments to each other on the agreed upon terms.

There are several factors that lead to a disagreement outcome in international watercourses: the existence of private information concerning relative capabilities and/or resolve and incentives to misrepresent such information, which prevent states from locating a mutually preferable agreement.[21] Each state has private information about strength and resolve, and this generates conflicting expectations about the other side's minimum settlement terms.[22] Furthermore, a state's tendency to misrepresent private information exacerbates watercourse dilemmas. In this environment, crises, the threat of the use of force, and low intensity military operations are among some of the means that reveal private information as tools of the bargaining process. The shifting domestic and international contexts also contribute to the conflicting expectations among states about each other's minimum terms of settlement, causing delays and failures. In addition to the existence of private information, incentives to misrepresent such information, and shifting domestic and international political contexts, the conveyance of private information credibly might also cause delays and failures.[23] All these variables feed and exacerbate states' conflicting expectations about the terms of settlement that they could get from the other states involved.

The issue of credible commitments is also central to bargaining. The credible conveyance of intentions to other sides in bargaining situations is crucial in overcoming informational asymmetries. Not only is successful bargaining all about the credible conveyance of intent to other parties but it is also a foundation of any negotiated settlement and a cure for a commitment problem. It would be impossible to reach a negotiated settlement if the credibility of one of the negotiating states is in question. Bargaining failures are often the result of a state's failure to convey its intents credibly to the other side. The inherent credibility of different threats and commitments vary in accordance with the importance of states' interests in the issue of dispute. Threats are often more credible if the issue is salient and the stakes are high.

## Credibility and Commitment Problems

In international relations, disagreement outcomes occur because all the interested parties have reservation values that preclude bargaining space. An upward/downward change in the minimum terms of settlement shifts states' goals and creates a bargaining space thus enabling states to reach a negotiated settlement. Among the three potential outcomes – namely, the negotiated settlement, the continuation of the status quo, and the escalation of the conflict – the last two imply the continuation of disagreement outcomes. In some cases, the continuation of the status quo leads to the emergence of a de facto water rights regime in the watercourse. Informal agreements can bring stability to the watercourse if at least one of the watercourse states is unwilling officially to commit itself to a water rights agreement and other watercourse states are not willing to use (the threat of the use of) force in addition to having their current demands adequately fulfilled. As I noted before, (the threat of the use of) force often is one of the last bargaining tool states employ in order to credibly convey their intents or extract concessions from other states.

Fearon sets forth three causal mechanisms that explain the use of force.[24] The first is related to two interconnected facts: (1) that states have private information about their capabilities and resolve and, (2) that they have incentives to manipulate, misrepresent, or withhold that information in order to maximize their leverage. The second causal mechanism derives from the problem of commitment under the conditions of anarchy, and the third relates to the problem of 'issue indivisibility,' which refers to the lack of mutually satisfactory outcomes. Often states cannot find mutually satisfactory outcomes, because in any bargaining situation, states have incentives to dissemble or manipulate information to increase their leverage over other parties. If it is the incongruity between the actors' true and perceived capabilities and resolve that prevents a change in bargaining position, then we should observe bargaining between an upper watercourse state and a lower watercourse state characterized by bluffing for various reasons. For example, to avoid appearing like a bully to third parties, an upper watercourse state might signal to a lower watercourse state that it does not demand as many policy changes as it really wants; this could lead a lower watercourse state to fail to reduce its own range of acceptable outcomes enough to placate the upper watercourse state. Or the lower watercourse state might exaggerate its ability to harm the upper watercourse state's interests in the hope of forcing it to release more water, but that bluff might cause the upper watercourse state to see the lower watercourse state's threats as non-credible and display its military capabilities to prevent the lower watercourse state's harmful policies.[25] An upper watercourse state can also easily underestimate the relative power capabilities and resolve of a lower watercourse state. In order to prove that a lower watercourse state is not as weak as an upper watercourse state assumes, a lower watercourse state can initiate war to change an upper watercourse state's position with respect to the water rights. Watercourse states will not change their positions if one or more actors denies the others information about its true capabilities and/or resolve. States always deny access to some information, which reduces the chances of finding an agreement space. In a competitive, self-helping international system, information is an instrument of strategic actors; it can be true or false; it always serves a purpose.

A lower watercourse state can try to reconstruct the choice situation by making it, for example, more costly to reject concession demands. There are several options available in such a case. First, a lower watercourse state can make an alliance with other lower watercourse states to present a strong front against an upper watercourse state. An upper watercourse state will likely give concessions in the face of a common front, which will limit an upper watercourse state's capabilities to exploit the differences between the lower watercourse states. Another option for a lower watercourse state is to exploit any internal instability in an upper watercourse state by supporting clandestine groups – ethnic, religious, or ideological. This is more likely if the other state does not have inclusive governing institutions. Offering issue linkages – compensations, free trade, preferred treatments for investors, cooperation in other areas – constitutes another possible policy option to change state's preferences.

Although none of the watercourse states would see this openly as a preference, another option is to decrease the dependency on water resources by altering the consumption structure. States need to be flexible to utilize different conceptual approaches to adapt to different factual contexts that the watercourse presents. Population growth, for example, puts enormous pressure on scarce natural resources and in the long run it might be best to use water resources in accordance with the logic of economic efficiency. This would mean, for example, a reallocation of water resources from agriculture to industrial and urban use, or an application of water efficient irrigation methods, such as drip irrigation or of dry land farming methods and drought resistant seeds. This is predicated on state capacity, and as we saw earlier, the inclusivity of governing institutions is also a pre-requisite.

The threat of the use of force and the use of force are options for states that should not be disregarded. Force and the threat of its use constitute a means of last resort through which states convey their resolve and intentions credibly and prove that other states underestimated their power capabilities and resolve. In international watercourses, if a threat of the use of force is credible and comes from a strong challenger who wants to reach a negotiated settlement, the emergence of water rights is more likely (Table 4.1). For example, if the distribution of relative power capabilities is in favor of the

Table 4.1. Conditions for the Emergence of Water Rights in International Watercourses.

| | Credible Threat | Non-credible Threat |
|---|---|---|
| Strong challenger | More likely | Indeterminate |
| Weak challenger | Indeterminate | Less likely |

lower watercourse state, which has a strong stake in a negotiated settlement, the position of a lower watercourse presents a powerful challenge to the upper watercourse states. Since a lower watercourse state has a strong stake in the sustainability of its water development projects and the current and estimated future water consumption, any threat of the use force coming from a lower watercourse can therefore be instrumental in bringing about a settlement of water rights. However, if the threat is not credible and comes from a weak challenger who wants to change the existing status quo, the emergence of water rights is less likely (Table 4.1). If the strong challenger makes a non-credible threat or a weak challenger makes a credible threat of the use of force, the emergence of water rights will be indeterminate.

International and domestic political conditions and any change in them would likely affect the cost–benefit structure of watercourse states. States' adaptive capabilities, which are also a function of their institutional capabilities, come to the fore when there is new information either favorable or unfavorable to their position in the watercourse, since the new information has an impact on the likelihood of the emergence of water rights in the watercourse. If the information is favorable to both upper and lower watercourse states, reaching a negotiated settlement becomes less likely (Table 4.2). On the other hand, if the information is unfavorable to both states, reaching an agreement would become more likely. An illustration of this is the signing of the 1989 treaty determining the water rights concerning the Euphrates between Iraq and Syria. In the face of

Table 4.2. States' Adaptive Capabilities: New Information and Water Rights.

| | Favorable new info for A | Unfavorable new info for A |
|---|---|---|
| Favorable new info for B | Reaching a negotiated settlement is less likely | Indeterminate |
| Unfavorable new info for B | Indeterminate | Reaching a negotiated settlement is more likely |

the threat from the upper watercourse state's near completion of a major dam, both Syria and Iraq managed to leave aside their differences and signed a treaty dividing the water coming from Turkey between them.

Table 4.2 indicates that if new information is positive for one of the two watercourse states, reaching a negotiated settlement would be indeterminate. It could either lead to the escalation or the continuation of the status quo depending on the configuration of a watercourse state's geographic position and power capabilities. If the new information is favorable for all watercourse states, a negotiated settlement would be less likely. Here 'favorable' means that the cost of non-agreement is reduced. The status quo will prevail. If new information is negative for all watercourse states, for example, the resource is in grave danger, a negotiated settlement would be more likely. Any negative new information would change states' willingness to concede and accept each other's minimum terms of settlement. Negotiated settlement occurs when there is formal agreement delineating water rights. The continuation of the status quo does not always indicate a lack of water rights. There is often a de facto, informal agreement regulating water rights. The escalation of conflict refers to situations where the threat of the use of force is issued or the use of force has occurred leading to a crisis in the watercourse. This is by its very nature an intermediate outcome; it could either lead to a formal agreement or to a continuation of the status quo ex ante.

A disagreement outcome occurs because bargaining states have reservation values precluding a bargaining space. An upward or downward change in the minimum terms of settlement shifts goals and creates a bargaining space, which enables states to reach a negotiated settlement. The expected benefit of any agreement on water rights depends on the domestic and international consequences of that settlement and it is subject to the effects of the developments in the international and domestic arenas. As benefit maximizers, states need to be responsive to input from the domestic and international systems. As a result, states adapt and utilize new information to make decisions to protect their interests.

The commitment problem in an anarchical system, that is, the difficulty of trust in the absence of reliable mechanisms to enforce agreements, is inherent to all international cooperation. Yet states do cooperate with each other. Indeed, states are capable of making credible commitments and the inability to do so often indicates a lack of incentives in negotiated settlements on the issues of conflict. The cost of disagreement outcomes is not high enough for states to force them to prefer negotiated settlement to other outcomes.

## The Role of International Institutions and Third Parties

Why should a watercourse state change its minimum terms of settlement and cooperate when it runs against its economic and domestic political interests? Cooperation in international watercourses, including a negotiated settlement of conflicts to achieve a mutually beneficial outcome, can take two different forms: coordinative/co-adjustment cooperation and coercive cooperation. The first type is likely to emerge if the distribution of power among watercourse states is more or less equal. In order to avoid sub-optimal outcomes, watercourse states are likely to prefer cooperation to the status quo or to the deterioration of the conflict into a wider one. In coordinative/co-adjustment cooperation, iteration and institutions facilitate watercourse states' efforts to overcome collective action dilemmas by making tit-for-tat bargaining strategies more effective, by increasing the influence of the shadow of the future on a state's considerations, and by reducing the transactions and information costs.

The clear power asymmetries among the watercourse states, on the other hand, make the coordinative/co-adjustment type of cooperation highly unlikely for Middle Eastern watercourses. The second form of cooperation, coercive cooperation, is likely to emerge if the distribution of power is asymmetrical and the stronger watercourse states have vested interests in the determination of water rights. In the absence of other incentives, it is unlikely that strong watercourse states will agree on water rights and refrain from water development projects that are deemed to be crucial for the advancement of their economic well being. To date, there is no indication of a comprehensive negotiated settlement of water rights in any of the Middle Eastern watercourses, which underlines the necessity of creating artificial incentives.

The norms and expectations established by the community of users leading to a voluntary submission to the rules seems to be an elusive one in international watercourses, since there is neither an idea of community *vis-à-vis* international watercourses nor urgency on the part of some watercourse states to establish water rights. Even for lower watercourse states that have strong interests in establishing water rights, there are some offsetting factors at present. For instance, each completed water project can provide grounds for acquired rights claims; accordingly, the absence of clearly defined water rights does not prevent lower watercourse states from planning and building water projects in their portion of the watercourse, which undermines the urgency of reaching an agreement. Indeed, in many international watercourses today, watercourse states with strong military and economic capabilities are trying to complete as many water projects as possible before the final settlement of water rights regardless of their geographic position. Furthermore, despite the stated requirements of international organizations, such as the International Monetary Fund, the World Bank, and so on, upper watercourse states are able to fund their water projects without obtaining the prior consent of lower watercourse states.

The role of international institutions has also been discussed in creating incentives and thus promoting cooperation among states. Political economists and regime theorists argue that institutions satisfy the functional need for agreements in an environment of ever-increasing international interdependence and help to lower transactions costs thus helping to overcome collective action problems better than any hierarchical solutions.[26] Institutions, once they are created, have an undeniable affect on state preferences and bargaining strategies. In fact, they are the by-product of interstate bargaining facilitating cooperation by providing information, which is crucial for reducing the uncertainties surrounding the issues of conflict, and by linking different issues thus creating a bargaining range.

Yet the very creation of these institutions is a collective action problem, and in the case of international watercourses it has proven to be a complicated one. In semi-arid and arid regions, international water resources generate interdependencies, vulnerabilities, and distributional tensions. One of the most important implications of this is that institutions, particularly on issues like water rights, may not be very effective in reconstructing and modifying state preferences, and thus securing the compliance of states. Therefore, the prelude to any discussion of the possible role of institutions is to assess the factors that initially help states to overcome collective action problems. In this context, hegemonic states clearly have enough political and economic leverage to play an important role in alleviating crises, preventing conflict escalations, and promoting cooperation in the international system.

The central importance of an external authority becomes clear when one considers the need for a clearly defined, protected, and enforced private property rights in the smooth functioning of the free market, which is based on the assumption that the rational pursuit of an individual's self-interest will lead to the efficient distribution of economic resources. Likewise, hegemonic stability theory, which considers international cooperation as a public good, underlines the central role of a hegemonic state in promoting cooperation, alleviating crises, and preventing conflict escalation.

As mentioned before, a state's geographic position and relative power capabilities are the primary determinants of a state's objectives and bargaining strategies that are available to states for attaining these objectives. Furthermore, under the prevailing conditions of uncertainty, watercourse states' choices on how to share and manage scarce water resources are interdependent; a choice of one strategy over others depends on what a watercourse state expects its counterparts will likely do. Accordingly, incentives to misrepresent information about states' relative power capabilities and resolve become prevalent and feed the conflicting expectations about the terms of a negotiated settlement, which in turn prevent states from reaching a settlement. In addition to this, the ongoing instability of the Middle East worsens states' ability to estimate their opponents' relative military capabilities and resolve and thus contributes to the conflicting expectations on all sides.

The role of third parties, especially in a hegemonic state, in preventing crises and promoting cooperation in international watercourses also comes to the fore in the context of watercourse states' inability to commit themselves in the hope of getting better terms and when at least one of the watercourse states has a strong preference to maintain the status quo over any terms of settlement. One can discuss the role of a hegemonic state in two different situations: the first deals with situations in which there is a bargaining range, and for whatever reason the watercourse states are unable to reach an agreement; the second deals with situations in which there is no bargaining range indicating there is no incentive for at least one of the watercourse states to agree on any terms of settlement. In these situations, the hegemonic state's role is to manipulate the existing context in such a way that it reduces the negative effects of variables, such as the transaction costs, or to create new incentives for states to reach a negotiated settlement on water rights.

The existence of bargaining space or range is a necessary condition for the negotiated settlement of water rights conflicts. In other words, the minimum terms of settlement for all sides should be compatible for negotiated settlement to be possible. As I noted before the expected benefits of a negotiated settlement should be greater than the expected benefits of the continued status quo or of the use of force. In order to examine how the state preferences change, one should identify the causes of change in expected benefits of these three possible outcomes.

If a bargaining range is already present in an international water rights conflict, the main source of disagreement can be the existence of private information about the relative power capabilities and resolve or the continuously shifting context, both of which generates conflicting expectations about the terms of a negotiated settlement. There are a variety of bargaining strategies available to states to reveal private information, and each bargaining strategy, including the use of force or the threat of the use of force, has different configurations of costs and benefits. The possible role of a hegemonic state in this type of situation is to help reveal private information through peaceful means. Note that there is no logical reason to assume that a hegemonic state has access to private information or has more capability to evaluate the situation. It is very likely that private information and shifting contexts also restrict the accuracy of a hegemonic state's strategic calculations. Thus, it is better for a hegemonic state simply to manipulate the strategies of revealing private information and resolve in favor of peaceful ones by altering the costs and benefits of the different strategies. A hegemonic state has enough economic and political leverage to increase the costs associated with some of the strategies, for example, the use of force, while lowering the costs for the more peaceful options. The use of force or the threat of the use of force are the most common means that states use in order to reveal private information, which in the final analysis leads to an overlap in bargaining range.

As we saw earlier, in international watercourses, a combination of geographic position and relative power capabilities determines the relative strength of states' bargaining positions. The hegemonic state's interventions can change the cost and benefits of strategies aiming to improve one's bargaining situation. For instance, increasing the cost of fighting or supporting terrorist movements in neighboring states is likely to prevent states from employing these strategies to improve their bargaining position. Also, increasing the cost of illegitimate bargains can narrow the number of possible equilibria, since it is entirely possible that the existence of multiple options along the bargaining range causes difficulties and thereby delays. Thus, narrowing down the possible bargaining strategies and outcomes can simplify the bargaining process and prevent delays. The cost of delay is distributed unevenly among watercourse states; a watercourse state that suffers the least is expected to get a better deal.

Secondly, in situations where there is no bargaining range, a hegemonic state can introduce artificial incentives. In this respect, issue linkages and side payments are the best tools for creating artificial incentives for establishing water rights in international watercourses.[27] The US, as a hegemonic power, can manipulate international economic and political institutions to change the costs and benefits associated with a particular course of actions. But, if the US is to play an active role in the establishment of a water regime in any of the international watercourses in the Middle East, it needs to present itself as a benign hegemonic state. As the only current super power, the US will greatly benefit from stability in the international system in general and in subsystems like the Middle East for a variety of political and economic reasons. Thus, it has an incentive to promote cooperation among Middle Eastern states. The proper way to do so is not through the direct imposition of the terms of settlement but the manipulation of the bargaining strategies that states use to reveal private information about each other's relative power capabilities, and the provision of incentives though issue linkages and side payments.

There are several cases of successful hegemonic state interventions in the history of Middle Eastern watercourse conflicts. The first water regime concerning the Nile waters, for example, was established under the auspices of Great Britain, which provided compensation packages, including technical assistance, for both Egypt and Sudan in the first half of the twentieth century.[28] Later, in 1959, Egypt and Sudan signed an agreement with the assistance of the Soviet Union, which helped to build the Aswan Dam. Likewise, the Soviet Union also provided technical know-how and assistance to Syria for building the Tabqa dam when both Syria and Iraq were its client states in the Euphrates/Tigris Basin. The US has played a major role in establishing the current regime governing the Jordan watercourse.[29] In the early 1950s, the US sent a special ambassador, Eric Johnston, to mediate the water conflict between the Arab states and Israel; the 1955 Johnston plan was a byproduct of this endeavor. Although, the Arab states did not ratify the Johnston plan for political reasons, they continued to adhere to the plans' water quotas. In subsequent years, the US conditioned its aid to Israel and Jordan for water related projects on adherence to the water quotas of the Johnston plan. Furthermore, the US brokered the 1994 peace treaty between Israel and Jordan by providing significant incentives for both countries. In the course of the following years, both Jordan and Israel received substantial foreign direct investment. Also, as a part of Jordan's debt reduction program, the US wrote off approximately US$ 700 million of the Jordanian debt in 1995 and helped with the modernization of the Jordanian military.

In international watercourses, coercive cooperation is particularly likely in two different scenarios of severe power asymmetries: if the upper watercourse state is also the most powerful militarily or if the lower watercourse state, which is highly dependent on the water resources, is much more powerful than the upper watercourse states. One of the most important implications of these scenarios lies in the verification of the centrality of force or threat of force in the bargaining process among states. Indeed the bargaining process among states includes not only negotiations but also the threat of use of force and the use of force as means to reach an agreement.

The third type of cooperation, co-adjustment or coordinative cooperation, appears when all states prefer cooperation to the status quo or want to prevent deterioration of the status quo into a wider/more violent conflict. Co-adjustment/coordinative cooperation would be more likely if the distribution of power among watercourse states is more or less symmetric or the cost of coercive cooperation is too high. States in protracted conflicts might especially fear that conflict over an international watercourse can spillover into a broader political and military conflict or even into a nuclear war. To avoid the negative effects of conflict over international water rights complicating and increasing tension in already tense relationship, watercourse states may prefer to change their minimum terms of settlement and cooperate.

Iteration, long time horizons, tit-for-tat bargaining strategy (which combines coercion and conciliation), the small number of states, issue linkages, and side payments are all highlighted in recent scholarship as conditions that are likely to lead states to cooperate.[30] In the absence of other forms of compensation, it is highly unlikely that powerful states will agree to cooperate and comply with the existing agreements if they are against their interests. Issue linkages, therefore, play an important role establishing and maintaining cooperation in international watercourses.[31] A survey of the existing international treaties complied by the Transboundary Freshwater database[32] indicates that the most common form of compensation is capital (30.3 percent), which refers to monetary compensation, including selling water, followed by land (4.2 percent) and other linkages (6.3 percent). Another important finding is that political concessions are very rare (1.4 percent). If we look at the issue linkages by the issue of treaty, we observe that capital is the most common form of issue linkage in treaties concerned with hydropower production (43.9 percent). The majority of the treaties do not have any issue linkages, but they are more common in bilateral treaties than multilateral ones. Also, the most common form of cooperation is partial: out of 149 international treaties, only 19 (13.3 percent) of them are multilateral treaties, and only three of these multilateral treaties (2.1 percent) regulate water supply as opposed to 46 (37.4 percent) bilateral treaties regulating water supplies. Most of these treaties (40.1 percent) are concerned with hydropower production suggesting that it is more likely and easier for states to cooperate on hydropower production than on the more delicate and conflict-prone issues of water rights.[33]

In terms of the problems of monitoring and enforcing compliance with agreed-upon rules, which have been rightly underlined as being a long-enduring detrimental problem of common pool resources, the survey results verifies their intractable nature. Only 51.7 percent of treaties have stipulations for monitoring; 79.7 percent of the treaties do not have any sort of enforcement mechanisms. This finding is consistent with the assumption that once states reach a negotiated settlement these settlements are self-enforcing. In the remaining treaties, the use of force/the threat of the use of force (1.4 percent), economic sanctions (0.7 percent), and council (18.2 percent) constitute the main enforcement mechanisms. In summary, most of the existing treaties in international watercourses are bi-lateral, and almost half of them are about hydropower production. Also, more than half of them do not have any stipulations for monitoring, and two-thirds of them do not have any enforcement mechanism. In order to shed light on our understanding of the sorry status of international water rights, as illustrated by these statistics, the Conclusion will focus on analyzing the modern history of the water rights conflict in the Euphrates and Tigris watercourse through the lens of the bargaining framework presented here.

# PART II

# CASE STUDY

# CHAPTER 5

# BARGAINING FOR WATER RIGHTS IN THE EUPHRATES AND TIGRIS WATERCOURSE

The Euphrates and Tigris watercourse extends from Turkey to Syria, Iraq, and Iran, creating one of the most extensive and fertile regions in the world, Mesopotamia, where some of the first advanced civilizations took root.[1] Given the enormously long history of the region, it comes as no surprise that it has repeatedly suffered from the same patterns of conflict over the competitive exploitation of water resources and the same patterns of environmental destruction, deriving from irrigation and the subsequent salinization of soil. The first recorded war that was fought over water took place in Mesopotamia around 2500 BC between the Sumerian city-states of Lagash and Umma, and lasted over 150 years. Though Umma's infringement of an age-old boundary agreement over a canal along the Tigris was the cause of warfare between the two city-states,[2] the history of this early conflict underscores how water has been used as a weapon since the emergence of the first civilizations in the region and has been a focus of territorial disputes. As we saw earlier, given the opportunity and means, modern states do not refrain from meddling in another state's water supply. Significantly too, Lagash and Umma signed the first treaty concerning the waters of the Euphrates and Tigris.

Aside from the detrimental impact of periodic spring flooding and the subsequent deposition of silt, historical records indicate that Mesopotamia may have suffered from recurrent environmental disasters following intensive agricultural activity and irrigation. The region is subject to the effects of rapid evaporation of surface water, which causes the salinization of the soil. While in the short run the application of water to the parched soil drastically increases agricultural output, in the long-run, it increases the salt content of the soil and consequently hinders agricultural activity, which in turn triggers political crises. This constitutes a formidable common challenge facing irrigated agriculture in arid regions, where high evaporation rates and poor drainage lead to the formation of salt layers on the surface of the soil rendering the land unusable for long periods until the soil recovers.

Not only did irrigated agriculture ruin the environment in Mesopotamia, but it also contributed to the collapse of these early civilizations. Ecological disasters in Mesopotamia indicate the difficulty of reversing the desertification process; the earliest collapse occurred *c.*4000 BC. A second agricultural collapse occurred between 1300 and 900 BC following an intensive period of irrigation. Around the seventh and eighth centuries AD another disaster occurred in Baghdad and its vicinity. At that time, to increase food production in order to feed an ever-increasing population, which peaked at one and half million, four main irrigation channels were constructed between the Euphrates and Tigris. The result was a repetition of what happened 3,000 years earlier: the salinization of the soil and the subsequent decline of the existing society. Thus, long before the Mongol conquest in the thirteenth century, Mesopotamia suffered from a decline: by the time the Mongol incursions started, the population in the region had shrunk to a mere a hundred and fifty thousand.

Modern inhabitants of the watercourse face similar challenges to that of the ancient inhabitants of Mesopotamia. Indeed, the major problems in the region have changed little throughout its long history. Soil quality and salinization remain critical problems, especially for the modern lower watercourse states, Iraq and Syria. What has changed, however, is technology, population sizes, the scale and intensity of human induced environmental change and international relations. This in turn has increased the enormity and the complexity of the risks involved in the failure to cope with the dilemmas facing watercourse states.

Conflicts over water resources have proven to be not only a matter of water deficit, but also a highly complex, multi-dimensional problem with ramifications touching on the environmental, social, economic, and political balances among states. The political, economic, and institutional capacity to manage water resources has more then ever become necessary for advancing long-term solutions to water crises and on-going environmental problems. Over the course of the last century, a comprehensive international agreement determining water rights in the Euphrates and Tigris basin has not been obtainable, despite the critical need for such an agreement. In what follows, I review in detail this more recent history of the pursuit of water rights institutions in the Euphrates and Tigris watercourse, and the ambitious unilateral attempts to develop water resources.

Although the emergence of comprehensive water rights institutions has proven to be unattainable, an informal water rights regime has emerged through a long and arduous bargaining process among the watercourse states. Several international agreements with provisions on the Euphrates and Tigris have been signed over the course of the last century. The first recorded provision concerning the Euphrates and Tigris was in a secret agreement between colonial France and Great Britain. With the 1916 Sykes-Picot agreement, France provided Great Britain with the right to access the Euphrates. According to a clause in the agreement France gave 'guarantee of a given supply of water from the Tigris and Euphrates in area (a) for area (b).' Again in 1920, France and Great Britain, as the mandatory powers in Mesopotamia, signed a treaty regarding utilization of the waters. Article 3 of this treaty provided that the two governments should set up a commission responsible for examining irrigation plans in the region. On 20 October, 1921, Turkey signed the Ankara Treaty with France, which was the first treaty signed by one of the current watercourse states. The Turco-French Protocol, signed in 1930, committed the Turkish and French governments to coordinating any plans for the use of the waters of the Euphrates. The principle of mutual cooperation over water development was extended in a Protocol annexed to the 1946 Treaty of Friendship and Good Neighborly Relations between Turkey and Iraq. The agreement encompassed both rivers and their tributaries. At that time Turkey and Iraq agreed to share related data and consult with each other in order to accommodate both countries' interests. The 1946 treaty mandated a committee to implement these agreements. Although none of this has yet occurred, if fully implemented, the 1946 Agreement would constitute a good starting point for cooperation between Turkey and Iraq today. Around 40 years later, in July 1987, Turkey and Syria signed two protocols, one of which has ensured an annual flow of a minimum 500 cubic meters per second of water from the Euphrates until the ultimate allocation of the river's waters. The second protocol was a security agreement where Syria pledged to end its support for the Kudistan Workers' Party (PKK) and other anti-Turkey groups. Turkey also made it clear that this water pledge was contingent on 'its right to first use.' Two years later, in April 1989, Syria and Iraq reached a bilateral agreement at the 13th meeting of the Joint Technical Committee. Accordingly, Syria agreed to release 58 percent of the flow of the Euphrates waters from Turkey to Iraq. Although both Syria and Turkey declared their intentions to reach a final solution determining the allocation of the waters of the Euphrates River before the end of 1993, the status quo has not yet changed. Water rights have become an issue on and off often following the announcement and construction of big water development projects.

In modern times, Al-Hindiyya was the first dam to be built on the watercourse in an attempt to control the Euphrates by the Ottoman Administration of Iraq in 1913.[3] The conflict over water rights, however, emerged much later, after both Syria and Turkey, now both sovereign states, simultaneously began to plan and implement large-scale water development projects in the 1950s, and at first not on the Euphrates or Tigris but on another and much smaller watercourse. Prior to the 1950s, both Syria and Turkey's economic development strategies and plans focused on their western regions, which also explains the latent attention paid to the Euphrates and Tigris. Syria was preoccupied by the Ghab project on the Orontes (Asi) watercourse, which precipitated the first water rights dispute between Syria and Turkey.

## The Orontes Watercourse

Three watercourse states share the Orontes, which rises in Lebanon and flows mostly through Syria before emptying into the Mediterranean Sea in Turkey. It travels approximately 248 km, of which 40 km lies in Lebanon, 128 km in Syria, and 80 km in Turkey. It has an approximate total discharge of 1.2 billion cubic meters (BCM).[4] An estimated 92 percent of its total annual discharge is contributed by Syria and the remaining 6 percent by Lebanon and 2 percent by Turkey.[5] Many small tributaries and springs along with two major tributaries, the Karasu River and Afrine River, feed the Orontes. Though detailed water use data is not available, Syria has in the past used approximately 90 percent of the total flow of 1.2 BCM and leaving only 120 million cubic meters (MCM) of heavily polluted water to cross into Turkey.

Syrian efforts to develop the Orontes date back to the 1930s when Syria was a French Mandate territory. The French Mandate Authorities drafted the first plans for the river, which were not implemented for political reasons.[6] After gaining its independence from France, Syria in 1950 resurrected the early plans for the drainage and irrigation of the Ghab Valley, situated in northwestern Syria. The Ghab project covers a total of 140,000 ha of land, including the drainage of 30,000 ha of swamp land and the transformation of 13,000 ha of rain-fed land into irrigated land. The construction of two dams, a weir, and two large drainage canals constituted the Ghab projects main installations.[7]

To finance the construction of the Ghab project Syria applied to the World Bank. The World Bank found the Ghab valley project attractive, yet required the consent of the other watercourse states, Lebanon and Turkey, before providing the loan. The lack of conclusive international law on the water rights issue, which often generated disputes among watercourse states, and the World Bank's desire to preempt controversial water development projects were behind this decision.[8] Having examined the legal and technical aspects of the Syrian proposal, the World Bank reached the following conclusions: (1) Lebanon, the upper watercourse state, did not constitute a threat to the project, and (2) the project would be beneficial to the lower watercourse state, Turkey. It would prevent disastrous floods by regulating discharge, which fluctuated greatly according to the seasons and years, and would also provide sufficient summer flow to the lower watercourse state. At first glance, the World Bank's preconditions seemed to have been met – the absence of threat from the upper watercourse state and protest from the lower watercourse state for the infringement on its existing and potential uses. However, just before the presentation of the loan to the World Bank Board, Turkey contended on technical grounds that it would be adversely affected by Syria's water development project. In return, Syria first deferred from further processing of the World Bank loan and later withdrew its request without attempting to negotiate it with Turkey. The water rights issue remained unsettled.[9]

Syria proceeded to complete the Ghab project with the assistance of the Soviet Union in 1968.[10] The two dams, the Rastan and Makerdeh, have storage capacities of 250 MCM and 65 MCM, respectively, generate hydroelectric power (HEP) for the cities of Hama and Homs, and irrigate 70,000 ha. Before the current civil war, Syria was using 90 percent of the Orontes waters, and it had plans for the construction of new dams and reservoirs on the watercourse. Among these proposed dams were the 17 April Dam, near the village of Ifrine (west of Aleppo), with a storage capacity of 220 MCM; the Zaita dam, near Homs, with a storage capacity of 80 MCM;[11] the Kremish dam on with a storage capacity of 275 MCM and proposed irrigation scheme of 25,000 ha; and another dam on the Afrine near the Turkish border with a 230 MCM storage capacity and proposed irrigation scheme of 20,000 ha. If all these plans eventually become reality, the amount of water flowing into Turkey would dwindle to 25 MCM from the current 120 MCM[12] and water quality would be adversely affected.[13] For example, the average discharge of the Afrine is 250 MCM a year, and according to estimates, Syria planned to use 200 MCM for irrigation of 20,000 ha. As a main tributary of the Orontes, any reduction in the Afrine's flow means a substantial reduction in the flow and quality of the water.[14]

Concerns about the future of the fertile Amik Plain due to the potential damages of the planned dams in Syria drove Turkey's attempts to negotiate for water rights in the Orontes watercourse. The Amik plain itself has been one of the most fertile agricultural areas in Turkey due to the special combinations of the hot climate and irrigation. The decline of the Orontes's flow from 125 MCM to 25 MCM would unquestionably desiccate the river leading to serious environmental and economic damages. The nature of bi-lateral relations in general, and to some degree the fact that Turkey and Syria were part of the different camps during the Cold War, did not allow the negotiations on the Orontes to proceed. Syria refused to acknowledge Turkey's water rights on the Orontes, since the acknowledgment would mean Syrian recognition of Turkish sovereignty in Alexandretta (Hatay).[15] As far as the Syrians were concerned, the Orontes completed its journey to the Mediterranean Sea in Syrian territory. Syria maintained this position until its implicit recognition of Alexandretta as a Turkish territory in a number of economic cooperation agreements, including a bilateral investment treaty[16] and a free trade agreement,[17] signed between the two countries in 2004. The case of Orontes illustrate how the intricate nature of international relations can inhibit states from cooperating on issues that some may consider to be of low political importance.

Though watercourse-wide cooperation has been possible in the Orontes much of the history, this did not preclude the upper and middle watercourse states, Lebanon and Syria, from concluding partial agreements on water rights. In fact, there has been an agreement in effect since 24 July 1972. The cooperation between the two countries has been facilitated by Syria's hegemonic position with respect to Lebanon and the physical nature of the Orontes watercourse. Most of the water originates and is consumed in Syrian territory. The 1972 agreement entitled Lebanon to 80 MCM and Syria to 320 MCM annually and regulated diversion times for irrigation.[18] The agreement was subsequently modified as a part of a series of economic agreements on 20 September 1994. The new agreement entitles Lebanon to 18 percent of the flow, which equals 72 MCM, slightly lowering the previous amount, for irrigation of the arid Northern Bekaa Valley.[19] Articles 5 and 6 of the agreement contain provisions through which Syria exercises control over Lebanese water development projects.[20] The terms of the agreement on water rights clearly points to Syrian hegemony over Lebanon, the relative unimportance of the Orontes for Lebanon and Lebanon for the Orontes, and a relatively even distribution of its tributaries among the upper- and mid-watercourse states. The blatant dominance of Syria over Lebanon, however, ostensibly came to a halt when Syria was compelled to withdraw from Lebanon in the face of a strong international pressure led by the US. In early 2005, Syria withdrew its army from Lebanon, yet it has continued to manipulate Lebanese politics in discreet ways. The outbreak of current the Syrian civil war in 2011 has the potential to change Syria's relative capabilities and its regime, but the impact of this on Lebanon's use of the Orontes is likely to be limited since only about 400 MCM originates in Lebanon.

The conventional explanation for Syrian Orontes policy has emphasized the requirements of domestic politics. The authoritarian rulers of Syria needed irredentist causes to reinforce the legitimacy of the regime by providing them with tools to divert the public's attention away from internal problems in order to mobilize public support. The oppressive policies of the current regime and its sectarian quality created a potential for an uprising by Sunni Arabs and other regime dissidents in the absence of external problems. Irredentism in this context then became an easy way for Syrian rulers to gain popularity and support under the conditions of pervasive communal tension within Syria, and to manipulate the pervasive feelings of discontent for the current boundaries of Syria. However, with respect to Alexandretta and the related water rights issue this argument seemed to be flawed. Syria did not really need Alexandretta as a driving force behind its irredentist policies, which were intended mainly to affect domestic politics, especially considering that the Golan Heights have continued to be under Israeli occupation and the responsibility for this fell more obviously on the Syrian government. Indeed, Syrian officials had often downplayed the issue of Alexandretta, while simultaneously avoiding giving any direct answers and putting the blame on others, especially Israel. On one occasion, a Syrian official responded to a Turkish journalist's question in a typically evasive way: 'I don't think the Turkish people are too concerned about this. I don't think they attach too much importance to it. The only thing the Turkish and Syrian people want is good bilateral-relations. This issue is occasionally exploited in certain newspapers under Israeli influence. They want to obstruct Turkish-Syrian rapprochement and to denigrate Syria.'[21]

Obtaining *de jure* Syrian recognition of Turkish sovereignty over Alexandretta was also suggested as a driving force behind Turkey's attempts to settle the water rights concerning the Orontes.[22] However, this fails to consider the fact that with or without Syrian recognition, Alexandretta has been recognized indisputably as Turkish territory. Turkey's continuing efforts to link the settlement of water rights in the Orontes with that of the Euphrates and Tigris has been more likely to be a result of strategic calculations – an attempt to strengthen its bargaining position – with respect to the Euphrates and Tigris. Indeed, Turkey insisted on the inclusion of the Orontes in the Euphrates and Tigris negotiations with no success during the 1980s and 1990s.

The drastic changes during the last two decades in the international relations of the Middle East point to the importance of the context in which foreign policy decisions are made. The changes in the leadership and international relations often create opportunities and pressures for the resolution of long standing conflicts. The period following Bashar Assad's ascension to power in 2000 till the outbreak of the Syrian civil war of 2011 represented a peaceful period in bi-lateral relations and cooperation in agriculture, transportation, energy, health, environment, and water. For example, on 23 December 2004, Syria and Turkey reached a consensus on the joint construction of a dam on the Orontes at the Turkish-Syrian border.[23] Turkey also granted Syrian request for pumping water from the Tigris and agreed to provide technical support. The gradual toughening of the US policy towards Syria after the invasion of Iraq in March 2003 was instrumental in the change of Syrian policies and the sudden desire to seek Turkey's alliance. Having resolved the problem of PKK terrorism originating from Syrian territories since 1999, the Syrian rapprochement was also a welcome development from the Turkish perspective. More importantly, the instability in Iraq, which paved the way for the re-insurgence of PKK terrorism in 2002, become a main concern for Turkey and a source of discontent towards the US Iraq policy at about the same time. The outbreak of the Syrian civil war ended the rapprochement in bilateral Turkish-Syrian relations. In sum, this brief history of the search for water rights in the Orontes watercourse over the last century again points to the importance of the strategic environment for the resolution of water conflicts. Whatever small steps Turkey and Syria may have made towards a resolution of this conflict over the last decades, these now have been turned back by the Syrian civil war.

## The Euphrates and Tigris Watercourse

Modern Turkey's first attempt to exploit the resources of the Euphrates and Tigris watercourse was made in mid-1930s by the General Directorate of

Electrical Power Resources Survey and Development Administration (EIE). Along the Euphrates, the EIE built gauging stations and conducted a preliminary survey of the Keban dam project in 1938. The authority to develop water resources was transferred to a new State Hydraulic Works (DSI) in 1953.[24] The Keban dam was built in order to prevent extreme fluctuations of the Euphrates' flow. It was designed to maintain a minimum flow of 450 cubic meters per second or a maximum flow of 1000 cubic meters per second and to generate 5,871 GWH with an installed capacity of 1240 MW. The hydrological data from 1937–64 indicated that the Euphrates flow ranged from a minimum of 16,871 MCM in 1961 to a maximum discharge of 43,456 MCM in 1963, while that of the Tigris at Cizre in the upper Tigris dropped to 7,891 MCM in 1961 rising by a factor of four to 34,340 MCM in 1969 at the Turkish-Syrian border. There were also steep differences between maximum and minimum monthly flows, which for the Tigris could be as much as 80 times and for the Euphrates 28 times as much.[25]

Recognizing the potential of the Euphrates in promoting the development of their countries, both Syria and Turkey began to plan large-scale dam projects for the utilization and control of the Euphrates in the 1950s. The water rights conflict gained momentum after both Turkey and Syria started to implement these plans in the 1960s. Different imperatives were instrumental in water development projects ranging from the need for hydraulic energy to the resettlement of populations, and from the creation of jobs to securing the allegiance of different ethnic groups. The dilution of population density in the western parts of Syria and the creation of jobs in agriculture, which usually is the main source of much needed foreign exchange in developing countries, were imperative. For rapidly industrializing and urbanizing Turkey, it was initially the insatiable need for electricity that led to the damming of the Euphrates.

In 1966, the DSI released the study 'Lower Euphrates Project,' which assessed for the first time the development potential of soil and water resources.[26] The project was an earlier predecessor of the Southeastern Anatolia Project (GAP) and its master plan was completed in 1970. Together with the Tigris project, which was completed in 1978, the Lower Euphrates Project constituted the two building blocks of GAP.[27] Today, if we look at the impact of the various DSI development projects, we see that the average annual growth rate for hydroelectric energy production has been around 15 percent. In 2013, the hydroelectric production constituted *c.*24.7 percent of Turkey's total electricity production with a total installed capacity of 22,289 MW up from 17.9 MW in 1950.[28]

As a first large dam built by Turkey for the regulation of the erratic Euphrates and hydroelectric power (HEP) production, the Keban dam introduced trilateral negotiations on water rights in the region and also the politics of international financing for dams in international watercourses. In order to comply with the requirements of international financing, like the consent of the lower watercourse states, Turkey held negotiations with Syria and Iraq in order to win their consent for the project, but the negotiations ended without an agreement. What made the loan from the United States Agency for International Development (USAID) and other donors – the European Investment Bank, French, Italian, and German governments – possible was the provision that, in case Turkey was unable to secure the consent of the lower watercourse states by the impounding period of the dam, it would guarantee a flow of a minimum of 350 cubic meters per second for the needs of the lower watercourse states in accordance with the program submitted to the creditors.[29] It is important to underline that the loan was approved before the consent of the lower watercourse states was provided. The construction of the Keban was completed in 1973 after eight years of construction; HEP production began soon after the impounding period of a year in accordance with the Lower Euphrates Project.

Since the Keban dam, Syria adopted an official policy of protesting all upper watercourse development projects even if they are for solely non-consumptive uses, such as power generation or flow regulation. The widely accepted explanation, or in some cases justification, for Syrian position was that each dam gives Turkey a strategic advantage and constitutes a direct security threat since supposedly Turkey could either cut the river's flow or drown Syria. The argument goes that if the waters of the Atatürk Dam were released at once – provided Turkey would be willing to destroy the Birecik and Karkamis Dams – then it could sweep Syria, figuratively speaking, all the way to the Gulf. Or, if the irrigation canals were opened simultaneously, it could to turn the whole area into swampland and therefore prevent the possibility of a land war.[30] The materialization of these scenarios is highly doubtful. Turkey, or any other country, cannot possibly hold onto running waters for long or release them at once without endangering its own infrastructure and population; the physical capacity of dams simply will not permit this. These types of accusations seem to reflect Syria's own policies, especially toward Iraq. In this regard the 1975 crisis with Iraq showed how the Syrian regime could use the Tabqa dam to achieve certain political objectives. Presumably, the simultaneous impounding in Turkey's Keban and Syria's Tabqa dams instigated the first crisis over water and almost led to the escalation of the conflict to military levels, as we now shall see.

### *The 1975 Crisis*

The Tabqa dam was built in 1974 on the Syrian portion of the Euphrates using Syrian capital and Soviet technical, material and financial assistance. During the first season of impounding, which coincided with that of the Keban dam, Iraq requested an additional 200 MCM of water from the Tabqa from Syria and threatening to bomb the dam if this did not happen; it also moved its troops to the Syrian border.[31] The Iraqi request was accepted by Syria and thus the first year of impounding in the middle watercourse states went without conflict. However, the second year of the impounding period resulted in open conflict between Syria and Iraq. Iraq protested the sharp reduction of the flow form 28 BCM to 21 BCM per year and declared its unease with Syrian water projects and fears about the potential decrease in water quantity. Syria officially protested and blamed Turkey for the reduction of the Euphrates' flow. Turkey rejected the validity of the Syrian accusations and continued with the planned impounding schedule and water development projects on the Euphrates.

The prior efforts of Iraq and Syria to reach an agreement on the allocation of water rights on the Euphrates were unsuccessful due largely to the lack of major hydraulic works undertaken by the upper watercourse states and the negligible adverse effects of implemented projects throughout the 1960s. Iraq and Syria formed a joint technical committee in 1962 to deal with water rights issues in regards to the Euphrates. However, attempts to reach a consensus on water rights and to forge a common front against the upper watercourse state, Turkey, failed. The political context of international relations was such that no matter how beneficial the partial agreement on water rights between the two Arab states, both ruled by the different branches of Ba'th party, agreement was not possible. In fact, the conflict over the regional influence between Iraq and Syria intensified after the Ba'th party came to power in Iraq on 30–31 July 1968.[32]

On 7 April 1975, Iraq summoned an emergency meeting of the Arab League foreign ministers blaming Syria for using its new Soviet-constructed dam at Tabqa to divert excessive quantities of water from the Euphrates, thereby endangering the lives of 3 million Iraqi farmers who were dependent on the river's waters for irrigation,[33] and for the failure of agreement on water rights 'due to a lack of response by the Syrian government to all the efforts exerted by the Iraqi government for years to reach an agreement, necessitated a consideration of national responsibility, justice, humanity, and the provision of international law.'[34] The reciprocal charges were followed by the accusations of the Syrian and Iraqi governments regarding the other's character and policies, and of reports of offensive actions of each government against the so-called proponents of the other's regime. On 9 April 1975, the Iraqi government threatened that: 'It would take whatever steps it deemed necessary to ensure the free flow of the Euphrates and would hold Syria responsible for the serious results which harnessing its waters have on Iraqi farmers.'

Meanwhile Syria accused the 'rightist Iraqi clique' for its alleged collusion with Iran and its 'betrayal of the causes of the Arab nation.' On 19 April 1975, Syria issued an official statement claiming that 'It had been seeking a definite agreement with Iraq and Turkey on sharing the waters of the Euphrates 'for many years' but had met with 'rejection and evasion' by Iraq, which has conducted bi-lateral negotiations with Turkey without informing Syria of what was discussed.' The official statement furthermore accused Iraq of procrastination over the agreement concerned with the Euphrates flow: 'In October 1973, Syria reached a provisional agreement with Iraq on the water flow for the 1973–74 winter season, stipulating that the figures would be revised when Turkey began to fill its own dam at Keban. However, when it had been established in late January 1974 that the filling of the Keban dam had begun, Iraq had 'procrastinated' about revising the agreement.'

Furthermore, Syria blamed Turkey for the erratic flow[35] and claimed that it still continued to release 71 percent of the Euphrates flow to Iraq on the orders of President Assad. In addition to this, when Iraq requested an additional 200 MCM of water from the Tabqa dam, President Assad consented in spite of the difficulties. Syria also asserted that it released 75 percent of the river flow coming from Turkey to Iraq during the winter of 1974–75. Iraq was not satisfied with Syrian response and the data. As a result, Iraq maintained that only about half of the water to which it was entitled had reached Iraq in the 1974–75 season, and the Tabqa reservoir had been filled above the level necessary to generate power. Iraq not only denied the validity of the Syrian figures, but also the claim of the release of additional flow from the Syrian share. Besides this, Syria also used the water for irrigation.[36] The accusations of erroneous figures about the amount of water achieved a prominent place in the crisis.

On 22 April 1975, the Arab League Council approved the establishment of a 'technical committee' to mediate the dispute between Syria and Iraq. Syria refused to participate in the meeting and continued to blame Turkey for the reduction of the Euphrates flow. A second failed attempt to mediate the dispute came from Saudi Arabia on 3 May 1975. The accusations made by Syria and Iraq about the each other's regime intensified and heightened their severity, and the tension was further aggravated when Syria closed its air space to Iraqi aircraft leading to a further Iraqi threat to bomb the Tabqa dam. The developments induced another attempt by Saudi Arabia in early June. This time, Saudi Arabia succeeded in its mediation effort.

Syria agreed to release additional water from the Tabqa reservoir as a 'gesture of goodwill' towards Iraq. The official Syrian statement on this issue was carefully worded: 'In the light of the good offices made available by the fraternal Kingdom of Saudi Arabia and in view of the fraternal Iraqi people's needs, particularly during the period in which Euphrates river water is scarce, the Syrian government has decided to supply from its own share the requirements of the fraternal Iraqi region regardless of the Iraqi regime's attitude. The Syrian government expects this to be helpful in promoting a permanent agreement before long on sharing the waters of the Euphrates.'[37] In the days to come, however, the amount of water that Syria agreed to release to Iraq was not materialized. The Iraqi irrigation minister rejected the Syrian claim of the release of new water from Syria's own share and argued that the decision by Syria had come too late to prevent the devastation of the summer crops. Syria responded accusing Iraq of having erroneous figures. The tension once again began to intensify with the propaganda war and mutual allegations. Iraq claimed that Syrian authorities had launched a ruthless campaign of suppression against internal opposition groups. In the meantime, Iraq agreed with Turkey in principle that the problems emanating from the use of the Euphrates waters should be settled in tripartite talks with Syria. The agreement on this issue was made public in July 1975 in Ankara.

Both the bilateral and trilateral negotiations held by Syria, Iraq, and Turkey on the Euphrates waters ended without reaching any formal agreement during the 1960s. The lack of agreement and conflicting figures of water data, besides other political, ideological, and strategic factors, brought Iraq and Syria to the brink of war in 1975. The 1975 crisis, according to scholars, would have been prevented if Syria and Iraq had revised the water figures of the crisis years, which were extremely dry, and in which the reservoir filling alone could not account for a low level of discharge.[38] Yet, this was not what happened under the tense bilateral relations of Syria and Iraq, indicating the complex nature of the water conflict in the watercourse emanating in part from the strategic, ideological, and political concerns of the states involved.

By April 1975, Iraqi-Syrian relations seriously deteriorated over the use of the waters of the Euphrates, yet the conflict had been brewing for sometime because of concerns deeply rooted in the strategic, ideological, and political realms. Seale analyzed the situation as follows:

> If Damascus and Baghdad had not been so much at odds, they might perhaps have been able to resolve their long standing dispute over the division of the Euphrates waters [...] Dam-building and irrigation projects in all three countries from the 1960s onwards caused a row to break out over the volume of water each was entitled to [...] The squabble over water rights grew into a vast bone of contention, not to be assuaged by mediation attempts, most notably Saudi efforts. From 1975 onwards the two countries began abusing each other over the airways – 'fascist right-wing criminal' was standard invective – arresting each other's sympathizers, moving troops threateningly to the border, setting off explosions in each other's capitals.[39]

The bitter rivalry between the two opposing Ba'ath Parties deepened the tension and distrust between Iraq and Syria.[40] Both governments sought to undermine each other and were rightly suspicious of each other's subversive activities and feared the other one was plotting to bring their downfall. The exclusive nature of domestic political institutions created opportunities to exploit internal tensions arising from ethnic and sectarian divisions. The conflict between the Ba'thist rulers of Syria and Iraq was the main culprit for the failure of negotiations.

The tension between the watercourse states, Syria and Iraq, had been on the rise following the nationalization of the Iraqi Petroleum Company (IPC). The Syrian demand for the increase in royalties in early 1973 and the subsequent closure of the oil pipeline that carried Iraqi oil to the Mediterranean Sea crossing Syrian soil did not help either.[41] Furthermore, Iraq signed an agreement with Turkey for the construction of an oil pipeline to transport Iraqi oil throughout Turkish lands to the Mediterranean Sea on 26 August 1973. Not only did Syria lose a substantial amount of oil revenues and alienated Iraq, it also gave Turkey an opportunity to develop its relations with Iraq and to gain a new source of revenue. Disturbed by the Iraqi oil policy, Syria accused Iraq of not following Ba'thist ideology, not keeping its promises about expanding the capacity of the Syrian-Iraqi oil pipeline, and of favoring Turkey – a non-Arab state. Iraq's good relations with Turkey concerning the Euphrates waters were also source of a concern for Syria. Indeed, Iraq did not express any displeasure throughout the crises towards Turkey and did not include Turkey in its protests of Syria during the 1975 crisis.

Another important source of tension between the two Ba'thist states was Israel. Since 1948, Israel has been a contentious issue among the Arab states. In 1975, Iraq firmly opposed to a partial Middle East agreement and was accusing Syria of being in the process of accepting such a peace agreement with Israel. The last straw in Iraqi accusations took place in May 1975, when Iraq proposed the creation of the 'Northern Military Front' against Israel. Iraq's policy at that time was likely designed to deepen the Ba'th party rule in Iraq and to steer the members of the Iraqi Ba'th Party away from any involvement with Syria.[42] Syria responded by charging Iraq with surrendering Arab land to Iran, the betrayal of the Arab people, and deriding Iraqi aid during the October war.[43] Furthermore, Syria retaliated by using its newly gained strategic advantage: manipulation of the water flow entering Iraq. Indeed, Syria reduced the water flow entering Iraq first in the spring 1974 and then in 1975, as we have seen. This led to the destruction of 70 percent of Iraq's winter crops[44] and also formed the basis to Iraqi claims of deliberately holding more water in the lake of the Tabqa dam.[45] Iraq also charged the Syrian Ba'th party with betrayal of the Ba'th party ideals. The short and long-term repercussions of Syria's vast usage of the Euphrates water, including the reclamation of 640,000 ha of land,[46] the evaporation of the water from the reservoir of the Tabqa dam, and the quality of water that flowed into Iraq, provided Iraq with good justification for its protests. Overall approximately 3 million Iraqi farmers of Shi'i origin suffered economically.[47] In some sources, the spread of the Shi'i underground movement, Al-Dawa, has been attributed to this water shortage.[48] This highlights a crucial dimension of the water rights conflict: minorities inhabiting the Euphrates and Tigris watercourse. Here one should also note that the majority of the Iraqi army was at the time of Shi'i origin.[49]

Every development concerning the Euphrates and Tigris water has important repercussions in domestic politics, especially in Iraq and Turkey. Following the Algiers Agreement in March 1975 between Iran and Iraq that helped Iraq to crack down on the Kurdish insurgence in northern Iraq, Syria attempted to instigate Shi'i unrest in order to weaken the Iraqi government's hold on power by reducing the Euphrates flow. For a number of reasons, Syria interpreted the Algiers agreement as a harmful development. First, Syria's position in the Arab world as an ardent antagonist of Israel might be undermined, because having settled its protracted dispute with Iran and re-established stability in northern Iraq, Iraq now had resources at its disposal to use against Israel. Iraq had already accused Syria of selling out to Israel and strongly opposed Syrian disengagement negotiations with Israel. Secondly, Iraq could undermine the Alawite dominated Ba'th rule by playing on the suspicions of the Sunni Arabs in Syria concerning the indifference of the Alawite regime to the struggle with Israel. At this point, Iraqi allegations were not groundless and appealed to Syrian Sunnis, who were already suspicious of Assad's regime, developing conspiracy theories about Assad and the collusion between his regime and the Zionists. Iraq and Sunni Arabs of Syria justified their claims by arguing that during the 1967 war Israel occupied the Golan Heights without a fight while Assad was the defense minister; furthermore, in 1970 Assad betrayed Palestine by refusing to allow the deployment of the air force in a Syrian expedition to assist the PLO against Jordan; the Assad regime also sabotaged the Iraqi attack against Israel in 1973. Accordingly, Syria implemented a policy of limited crisis with Iraq and adopted an unyielding position against Israel. By doing this, first of all, Syrian rulers anticipated to fortify their hold on power and to make their rule admissible to the majority of the population. Water rights proved to be a good opportunity for Syrian leaders, through a limited international crisis, to strengthen the Syrian Ba'th regime's hold on power. The possibility of war with Iraq aroused anti-Iraqi feelings among the Syrians and provided an opportunity to the Ba'thist ruler to purge approximately 200 Sunni members of the Ba'th party on a charge of plotting against the government, and of being sympathetic to the historic leadership of the Ba'th in exile in Baghdad.[50]

As feared by Syria, with the Algiers agreement, Iraq gained considerable advantage towards becoming the leader of the region. Under the terms of this agreement, Iran would cease to support the Kurdish insurgency and would withdraw its arms and military equipment from the Kurdish area in the northern part of Iraq.[51] The Kurdish revolt impeded Iraq's participation in the Arab-Israeli conflict by tying down Iraqi troops in Northern Iraq.[52] This enervating role of the Kurdish rebellion in Iraq was described by Kissinger, the US special national security adviser and foreign minister, in 1972, as follows: 'The benefit of this decision [the US' decision to support Kurds as a response to Iran's request] was apparent in just over a year: only one Iraqi division was available to participate in the October 1973 Middle East war.'[53] This also explains why Iraq was so eager to sign an agreement, which ceded some part of Iraqi territory to Iran by accepting to move the boundary to the thalweg in exchange for the cessation of Iranian support of Iraqi

Kurds in 1975.[54] The Kurdish resistance was suppressed for the time being and Iraq got a chance to reallocate its resources to more profitable ends.[55] Under these propitious circumstances, Iraq attempted to undermine Syria's privileged position in the Arab-Israeli conflict. From the strategic point of view, the dwindling amount of the Euphrates water presented a suitable opportunity for Iraq to exploit.

The 1975 crisis revealed some of the persistent characteristics of the conflict over Euphrates and Tigris water: the parties could not concur on the water rights and accused each other of having erroneous figures. Secondly, all the parties backed their positions with the principles of international law, at least those portions that best suited their interests. Iraq has long insisted on acquired rights on the Euphrates' waters and on the priority of agricultural lands already under use. Iraq needs to persuade both Turkey and Syria that they are under the obligation of not causing a change in the natural integrity of the resource without the consent of downstream states. The developments of the last couple of decades have indicated that both Turkey and Syria are far from accepting Iraq's acquired rights claims. Syria has argued that it has limited water resources in comparison to Turkey and Iraq and that Iraq can use the Tigris to offset any reduction of the Euphrates. Yet, Syria claims that it has also acquired rights over the Euphrates derived from prior usage. Turkey's response to acquired rights claims is that prior usage of water by downstream countries on a river is just one of many factors which have to be taken into account when trying to reach an agreement based on equitable and fair use. After the initial failure, the Arab League served as an intergovernmental organization through which Syria and Iraq have put pressure on Turkey about water rights on the Euphrates and Tigris watercourse. Syria hoped to have all-Arab support behind it on the water issue; Syrian officials pleaded that 'the economic, politic, and security implications of the cutting of the river flow to the downstream countries required to be dealt with jointly by the Arabs rather than by Syria and Iraq separately.'[56] By insisting on the Euphrates and Tigris water as 'Arab waters,' Syria issued a call for the creation of a unified Arab strategy. The goal was to discourage separate agreements, to halt the inter-Arab conflict, and to encourage Arab reconciliation. It was hoped then that the perceived exploitation of Arab waters rendered it impossible to separate economics from politics in the Arab media. This later paved the way for the 1993 decision by the Arab League concerning the formation of a political committee on water issues. Besides the selective use of international law and claims of bad data, accusations of inefficiencies in the use of water have been made by the watercourse states. Syria accused Iraq of dereliction in updating its irrigation methods and in turn was subject to similar accusations by Turkey. According to a Syrian statement on 9 April 1975, the Iraqi government had failed to take steps to modernize irrigation methods used in Iraq in order to utilize the actual water flow more effectively. Turkey has used similar charges against both Syria and Iraq at later dates.

The 1975 crisis also showed how water rights issues might become entangled with other important issues, such as ethnic or oil conflicts. As we have seen, the exploitation of dissident religious and ethnic groups has been another feature of the water conflict. Both Syria and Iraq have exploited the regime dissidents as political leverage against each other. During the heated months of the 1975 crisis, Syria openly stated its support for the Iraqi internal opposition groups. In fact, the foundation of PUK's (Patriotic Union of Kurdistan) permanent office in Damascus in June 1975 was a clear manifestation of Syrian policy. The exploitation of regime dissidents was later used against Turkey first by Syria at the beginning of the 1980s and later by Iraq at the end of the Gulf war. In 1975, Iraq succeeded in securing Turkish concessions on the Euphrates and collaboration against the Kurdish threat in exchange for oil. The repercussions of this were not limited to Turkish-Iraqi bilateral relations. At a minimum this cost Syria some oil revenues, at a maximum the loss of strategic advantage, since now Iraq had another outlet to send its oil to the world market. Up to that point Turkey had been able to maintain its policy of separating water issues from other issues, such as ethnic and oil. In retrospective, these developments were early precursors of what was to come in the following decades.

The apportionment of the Euphrates waters on a proportional basis between Iraq and Syria on the basis of the Saudi proposal did not materialize until April 1989. Even during the rapprochement period following the Camp David Agreement in 1978–9 no progress was made on the issue. Meanwhile, Iraq continued to protest against the Syrian withdrawal of water, especially during the drought prone years of the 1980s. Iraqi-Syrian relations remained tense throughout the 1980s. This was due partly to Syria's open support for Iran during the Iran-Iraq war, which stirred the mediation efforts by Saudi Arabia and Jordan both of which desired to prevent inter-Arab conflict. According to Seale, the emergence of the Islamic Republic in Iran 'put paid once and for all to any hope of a Syrian-Iraqi entente,' on the contrary, it 'sharpened their antagonism.'[57] The two Ba'thist regimes held diametrically opposing views about Iran. Syria welcomed the rise of Shi'i Islamic Republican Iran and eventually ended up on Iran's side during the long Iran-Iraq war, which deepened the animosity between the leaders of Syria and Iraq. Saddam Hussein, on the other hand, perceived a threat to Iraq's territorial integrity and concerned with the ongoing Shi'i dissent in the south of Iraq.

Last but not least, the 1975 crisis illustrates how the nature of the institutions, informational asymmetries, and the confluence of domestic and international context determine watercourse state polices given their relative power capabilities and the geographic position. As we have seen, the requirements of acquiring and maintaining legitimacy under exclusive institutions incentivizes governments to adopt policies that interfere other states internal affairs, exploit domestic conflicts for their own goals, and lead them to misrepresent private information about water data and water and other policies of facilitating opposition groups. In the end, this increases transaction costs and also makes the states vulnerable to similar policies adopted by rival watercourse states.

### *The 1980s: In Search of Cooperation*

In 1980, Turkey combined the Lower Euphrates Scheme and the Tigris River Projects under the Southeastern Anatolia Project (GAP). Turkey steadily continued to harness the waters of the Euphrates for HEP and irrigation (see Table 5.1). The second major dam project further downstream from the Keban dam, the Karakaya dam, was completed in 1987 and was financed in part by the World Bank on condition of Turkey's unilateral guarantee of 450 cubic meters per second to the downstream users. While work on the Karakaya dam was in progress, the construction on the third dam, the Atatürk dam, was initiated in 1983 this time without asking for international funding. The potential for credit blockage by Syria and Iraq, and Turkey's experience with the previous two dams that left the impression that international funding agencies were in favor of the rights of lower watercourse states, were thought to be instrumental in this decision.[58] The possibility of the water rights agreement was close to nil at the time given Turkish position that Iraq and Syria had not calculated their water needs based on objective criteria and their exaggerated amounts were unjustifiable especially under the wasteful practice of traditional water use and development patterns. To avoid international pressure in reaching an agreement on water rights and probably also to showcase its capabilities and growing power, Turkey opted to construct the Atatürk dam and the Urfa tunnels with domestic capital, technology, and human resources.[59]

GAP master plan projects consumption of 52 percent of the Euphrates flow and 32 percent of the Tigris flow. Only a minor part of the flow will

Table 5.1. GAP (The Southeast Anatolia Project).

| Project Name | Completion Date | Installed Capacity (MW) | Average HEP (GWh) | Irrigated Area (ha) |
|---|---|---|---|---|
| **The Lower Euphrates Project** | | **2,450** | **9,024** | **691,858** |
| Atatürk Dam and HEP | 1993 | 2,400 | 8,900 | |
| Sanlıurfa irrigation tunnel HEP | 2002 | 50 | 124 | |
| Sanlıurfa irrigation tunnels | 1993 | | | **376,699** |
| a. Urfa-Harran irrigation project | 1996 | | | (151,419) |
| b. Mardin-Ceylanpinar gravity irrigation | | | | (109,184) |
| c. Mardin-Ceylanpinar pumped irrigation | | | | (116,086) |
| Mardin-Ceylanpinar irrigation | | | | 111,939 |
| Siverek-Hilvan irrigation project | | | | 158,053 |
| Bozova irrigation project | | | | 45,167 |
| **Karakaya Project** | | **1,800** | **7,354** | |
| Karakaya Dam and HEP | 1987 | 1,800 | 7,354 | |
| **The Euphrates Border Project** | | **861** | **3,168** | |
| Birecik Dam and HEP | 2000 | 672 | 2,516 | |
| Karkamıs Dam and HEP | 1999 | 189 | 652 | 53,030 |
| **Suruç-Baziki Irrigation Project** | 2007 | | | |
| Energy project | | 44 | | |
| Irrigation project | | | | 146,500 |
| Yaslica tunnel | | | | |
| **The Adıyaman-Kahta Project** | | **195** | **437** | **77,631** |
| Camgazi Dam | 1998 | | | 8,000 |
| Gömikan Dam | | | | 7,243 |
| Kahta Dam and HEP | 2009 | 75 | 171 | |
| Koçali Dam and HEP | 2014 | 40 | 120 | 17,761 |
| Fatopasa HEP | | 22 | 32 | |
| Sirımtas HEP | 2013 | 19 | 87 | |
| Büyükçay Dam and HEP | | 30 | 84 | 12,322 |
| Bulam regulator and HEP | | 9 | 43 | |

Table 5.1. *continued*

| Project Name | Completion Date | Installed Capacity (MW) | Average HEP (GWh) | Irrigated Area (ha) |
|---|---|---|---|---|
| Atatürk Dam Lake irrigation project | | | | 23,998 |
| Samsat irrigation project | | | | 8,307 |
| **The Adıyaman-Göksu Project** | | **12** | **52** | **70,968** |
| Çetintepe Dam | 2013 | | | |
| Adiyaman-Goksu Araban irrigation | | | | 70,968 |
| Erkenek HEP | 2009 | 12 | 52 | |
| **The Gaziantep Project** | | | | **140,903** |
| Hancagiz Dam | 1989 | | | 6,945 |
| Kayacik Dam | 2005 | | | 20,000 |
| Kemlin Dam | 2010 | | | 3,088 |
| Seve Dam (drinking water) | 2005 | | | |
| Blekis-Nizip irrigation | | | | 10,964 |
| Birecik Dam Lake irrigation | | | | 95,976 |
| Bayramli regulator and irrigation | | | | 3,783 |
| **Individual projects** | | | | |
| Çagçag HEP | 1968 | 14.4 | 42 | 90,072 |
| Small water works | | | | 5,839 |
| **The Euphrates Total** | | **5,332** | **20,077** | **1,190,690** |
| **The Dicle-Kralkızı Project** | | **204** | **442** | **119,755** |
| Kralkızı Dam and HEP | 1997 | 94 | 146 | |
| Dicle Dam and HEP | 1997 | 110 | 298 | |
| Tigris right bank gravity irrigation | | | | 50,743 |
| Tigris right bank pumped irrigation | | | | 69,012 |
| **The Batman Project** | | **198** | **339** | **34,421** |
| Batman Dam and HEP | 1998 | 198 | 483 | |
| Batman left bank irrigation | | | | 15,828 |
| Batman right bank irrigation | | | | 18,593 |
| **The Batman-Silvan Project** | | **160** | **623** | **235,048** |
| Silvan Dam and HEP | UC[60] | 160 | 623 | |
| Kayser Dam | | 90 | 315 | |

Table 5.1. *continued*

| Project Name | Completion Date | Installed Capacity (MW) | Average HEP (GWh) | Irrigated Area (ha) |
|---|---|---|---|---|
| Tigris left bank gravity irrigation | | | | 169,321 |
| Tigris left bank pumped irrigation | | | | 65,727 |
| **The Garzan Project** | | **55** | **199** | **39,164** |
| Garzan Dam and HEP | 2012 | 55 | 199 | |
| Garzan irrigation | | | | 39,164 |
| **The Ilısu Project** | | **1,200** | **3,833** | |
| The Ilısu Dam and HEP | UC[61] | 1,200 | 3,833 | |
| **The Cizre Project** | | **240** | **1,280** | **121,000** |
| Cizre Dam and HEP | PR | 240 | 1,280 | |
| Nusaybin irrigation project | | | | 89,000 |
| Silopi irrigation project | | | | 32,000 |
| **Individual projects** | | | | 3,548 |
| Small water works | | | | 3,258 |
| **The Tigris Total** | | **2,057** | **6,776** | **589,194** |
| **GAP TOTAL** | | **7,389** | **26,853** | **1,779,884** |

UC: Under Construction
PR: Project Ready

Source: DSI 2014

have a lesser quality: 22 percent in the case of the Euphrates and 9 percent in the case of the Tigris.[62] As one of Turkey's prominent economists, Ziya Özis, has argued 'the Mesopotamian part of the Middle East water crisis appears to be an irrelevantly exaggerated problem, since the co-operation options are far more dominant than the conflicts, when reason and goodwill are sought and brought.' For example, Turkey could release a portion of the water, which exceeds the natural discharge in dry seasons, to the lower watercourse states. The construction of large reservoirs in Turkey also allows for the effective regulation of the flow and less losses to evaporation benefiting all watercourse states. As a result of such externalities, Turkey could ask financial contributions from lower watercourse states in return for such indirect benefits. In extremely dry periods, Turkey might partly refrain from irrigation and release the more water in return for economic/financial

Table 5.2. Syria's Water Projects on the Euphrates.

| Project Name | Construction Completed | Installed Capacity (MW) | Storage Capacity (MCM) | Irrigated Area (ha) |
|---|---|---|---|---|
| Tabqa Dam HEP and irrigation | 1975 | 800 | 1,410 | 640,000[66] |
| al-Ba'th Dam | 1987 | 64 | 90 | |
| Tishrine Dam | 1999 | 1.6 | 19 | |
| Irrigated area | as of 2010 | | | 206,987[67] |
| Upper Euphrates (Aleppo) | | | | 75,468 |
| Lower Euphrates (Deir ez Zor) | | | | 33,952 |
| Middle Euphrates (Raqqah) | | | | 97,567 |

incentives. There is still a possibility of supplying water from other watercourses in Turkey to the lower watercourse states of the Euphrates and Tigris.[63] It does not seem unfair for Turkey to utilize one-half of the water generated within its borders.[64]

Yet, the scale and the ramifications of the use of the waters of Euphrates, and more importantly Turkey's ability to finance the project without major loans from the international agencies, gave rise to concerns and resentment in the lower watercourse states. Syria, for example, was concerned with the impact of GAP on the future of its own water projects during the mid-1980s. At the time, Syria was building al-Ba'th dam further downstream from the Tabqa dam, and was studying the construction of yet another dam, Tishrine, on the Euphrates.[65] Iraq, on the other hand, was concerned about both GAP and Syria's water projects (see Table 5.2 for detailed information about Syrian projects). Consequently, the endeavors to procure a tripartite Turkish, Syrian, and Iraqi agreement on the Euphrates waters acquired new stimulus in 1980s and led to the formation of the Joint Technical Committee.

In 1980, with Iraq's initiation, Turkey and Iraq set up a permanent Joint Technical Committee (JTC) and Syria joined it three years later in 1983.[68] The main objective of the JTC was to determine the methods and procedures through which fair and reasonable settlement of the Euphrates and Tigris water rights could be attained. Aside from this ambitious objective, its objectives included the exchange of hydrological and meteorological data, the exchange of the plans of dams and irrigation projects, and naturally the discussion of initial plans for the filling of the lakes behind the Karakaya and Atatürk dams. Besides two meetings, which were held at ministerial level, the JTC convened 16 times from May 1982 until June 1993. The JTC eventually collapsed due to the Syrian opinion that the JTC could not meet its expectations and that the water rights issue should be solved at a political level.[69]

The JTC meetings were different than its earlier predecessors, which were convened on an *ad hoc* basis. The idea behind the formation of the JTC was that a peaceful solution could be attained if the means were discovered for conflicting states to collaborate in technical and other non-political matters. It was hoped that as time elapsed continuing co-operation in technical areas would bind the states together in such a way that the political differences would eventually vanish. The former antagonists would realize that it was notably more beneficial to have peaceful relations.[70] The JTC provided a regular channel to exchange hydrological and metallurgical data but failed to eliminate the differences among watercourse states on how to settle the water rights in the Euphrates and Tigris.[71]

In 1984, Turkey proposed a three-staged plan for optimum, equitable, and reasonable utilization of the Euphrates and Tigris watercourse.[72] The main goal was to tackle the problem of the lack of reliable data on the quality and quantity of water and land resources in the Euphrates and Tigris watercourse. The only way to achieve efficiency in water and land uses and in planning was through reliable data. The plan had three stages. The first stage was called an inventory study for water resources. At this stage, the activities pertaining to data collection on water resources and the synchronization of the quality and the quantity of the flows of the Euphrates and Tigris were covered. The goal was to synchronize the methods of data collection and the interpretation so that during the negotiations all watercourse states would have the same data, which would facilitate the solution of the controversy. The second stage called for inventory studies of the land resources covering the whole watercourse. The main goals were identified as the classification of soil and drainage conditions according to same criteria by all the watercourse states, exchanging all the available data concerning soil classification methods and drainage system, securing consistency in the implemented methods, and the evaluation of the most suitable crop patterns and irrigation methods. Finally, the third stage was the evaluation of water and land resources summarized in the work of the first two stages. Among the specified goals of this stage were the development of the most suitable and economically efficient methods of irrigation, crop patterns, cultivation techniques, and of plans for the development of water and soil resources; the modernization of the existing irrigation projects in order to minimize water losses; and achieving a balance between water supply and water demand by setting up simulation models.

The proposal, and the silent treatment it received from the lower watercourse states, showed how far apart the Euphrates and Tigris watercourse states were from each other.

During the JTC meetings, the major issues of contentions were both the subject and the object of negotiations. Iraq and Syria consider the Euphrates and the Tigris to be international rivers and insisted on limiting the determination of water rights on the Euphrates. Iraq and Syria did not even respond to the Turkish proposal for optimum, equitable, and reasonable utilization of the Euphrates and Tigris watercourse. First of all, the plan was based on the premise that the Euphrates and Tigris constitute one single watercourse system. Secondly, the implementation of the plan would be more beneficial to Turkey. Indeed, the best places for the construction of dams and water installations were in Turkey. The quality of soil in Turkey was also higher. As the poor soil conditions in Iraq and Syria have already made it necessary that there be further expenditures on the drainage systems and on the desalinization of an already highly salinized soil.[73] This was and still is mostly a result of lack of incentives and capacity to maintain water and land projects as opposed to developing them in both Syria and Iraq. In addition to these factors, the implementation of the plan implied the restriction of state sovereignty over the natural resources within watercourse states' territories. It was obvious that since the most suitable lands for irrigation and dams are located within the Turkish portion of the watercourse, the basin wide efficient use of land and water resources was likely to favor the upper watercourse state, forcing Syria and Iraq to reconsider some of their water and land resource development projects.[74] Notwithstanding the scientific merits, this plan was blatantly in favor of the upper watercourse state and appeared as self-interested as the lower watercourse states' indiscriminative anti-GAP positions. This proposal still constitutes the backbone of the Turkish position on water rights issues with respect to the Euphrates and Tigris watercourse.[75]

In legal terms, Turkey defines the Euphrates and Tigris as a single transboundary watercourse system. It objects to Syria and Iraq's absolute territorial integrity claims that an upper watercourse state is under the obligation not to cause a change in the natural integrity of the resource without the consent of lower watercourse states. Non-interference by upper watercourse states to water flow suggests that a formerly used amount of water gains the property rights status has thus become the basis of acquired rights claims. Accordingly, a 'prior appropriation' impedes the utilization of waters by upper watercourse states,[76] since any reductions in water flow will likely cause a significant harm to lower watercourse states. Rightly so,

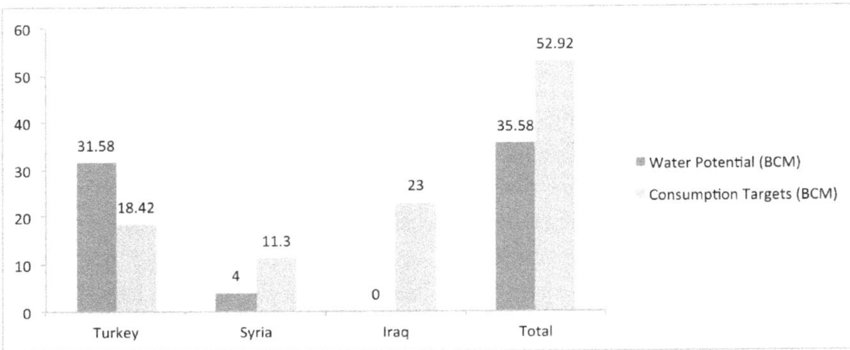


**Figure 5.1.** The Euphrates: Water Potential and Consumption Targets (billion cubic meters per year).

Turkey argues that prior usage of water by lower watercourse states is only one of the many factors that have to be taken into account when trying to settle water rights claims.[77]

The annual yield of the Euphrates and Tigris basin is 84.25 BCM. The Euphrates, which is formed by the Murat and Karasu rivers, has a flow of 35.58 BCM and a length of 2,935 km. The Tigris, which is formed by the Batman, Sason, and Yanar rivers, has a flow of 48.65 BCM and a length of 1,658 km. The consumption targets of Turkey, Syria and Iraq for the Euphrates are 18.42 BCM (51.80 percent), 11.50 BCM (31.8 percent) and 23.00 BCM (64.60 percent), respectively, while their contributions are 31.58 BCM (88.7 percent) in Turkey, 4.00 BCM (11.3 percent) in Syria, and none in Iraq (see figures 5.1 and 5.2). Whereas for the Tigris river, these consumption targets and contribution of water are 6.87 BCM (14.1 percent) and 25.0 BCM (51.90 percent) in Turkey, 2.60 BCM (5.4 percent), and no contribution in Syria, and 45.00 BCM (92.5 percent) and 23.43 BCM (48.1 percent) in Iraq, respectively. So the combined demands of the watercourse states amounts to 148 percent of the total flow capacity of the Euphrates and 111 percent of that of the Tigris.[78] The reconciliation of these demands has not proven to be easy. All the watercourse states, including the upper watercourse state, Turkey, would like to reach some sort of agreement, but so far unable to locate one.

Once it became clear to the lower watercourse states that Turkey would utilize more water from the Euphrates than from the Tigris for irrigation purposes, Syria and Iraq claimed acquired rights on the Euphrates' waters. During the negotiations, Syria argued that unlike the Euphrates, the Tigris did not have the same importance for meeting the potential water needs of

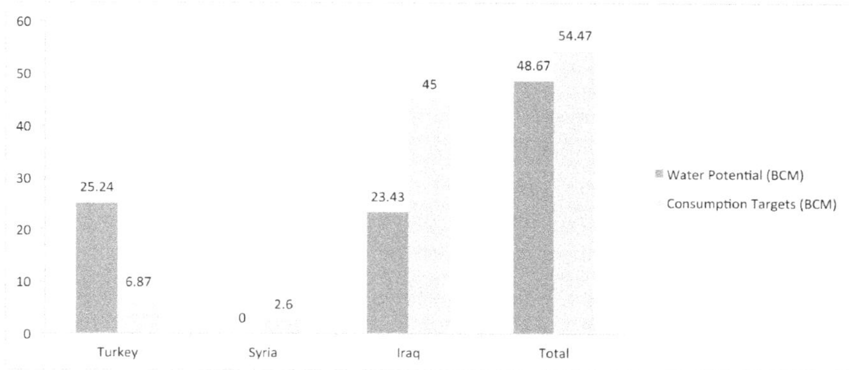


**Figure 5.2.** The Tigris: Water Potential and Consumption Targets (billion cubic meters per year).

Syria. As a middle watercourse state, Syria was still going to benefit from the negotiations if Iraq managed to get 700 cubic meters per second, which is about two thirds of the Euphrates flow. Also, the physical characteristics of the Tigris do not allow Syria to use the Tigris waters other than possibility for pumping water into Khabur. On the other hand, since both Syria and Turkey's plans for expansion of irrigated areas mostly involved the Euphrates, Iraq chose to focus its demands on the Euphrates. Thus for different reasons, the positions of Syria and Iraq converged on the demand for separate negations on water rights for the Euphrates and the Tigris. Most importantly, however, the imminent impounding of the Atatürk dam and Turkey's plans to irrigate *c*.1.7 million ha played a key role in the materialization of a water rights agreement on the Euphrates. On 17 April 1989, Iraq and Syria concluded an agreement according to which Syria would receive 42 percent and Iraq 58 percent of the flow entering into Syria from Turkey and a joint technical committee would be formed to settle technical and management problems arising from the application of the agreement.

Turkey interpreted this agreement as just a water-sharing plan and far from achieving optimum, equitable, and reasonable utilization of the resources of the watercourse, and as an all-Arab attempt to force Turkey into a trilateral agreement. Furthermore, Turkey met the Syrian submission to have less than 60 percent of the Euphrates flow with suspicion. In 1972, Syria insisted that Iraq should agree to give 60 percent of the Euphrates waters to Syria. When Iraq offered 45 percent, it was turned down and a subsequent offer of 50 percent was also rejected by Syria.[79] From the Turkish perspective, it seemed that Syria consented to have only 42 percent, which constitutes as substantial reduction from the earlier demands of 60 percent of the Euphrates water in order to forge a common front against Turkey. Since a few years earlier, as part of the 1987 Security Accord, Syria and Turkey signed a protocol of Economic Cooperation with stipulations on the water issues related to the Euphrates. In article 6 of the protocol, Turkey promised to allocate a minimum average of 500 cubic meters/second of the Euphrates flow at the Turkish-Syrian border during the impounding period of the Atatürk dam until the final allocation of the Euphrates. Article 7 of the protocol stipulated that Turkey and Syria would work together to allocate the Euphrates and Tigris waters within the shortest possible time, and article 9 stated that Turkey and Syria agreed in principle to construct and operate jointly irrigation and HEP projects.[80] On 20 July 1988, the Turkish-Syrian joint economic committee protocol, in accordance with the stipulations of the 1987 agreement, was signed in Ankara. Under the terms of the protocol, the two countries agreed jointly construct a dam on the Euphrates at the Turkish-Syrian border, exchange electricity, and technological exchange in the fields of sugar, cement, agricultural machinery, textiles and the medical industries.[81]

These two agreements led to the emergence of the current de facto water rights regime in the Euphrates watercourse: Turkey is obligated to release 500 cubic meters per second and Syria is obligated to release 58 percent of that to Iraq. However, the relations between the watercourse states remained tense due mostly to the exploitation of regime dissidents. Iraqi support for the Syrian opposition groups deteriorated the Iraqi-Syrian relations. On 21 February 1990, Syrian opposition groups formed the Patriotic Front for National Salvation. The Front was composed of the political and religious organizations and parties based in Iraq and Jordan, including the Muslim Brotherhood, which had never co-operated with nationalist and regionalist groups until that time, at least not without preconditions. The Front based in Baghdad aspired to oust President Assad 'by armed struggle if the people wish' and establish a multi-party parliamentary system. It also had financial support from Iraq. Before the announcement of the Front, Iraq rejected reconciliation efforts with Syria on the grounds of the impossibility of 'ethical, principled, and realistic understanding of and dealings with the President Hafez al-Assad's regime.'[82] Iraq declared that any moves towards rapprochement would have to precede a change in the policies of President Assad.

The Turkish-Syrian bilateral relations were not any better. Turkey's main concern at this time was the PKK-instigated Kurdish insurgency, which found support in Syria. It is widely believed that Turkey signed the 1987 accord in exchange for Syrian co-operation on border security issues. This belief seems to find support in Prime Minister Özal's remarks on 1 October 1989 against the continued support by Syria of the PKK: 'If Syria did not stick to the requirements of the 1987 Accord, Turkey would also see itself not bound by the requirements of its 1987 promise which stipulated that Ankara should deliver 500 cubic meters per second.'[83] Syrian-Turkish relations soured when a Turkish civilian aircraft was shot down 20 km inside Turkish territory by Syrian jets on 21 October 1989. The event resulted in the death of five people and the deterioration of bi-lateral relations. The tension worsened further when some of the Members of the Turkish National Assembly threatened the Syrian government with cutting the Euphrates flow unless Syria ceased its tacit support for the PKK, which was in full contradiction of the agreement of 1987. A special commission, which was set up by Syria to investigate the shooting down of the Turkish civilian aircraft, concluded that pilot error had caused the accident. Accordingly, the Syrian government agreed to pay compensation.[84] Shortly after the souring of the bi-lateral relations between Syria and Turkey, a crisis broke out over the Euphrates.

### *The Atatürk Dam Crisis*

A significant drop in the Euphrates flow occurred when Turkey diverted the river flow in order to fill the lake behind the Atatürk Dam for a month between 13 January and 13 February 1990. Both Syria and Iraq protested to Turkey about the damage that had occurred to their economies and mobilized the Arab world against Turkey.[85] The ensuing crisis suggests the existence of reasons other than so-called economic damage as likely the cause of the disproportionate response.

The official notification about the impounding of the Atatürk Dam was given to Syria and Iraq on 20 November 1989 along with some technical information. Following the notification, the Iraqi oil minister, Al-Chalabi, demanded a shorter, two weeks, impounding period during his meeting with President Özal on 14 January 1990. A day later the Syrian foreign minister made similar demands to the Turkish ambassador in Damascus and complained about the damages to Syria's water and electricity supplies. In return, Turkey offered Syria to supply any shortfall in electricity production, but declined to bargain over both the amount of water to be released during the impounding period and the length of the period of impounding.[86] President Özal also declared that Turkey had taken the needs and concerns of its neighbors into account and further pledged that Turkey would never use the control of water to threaten Syria and Iraq.[87]

Iraq and Syria interpreted the Turkish refusal as a verification of the claim that the filling of the Atatürk Dam was not the real reason and the technical considerations did not play any role in both the decision to impound and its length. Syria and Iraq claimed that the two week period was enough to fill the reservoir behind the Atatürk Dam and therefore Turkey's real intention was somehow to pressure Syria and Iraq. Some commentators even argued that Turkey was using water to create pressure on Syria, and to limit Iraq's enhanced influence due to its 'victory' in the Iran-Iraq War.[88] However, none of these claims held up under close scrutiny. It is more likely that Syria and Iraq were more concerned by their limited options in responding to what appeared to be a unilateral upper watercourse action and its symbolic and material meanings than the minimal economic losses.

Indeed, Turkey took precautions to keep the adverse effects of its action to a minimum level. The date of the impounding was determined by considering the time when the water requirements of Syria and Iraq were at the lowest level.[89] By choosing winter, when precipitation was at its highest and evaporation at a minimal, the loss to Iraqi and Syrian agriculture would be kept at its lowest. Furthermore, the discharge of the Euphrates had been increased to compensate the decrease prior to the cut off period. The total amount of water released to Syria between 23 November 1989 and 12 February 1990 was 3.6 BMC corresponding to an average of 509 cubic meters per second. This was slightly above the agreed amount of the 1987 protocol between Turkey and Syria.[90]

Immediately after the impounding period began, Syria sent a diplomatic note demanding a shortened impounding period and an increase in the amount of water entering Syria.[91] Syria also summoned the Arab League, which issued a statement in line with Syrian demands and called for a just apportionment of the Euphrates waters among the watercourse states. Furthermore, Syria turned to clandestine means that were less than acceptable and upsetting for both Turkey and Iraq: the use of the Kurds as a policy tool.

On 8 January 1990, a group of PKK militants tried to infiltrate Turkey from Syria. The encounter between Turkish security forces and the militants ended up in the death of nine terrorists who were carrying Syrian identity cards. According to Bölükbası, 'One cannot with certainty ascribe this infiltration attempt to Hafez Assad's anger over the diversion issue and his desire to get even with Ankara. But, in the past, Damascus has usually chosen to show its displeasure of unfavorable events by using clandestine methods.'[92] Despite official Syrian denial, Syria's record as a sponsor of terrorist organizations is well documented. It would be of no surprise if Bölükbası's assessments were correct.

Syria also allegedly claimed to release water from the Lake Assad for Iraq's benefit during the impoundment period. This change in Syrian attitude was linked with a transformation of the international context with the decline of the Soviet Union, which resulted in a decrease in the amount of assistance Syria got. Subsequently, Syria felt the need for improving its relations with the Arab world by working on its relations with Iraq first.[93] On the other hand, this meant little in real terms to Iraq and did not in fact take place. Since during the same period, Turkey released 3.6 BCM and Syria only allowed 860 MCM (less than 23.9 percent) of it to flow to Iraq. This was far less than the 58 percent stipulated under the 1989 agreement between Syria and Iraq.[94]

Concerned with the likelihood of further disruptions and the long-term adverse effects of Turkish and Syrian water development projects, Iraq made it clear to high level Turkish officials during the Turkish Prime Minister's visit to Baghdad on 5–7 May 1990 that the allocation of the Euphrates was the most important issue between Iraq and Turkey. Throughout the meetings, Iraq insisted on a trilateral agreement on the Euphrates and an increase in the amount of water flowing into Syria to 700 cubic meters per second. Turkey maintained its position that if used efficiently, the amount stipulated in the 1987 Protocol, 500 cubic meters per second, was just and sufficient for Syrian and Iraqi needs. In retaliation, Iraq refused to renew the 1984 security protocol, which allowed Turkish military forces to conduct cross-border operations up to 5 km within Iraqi borders in pursuit of PKK terrorists.[95] Following this, Turkey radically changed its policy towards its Kurdish citizens in line with the European Union's laws and regulations on human rights.

In retrospect, the Atatürk dam crisis revealed indications of Iraq's power[96] and its regional aspirations. The crisis also once again indicated the deeply entwined nature of water rights issues with ethnic conflicts and oil politics in the region. The rejection of the renewal of 1984 Security Accord constituted a turning point in bilateral Turkish-Iraqi relations, which were mostly based on mutual understanding and cooperation until that time.[97] Clearly by the late 1980s this was not the case. Iraq was no longer at war with Iran and its dependency on Turkey for exporting Iraqi oil was weakening. During the Iran-Iraq war when the Gulf route was closed to oil tankers, the only outlet for Iraqi oil was the Yumurtalık pipeline through Turkey. Considering the fact that oil constituted 96 percent of Iraq's national income, the importance of cordial relations with Turkey becomes apparent. Turkey was also Iraq's principal import source providing up to 75 percent of its food imports. Iraq's dependency on Turkey during the Iran-Iraq war for its oil export and imports in general explains Iraqi silence during the 1980s regarding Turkish water projects. Furthermore, by the end of the Iran-Iraq war, Iraq had accumulated a substantial amount of debt, about US$ 80 billion, and owed Turkey about US$ 2.5 billion. This amount seems an insignificant cause for further tensions in bilateral relations yet of this amount Iraq paid off 600 million dollars and made the payment of remaining amount contingent upon the resolution of the water rights conflict over the Euphrates.[98] By the late 1980s, Turkey represented a risky dependency for Iraq *vis-à-vis* oil and water.

At this low point of extremely sour relations among the watercourse states, the first Gulf War broke out following Iraq's invasion of Kuwait in the summer of 1990. Not only did the Gulf War curtail Iraq's burgeoning power and strategic aspirations, which were likely going to cause problems for Turkey and Syria, but also the continued instability in Iraq and its spread made any possibility of a negotiated settlement on water rights highly unlikely.

### *The 1990s: At the Crossroad of Ethnic, Religious, Water, Oil, and Border Conflicts*

The early 1990s was the beginning of extreme instability in the region and the concurrent failure of the Euphrates and Tigris watercourse states to reach a conclusive settlement on water rights despite the existence of growing concerns and feelings of urgency over Turkey's GAP development project. By the late 1980s, Turkey not only continued its progress on the implementation of the Southeastern Anatolia Project (GAP), but also succeeded in securing international funding by transforming GAP into an integrated sustainable development project in accord with the guidelines of the United Nations Development Program (UNDP).[99] In fact, the International Water Resources Association (IWRA)[100] gave GAP the Millennium Award for its concept of development as a human centered effort addressing social, economic, cultural, and environmental dimensions of economic development. This change in the attitude of international organizations requires an explanation other than the transformation of GAP from a water development project into an integrated development project. The general context of Middle Eastern politics provides us with clues to understand what really happened.

As a close ally, the pressure of the US on these organizations may partly explain the change in the policy of major international donors. The 1991 Gulf War reinforced Turkey's role as an ally of the US in the Middle East and has continued despite Turkish-US problems over first Iraqi invasion routes in

2003 and most recently about the Syrian regime. Turkey's Gulf War policy provided an opportunity to demonstrate its crucial geopolitical and geostrategic importance in the ever volatile Middle East. The 1980s were difficult years *vis-à-vis* Turkey's relations with the European Union (EU). Its membership bid to the EU faced obstacles concerning the stability of Turkish democracy, the army's role in domestic politics, civic freedom and individual rights even when Turkey fulfilled the membership conditions, including the reduction of subsidies and customs duties, and restrictions on agriculture and emigration to EU countries. The Gulf crisis provided an opportunity for Turkey to improve its standing with Europe. Not only did Europe support Turkey's diplomatic incursions in the Turkish speaking republics of the former Soviet Union, but it also provided several billion dollars in aid to Turkey. Furthermore, Turkey received US endorsement for its policy towards the Turkish speaking republics of the former Soviet Union, support for the Baku-Tbilisi-Ceyhan oil pipeline, as well as considerable tariff concessions especially for textiles and military equipment and investments from the US.[101] Considering the geopolitical context during this decade, the change of attitude towards GAP among the international organizations could be seen as the extension of increasing US support for Turkey for strategic reasons.

Following the crisis of 1990–1, Iraq became a pariah state. The United Nations (UN) imposed strict sanctions on Iraq further debilitating the country. The allied forces devastated most Iraqi infrastructure, including water, imposed embargoes and created security zones.[102] Widespread infrastructure destruction hurt the Iraqi population the most. More than a decade later, electricity production had still not reached its pre-war levels. The collapse of the electric power grid and water and sanitation systems ensured the collapse of public health by causing outbreaks of dysentery, cholera, and water-borne diseases. The destruction of water treatment facilities caused sewage to flow directly into the Tigris contaminating the drinking water exacerbating the problems. It was estimated that the attacks against Iraqi infrastructure cost an estimated minimum 110,000 civilian deaths between 1991 and 2003. Iraq also lost control of its northern territories including some portion of the Tigris watercourse and witnessed the revival of a distinct sense of ethnicity in the Sunni-Shi'i-Kurdish divide.[103]

Turkey's economic losses from the war were heavy, estimated at between US$ 9 billion to US$ 40 billion due mostly to the loss of Iraqi oil royalties and Iraqi markets. Yet the most drastic effect of the Gulf War was on the Kurdish issue and PKK terrorism. In the aftermath of the war, Turkey found itself harboring an estimated 500,000–700,000 Kurdish refugees. The safe zone created in Iraq provided the PKK with an alternative home to conduct terrorist attacks against Turkey. In the current situation, however, northern Iraq has now become the main center for Kurdish dissidents after the purge of the PKK from Syria.

Throughout the 1990s, Turkey tried to halt Syrian support for the PKK with all the means at its disposal ranging from economic incentives to disguised threats. In 1992, Turkey directly accused Syria of supporting the Kurdish insurgency in Southeast Anatolia since the early 1990s following the Atatürk dam crisis, and initiated a diplomatic campaign against Syria. In January 1992, the Turkish interior minister singled out Syria and Iraq among the states that were accountable for contributing to the separatist movement among the Turkish Kurds. The accusation was publicized a few months before the interior minister's Damascus visit during which Turkey and Syria signed two protocols aimed at revitalizing the security agreement of 1987, which Syria had failed to carry out.[104] Under the terms of the agreement, both countries condemned terrorism and pledged to undertake intervention against any illegal activity threatening each other's stability, to strengthen the security along the borders, and to exchange information likely to lead the capture of criminals. Turkey claimed that 7,000 out of 10,000 PKK guerrillas were based in Syria and northern Iraq.[105]

On 2 August 1992, the Turkish Foreign Minister Hikmet Cetin visited Damascus to negotiate the water issue in order to ease the increased tension between Syria and Turkey because of words spoken by Prime Minister Demirel on the eve of the inauguration of the Atatürk dam on 25 July 1992. Demirel had declared that Iraq and Syria could not make a claim on the water Turkey drew from the Euphrates and Tigris. At the end of the negotiations, a joint communiqué was issued. In this communiqué, both governments reiterated their adherence to the security protocol of 1987. A co-operation agreements which included agreements in various areas, including economy, trade, transportation, drug policies, technical affairs, and culture, was also signed[106] as a part of Turkish policy to give as many economic incentives as possible to Syria in order to deter Syrian support for terrorism on Turkish soil and to secure peaceful relations.

However, bi-lateral relations worsened only a few months later. The first prognostication of heightened diplomatic tension was Syria blaming Turkey for the failure of a trilateral meeting on water issues held by Syria, Iraq, and Turkey in October 1992 in Damascus. Nevertheless, the most severe reaction from Syria occurred in December 1992, as work on the construction of the Birecik dam began, which is located 20 km north of the Turkish-

Syrian border. An international consortium of French, Italian, German, Austrian, British, and Belgian firms undertook the construction on a Built-Operate-Transfer (BTO) basis. Syria complained to the Arab League and demanded the withdrawal of the international consortium. Turkey was as usual expecting some reaction from Syria, but it still found the Syrian response rather severe.[107]

Another important development with implications for the Euphrates and Tigris was the Iraqi inauguration on 7 December 1992 of the Saddam or the Third River, a 565 km canal with a discharge of 210 cubic meters per second between the Euphrates and Tigris. The main purpose of the manmade river was to remove saline water from an approximately 1,500,000 ha of land, of which 300,000 ha had been reclaimed. The opponents of the project claimed that the real goal was to drain the Southern Marshes that served as a refuge for the Shiite opponents of government. Another allegation about the project's goal was the development of proven oil reserves – estimated at about one-third of Iraq's total oil reserves – adding 2,200,000 barrels per day (bpd) to production through the drainage of the marshes.[108] One of the most significant implications of the Third River was the substantiation of Turkish and Syrian positions on the utilization of the Tigris waters to compensate the dwindling Euphrates waters due to upper watercourse development projects. For the first time, Turkish and Syrian claims found tangible support in the actual capacity of the canal linking the Tigris to the Euphrates.

Turkey's efforts to end Syrian support for the PKK continued in 1993. Prime Minister Demirel visited Syria on 19–20 January 1993. The agenda focused the issues of security cooperation, namely Syria's alleged support for the PKK, the situation in northern Iraq, and water disputes. During the talks, Prime Minister Demirel and the Turkish Foreign Minister Hikmet Çetin made it clear that 'it is not possible to make a bargain on water by provoking terrorism. Turkey can cope with terrorism even if it takes longer to (get) rid of it without Syrian cooperation, but Syria will never get the water deal it seeks by using terror as an instrument' and that 'it is not possible to claim right (over the waters) and obtain this right by giving support to terrorism because the Republic of Turkey will sooner or later defeat terrorism.'[109] Turkey and Syria also agreed to reach a conclusive agreement on the apportionment of the Euphrates water until the end of 1993. The next meeting held on 17–20 May 1993 ended with the refusal by Syria to discuss the inclusion of the Orontes river in the negotiations and the scheduling of another meeting for 21–24 June 1993. Only Iraq attended the June meeting and repeated its demands for the release of 700 cubic meters of water per second.

Meanwhile, when Turkey declared that it would not permit the usage of terrorism for procuring a water rights agreement, Syria retaliated by appealing to the Arab League. On 18–19 April 1993, the Arab League Council, which is the Arab League's supreme organ, convened for its 99th ordinary meeting. At the end of the meeting, in addition to forming a political committee on water issues, the Arab League Secretary, General Adel Meguid, issued a statement that 'Arab water security was an important question requiring political attention and security measures.'[110]

A few months later on 9 November 1993, President Demirel inaugurated the 26 km Sanliurfa Tunnels, which are the longest of their kind in the world and carry water from the Atatürk dam southwards to the productive, but parched Harran plain. The Syrian and Iraqi government used the occasion to reiterate their opposition to GAP; they claimed that GAP would affect large areas in each country and would deprive Syria and Iraq of substantial amounts of water from the Euphrates/Tigris rivers.[111]

The next controversy erupted over the Birecik dam. The dam was designed purely to regulate water levels and to generate hydroelectric power. In the spring of 1996, Syria repeated its demand and warned the companies involved in the construction of the Birecik dam that it would resort to legal action including compensation claims and boycotts if they did not withdraw from the project. Syria called on the financing companies and countries to suspend works on the Birecik dam until Turkey, Syria, and Iraq could reach an agreement on water sharing. In addition to the Birecik dam project, construction works was initiated on the southern most part of the Euphrates Border Project, the Karkamış dam and HEP. This was located approximately 4.5 km north of the Turkish-Syrian border. An Austrian led consortium won the US$ 170 million contract and planned to complete it in four years. On 3 December 1995 Syria formally protested against Turkey's program for the harnessing of the Euphrates. A few months later, on 8 January 1996, an Iraqi diplomatic note, the equivalent of the Syrian note, was sent to Ankara. They argued that Turkey's dam projects would prevent them from receiving their rightful share from the Euphrates, would infringe upon international law, and would relinquish Turkey's prior pledges.[112]

In April 1996, the Arab League siding with Syria and Iraq once again admonished Turkey. It accepted a resolution concerning the Euphrates/ Tigris waters. Under the terms of the resolution, the Arab League declared its support for the Arab states, Syria and Iraq, concerning the waters of the Euphrates and Tigris and their efforts for reaching a trilateral final agreement in accordance with the international law on international rivers. The Arab

League also decided to play an active role in pressuring the international funding institutions to link the provision of any aid or financial loan for the projects constructed on the Euphrates and Tigris in Turkish territory to the attainment of a prior agreement with the other watercourse states. The Turkish government was called upon to stop the measures related to the construction of dams and other projects on the Euphrates and Tigris watercourse without the consultation of the lower watercourse states, and also to stop the flow of polluted waters to Syria. To follow the implementation of this policy, the Arab League appointed a secretary general. The resolution was the sharpest reaction of the Arab League to Turkey's water projects and was motivated by issues beyond the Euphrates water rights. Thus, the resolution should be examined in the general context of Middle Eastern politics.[113]

Indeed, in mid-March 1996, Turkey and Israel signed a military co-operation agreement during the Turkish President Süleyman Demirel's visit to Israel. This was particularly vexing development for Syria and Iran, and generally for the whole Arab world. The Turkish-Israeli military accord was interpreted by Syria to be mainly targeting Syria and Iran, and led to the Syrian rapprochement with Iraq in order to counterweight the accord. The meeting was interpreted as a harbinger of the rapprochement between Syria and Iraq. But with the power of hindsight, the competition between Syria and Iraq in trying to attain regional hegemony significantly constrained the extent of this presumed rapprochement. At the time, Turkey was also actively lobbying for Iraq to promote UN resolution 986, which called for 'Oil for Food,' allowing Iraq to export US$ 2 billion worth of oil every six months in return for the import of food and medicine. The passage of the resolution reduced the economic pressures on Turkey since the 'Oil for Food' deal was estimated to bring Turkey about US$ 500 million a year.[114]

About six weeks later in May 1996, a meeting between Syria and Iraq was held to discuss the Turkish-Israeli military accord, Turkey's water projects for harnessing the Euphrates, and Arab solidarity.[115] During the secret meeting, Syria argued that the water weapon being used by Turkey damaged both the interests of Iraq and Syria, and that Turkey was collaborating with Israel and the US, who were trying to impose their hegemony over the Mediterranean and Red Sea. Although Iraq agreed with the Syrian analysis, it argued that the Israeli aircraft in Turkey were aimed at Iran not Iraq.[116] Turkey's permission for Israeli aircraft to train in its air space opened a new front against Syria in the north, and could be perceived as a way to pressure it to abandon its support of the PKK.

Throughout the 1980s and 1990s, Syria supported first Armenian and Turkish left-wing extremists, and later Kurdish separatists.[117] However, the Syrian efforts to link its support of terrorist organizations to the water issue eventually failed when Turkey forced Syria, by threatening to use military force, to sign an agreement in October 1998 that stipulated the termination of Syrian support for the Kurdish Separatists movement.[118] As noted earlier, the end of PKK terrorism originating from Syria removed one of the most contentious issues in the bilateral relations. It also provided an opportunity to develop relations in economic, commercial, scientific, and technical fields. In May 2000, Turkey and Syria held a Joint Economic Commission meeting for the first time since 1988.

The moderation of the Syrian position with respect to water rights issues became clear during the severe drought conditions of 2000. In mid-January 2000, Dogan Altınbilek, head of the DSI, expressed concerns over the worst drought of the century to hit the region and pledged that the amount of water released to the lower watercourse states would not decrease unless Turkey's own resources fell to such an extent that it could not supply 500 cubic meters per second. On 6 August 2000, Turkey reduced the water flow to 500 cubic meters per second from 1000 cubic meters per second due to the heavy drought conditions. By the end of September 2000, the Euphrates flow decreased to 300 cubic meters per second. As a clear indicator of Syria's new stance, Syria did not complain or protest the reduction in the Euphrates flow below the amount stipulated in the 1987 protocol. By mid-October 2000, the Turkish government issued emergency measures to save energy. The water levels in hydroelectric power plants reached the lowest levels in ten years due to below average rainfall, with the result that the three main dams on the Euphrates in southeast Turkey curtailed power production. In fact, the water level in Atatürk dam, which accounts for the 20 percent of Turkey's hydroelectric power, fell to 526.6 meters (1,738 feet). This was only 60 centimeters above the minimum level required for power production and as a result HEP plant was operating on full capacity only one hour a day.[119]

Another indication of the moderation of Syrian policy was cooperation between GAP-RDA and Syria's General Organization for Land Development (GOLD). A Joint Communiqué, which envisioned cooperation between Syria and Turkey in the sustainable utilization of land and water resources of the Euphrates and Tigris watercourse, was signed between GOLD and GAP-RDA on 23 August 2001. This cooperation also included areas of training and joint constructions of dams. Due to GAP, Turkey had developed good know-how skills for dam construction, which could be of use to Syria. Indeed, in June 2002, a Syrian dam near Zeyzoun broke and the ensuing flood destroyed hundreds of homes and killed at least 20 people. The dam was built just six years earlier in 1996 to store water for irrigation purposes. At the time of the incident, the dam was full and nearly all of 71 MCM was unleashed onto the surrounding 60 square km of land.[120] While the Zeyzoun case was much worse than the technical inefficiencies the Tabqa dam suffers from,[121] which include pollution and water management problems, the overall trend implied serious technological and institutional capacity problems for Syria at the turn of the century.

The history 1990s again illustrates how the nature of the institutions, informational asymmetries, and the context of domestic and international relations shape watercourse state polices. As the new century dawned, a fresh controversy erupted over the Ilisu Dam project on the Tigris and pointed to new international dynamics and the growing role of transnational environmental movements in water rights politics.

### *The Contentious Politics of Building Dams in the Twenty-First Century: The Ilisu Dam Controversy*

The last quarter of the twentieth century witnessed the emergence of a transnational network of anti-dam activists, which transformed the international politics of water infrastructure projects around the world. International River Network was formed in 1985 and became a powerful voice of protest by the 1990s. The escalation of international controversies over large dam projects led to the formation of the World Commission on Dams, a global multi-stake holder body in 1998 by the World Bank and the International Union for Conservation of Nature. The newly minted World Commission of Dams released an influential report, *Dams and Development: A Framework for Decision-Making*, in November 2000, which identified equity, efficiency, participatory decision making, sustainability, and accountability as core values for decision making and provided recommendations for dam building.[122] With mounting push-back against dam projects, the construction of the most recent large dam project on the Tigris, the Ilisu dam, quickly became the focal point of a high profile transnational dam controversy, as international non-governmental organizations (NGOs) raised concerns about the project and its environmental, social, and cultural impacts.[123]

The growing importance of non-state actors became evident in the controversy when the international consortium supporting the project withdrew on two occasions.[124] First, Skanska, the Swedish member of the international consortium withdrew after the release of the World Commission on Dams report in December 2000. Skanska, a financial contributor to the World Commission on Dams, cited international arbitration as its formal reason for withdrawing and highlighted concerns over resettlement, environmental quality, and submergence of parts of the ancient city of Hasankeyf, as well as the dispute over the Tigris between Turkey, Syria and Iraq. Subsequently, the British construction group Balfour Beatty, the leader of the international consortium, dropped the project on 13 November 2001 citing commercial, social and environmental issues and problems of getting the backing of nine export credit departments, Austria, Germany, Italy, Japan, Portugal, Sweden, Switzerland, the UK, and the US.[125] The loss of funding however was not the end of the story. Turkey updated the environmental impact assessment and the resettlement plan and awarded the project to a consortium of Turkish, German, Swiss, and Austrian construction firms in 2005. Again due to concerns over meeting international standards, specifically the World Bank Environmental and Heritage standards, the German, Swiss, and Austrian Export Credit Agencies withdrew funding on 7 July 2009. Continued work on the project led to sharp criticism from Iraq. The NGOs, the United Nations Environmental Protection Agency (UNEP),[126] and the United Nations Economic and Social Commission for Western Asia (UN-ESCWA) continue to have issues with various aspects of the project.

The NGOs were part of the larger transnational environmentalist movements against dam building and the marketization of water.[127] The majority of the world's large dams were built in the second half of the twentieth century.[128] After decades of building these large water infrastructure projects, some of their negative impacts on environment, biodiversity, and human settlements have become more visible at the turn of the century and driven the formation of transnational environmentalist movements against the manipulation of the world waters and the environment.[129] Overall, there has also been a growing concern, particularly in first world countries, over the impact of development on natural resources and environmental change. Also, the idea that each individual has a stake in conserving the earth's resources has taken off leading to calls for global governance structures that bring together multiple stakeholders in projects like dams, including governments, social activists, water experts, local people, and so on. Global environmental governance, however, is not feasible under the current political organization of the world order, which is based on the sovereign equality of territorial states. In the meantime, thanks to the work of water experts and their global networks, we know the importance of a holistic approach to water resources management encompassing the entire watershed for the long-term sustainability of critical ecosystems. These networks of water experts formulated Integrated Water Resources Management (IWRM) as a blueprint for regime building for governing water. Despite these efforts, IWRM has had little impact in international rivers, a testament to the difficulties posed by the geographic spread of watersheds across political boundaries where states cling to their sovereign rights. These difficulties grow exponentially in developing countries where the preconditions for democracy, let alone watershed democracy, to take hold are still just beginning.

Furthermore, a global market failure in environmental protection poses challenges for reconciling conflicting interests among various stakeholders. Currently, there is no way to capture the value provided by conservation. The creation of a market for the 'services' provided by nature, such as biodiversity maintenance, in rainforests, wetlands, and critical ecosystems, is in its infancy. At the same time, in developing countries both states and local people have strong economic incentives to exploit existing natural resources no matter the conservation costs. Turkey's GAP, for example, was conceived as an integrated sustainable economic development project launched to improve the living standards of those inhabiting one of the poorest regions in the country, which had negative population growth despite having the highest birth rate in the country due to outward rural emigration and prevalent poverty. The dam projects also have linkages to other infrastructure investments like better roads. Moreover, the promise of dams and their benefits gets politicians elected thus providing strong political incentives as well.

The conservation of the environment is not one of the primary concerns of the poor as the awful environmental quality of many developing countries indicates. Income levels have a direct impact on what societies value and their discount rate of the future. In low-income developing countries current consumption has a high value and environmental protection on the other hand has a low value, especially given the high cost of environmental protection in developing countries due sometimes to technological and other capacity and implementation problems. The opposite holds true for high income developed countries, where the value of current consumption is low and the demand for environmental quality is high. In the short run, this conflict of interests makes it challenging to find a common ground for developing and developed countries on the contentious issues of environmental protection. At one level, the analysis comes down to how we respond to the question of whether developing countries should have the same rights to make the choices that developed countries had when they were in the early stages of development, which lead in the process to some degree of environmental degradation. As long as developing countries maintain weak sustainability, in other words as long as decreases in natural capital, in our case water and land resources, is compensated with increases in other forms of capital, namely physical and human capital, then the answer probably should be a qualified 'yes'. This is because the aggregate capital, including natural, human, and physical, will be increasing over time enabling virtuous cycles of sustainable development, which in turn lead to higher income levels that provide a solution to the problem since development generates higher living standards and more resilient societies.[130]

Unfortunately, natural resource based development is sometimes economically the most efficient one for developing countries that characteristically suffer from low levels of human and physical capital but relatively high levels of natural capital. With development comes institutional capacity and resilience to adverse shocks through embedded incentives to find innovative ways to address scarcity problems. The best long-lasting solution to high population growth rates and the elimination of poverty comes through development. If ecological problems arise later on because of development projects, then states would also likely have the capacity and resources to redress these problems, since the total available capital stock in the form physical and human capital would be much higher. For example, Israel in 1993 initiated a US$ 25 million environmental project to restore portions of the drained Huleh marshes,[131] a restoration deemed successful in dealing with some of the negative effects of draining that took place in the 1950s.[132]

In this context, the best approach to environmental conservation in developing countries is designing incentive mechanisms that highlight the costs related to environmental degradation, that increase their technological and other capacities to conduct environmental impact analysis, and that encourage the creation and implementation of policies minimizing the negative externalities of development projects. Although there are political challenges, incentivizing the use and easing the transfer of new technologies that minimize the negative impact of development projects on the environment holds greater promise for equitable solutions to environmental problems, especially those that pits various stakeholders against each other. In the case of dams, if one of the major negative impacts is the depletion of available water resources because of irrigated agriculture, this can be mitigated by technologies including the use of modern more efficient irrigation techniques, improved drought resistant seeds, agricultural practices and technologies that minimize the consumption of water resources. The problem for developing countries often lies in the cost of acquiring these technologies and also of successfully educating farmers to adapt to the new practices.

Returning to the Ilisu controversy, within international circles, there is a strong somewhat distorted concern about the impact of GAP in general and the Ilisu project in particular on the Mesopotamian marshlands. Indeed, the United Nations Environment Programme 2001 report entitled 'The Mesopotamian Marshlands: Demise of an Ecosystem' squarely blamed upstream damming in addition to the drainage work implemented by the Iraqi government in the 1980s and 1990s for the devastation of the marshlands.[133] The drainage of the Mesopotamian marshlands had been undertaken since the 1950s initially for land reclamation and water management purposes and later for oil exploration and extraction purposes. The marshlands were completely drained by the Iraqi regime in the 1990s, as noted earlier, for mostly strategic, military, economic, and political reasons; to what degree the upper watercourse projects are responsible for the devastation of marshlands needs to be assessed.[134] More specifically, for the Ilisu dam, the 2013 UN-ESCWA report, 'Inventory of Shared Water Resources in Western Asia', stated a projected irrigated area of 313,000 ha and claimed that it would be the largest hydroelectric power plant in GAP with a hydropower capacity of 1,200 MW, producing an expected 3,800 GWh per year.[135] It will have the third largest hydroelectric power plant, after the Atatürk (2,400 MW) and Karakaya (1,800) dams, of GAP. The report also claimed that GAP has led to increased salinity of irrigated soils. Turkish plans for the Ilisu dam, however, make no reference to the projected irrigated area (see Table 5.1, pp. 134–6).[136] Because, there are no plans for irrigation, aside from the impounding period of the reservoir behind the dam, there would be no change in the water quantity and quality of the Tigris.

The two potential downsides for lower watercourse states are that the completion of the project makes the last GAP dam project on the Tigris, the Cizre project, with plans to irrigate 121,000 ha feasible[137] and that due to high hydroelectric power production capacity of the HEP, Turkey would buy less natural gas from Iraq, though it is not clear if this is even a concern. The irrigation of Nusaybin and Silopi as part of the Cizre project is troubling for Iraq but still manageable, since Turkey's projected consumptive use of all projects on the Tigris amounts to only 6.87 BCM. Considering that approximately half of the total flow of the Tigris – about 25 BCM – originates in Turkey,[138] this consumption does not seem to be an unreasonable or unfair amount. In fact, this low figure explains why Iraq has long objected to the inclusion of the Tigris in water rights negotiations along with Syria[139] and has chosen to focus instead only on the Euphrates. This along with the greater degree of control that Iraq has over the Tigris also explains why Iran had not been made part of water rights talks throughout the twentieth century and why Turkey has never made any commitments on the Tigris, except for the 2009 protocol with Syria verifying the prior 2002 agreement between Syria and Iraq. Iraqi complaints of the Ilisu dam project to European countries and the US followed a general pattern of protesting Turkish dam projects on the Euphrates and Tigris, and seemed unnecessarily elevated due to the support it received from the US. All the while, the US played an important state-building role in Iraq and was a sponsor of the newly minted Iraqi government as we shall in the next section.

Turkey's growing energy needs has been the primary driving force behind GAP. This is shown by the fact that nearly all completed dams have had hydro-electric power plants installed, while only 22 percent of irrigation projects have been completed to date. For Turkey, the alternative to hydroelectricity is natural gas. But gas is much more expensive and has environmental costs as it emits greenhouse gasses.[140] Turkey is like other developing countries in that it faces international pressure to reduce green house gas emission.

The controversy over the Ilisu dam and its social and environmental impact led Turkey to take further precautions to alleviate concerns about water quality and archeological and historical heritage. One result of this is that Turkey has begun to emphasize its work on new sewage treatment facilities to be built in the towns along the Tigris. The main threat to the quality of Tigris waters comes not from salinization, at least while it flows within Turkey, but the growth of cities, like Diyarbakir and the release of untreated sewage into the rivers and water sources, which will only increase with the population growth projections in GAP cities. Sustainable land and water use practices already require extensive and costly drainage and conservation works, which include infrastructure for water sanitation and treatment. Even the 1989 GAP Master Plan, written before the project's transformation into an integrated sustainable development project, included these infrastructure projects, which Turkey has been working to complete since 1982.[141] In addition, Turkey has facilitated the work of archaeologists and scholars from Turkey and other countries in excavating, recording, and preserving as much of the archeological heritage as possible. The projected flooding is also now planned to be restricted to lower parts of Hasankeyf, an important historical site, with its citadel staying above the flood line.

Strategically, the main downstream discontent seems to emanate from the reservoir behind Ilisu, which would be the largest one on the Tigris with a capacity to store 10.4 BCM and would give Turkey more control over the river's flow. The physical characteristics of the Tigris ease the impact of this alleged control. As we saw earlier, the main tributaries of the Tigris, the Greater Zap, the Lesser Zap, the Adhaim, and the Diyala, are not in the upper watercourse as they originate in Iran and Iraq. Turkey could hypothetically draw waters from the headwaters of the Greater Zap, but the geophysical conditions would make this extremely costly at least in this century. The cost–benefit structure of development projects explains the reasons why the majority of GAP focuses on the Euphrates and the surrounding areas. Indeed, the geographic conditions exercise significant influence on the cost–benefit structure of the development projects given the financial constraints on developing countries, including Turkey, to fund such projects. Often the poor state of infrastructure is directly correlated with a country's development level. Similarly, as countries grow and become more developed environmental problems are likely to lessen, as noted above.[142]

Furthermore, the recent prolonged droughts in the region and climate change projections underline the importance of a comprehensive reservoir strategy to hold water and release it during dry months. Turkish reservoirs have in the past provided much needed water at critical moments for both Syria and Iraq. During the last drought, from 2006 though 2011, there were frequent requests for more water by both lower watercourse states and Turkey acted in good faith and obliged when it could.[143] GAP dams alleviated the costly consequences of irregular flow and increased the overall supply of usable water, which was distributed throughout the year. A further regularization of the Tigris flow would be beneficial to Iraq. During summer months when the discharge is reduced, the combined impact of salinization, contamination and pollution due to poor infrastructure, and the extensive damage caused by economic sanctions[144] are exacerbated. A more regular flow would ease these pollution problems to a degree. Iraq still needs to undertake extensive water infrastructure work, including the construction of water treatment facilities, to make water usable for agricultural purposes by reducing salinity levels and removing contaminants related to human and industrial waste, especially below Baghdad.

During the last decade, the droughts along with the mismanagement of already limited funds, bureaucratic inefficiency, and sectarian politics hampered Iraq more than anything else *vis-à-vis* water management. This has often led Iraqi officials, such as the Minister of Irrigation, to blame upper watercourse states for the lack of water availability and quality problems. Yet at the headwaters only a fraction of the planned irrigation projects have been completed and the majority of them are on the Euphrates. This limits the role of upstream development projects on the water quality and availability problems in Iraq. The water quality in both rivers is quite high especially during the high flow season, though there is an increase in the salinity levels in some areas on the Euphrates. This has been recognized and Turkey has implemented works to alleviate the salinity problems arising from the return of applied water to the rivers and has begun an education campaign to train farmers on better irrigation techniques, including the dangers of water-logging and other problems. It appears also that Turkey's stated water demands on both the Euphrates and Tigris for irrigation purposes might include the water needed to deal with salinization problems, losses to evaporation, and unforeseen future demands. A number of scholars have pointed out that the projected future water demand seems more than the amount of water needed to irrigate *c.*1.8 million ha of land. For example, in the Euphrates, the official figure is 18.42 BCM while the planned irrigation area on the Euphrates only amounts to 1,083,000 ha. A realistic calculation of 10,000 cubic meters per ha gives a total water demand figure of 10,830 MCM for irrigating 1,083,000 ha. 12,000 cubic meters per ha gives a maximum demand of 12,996 MCM. The addition of evaporation losses from the major dams on the Euphrates, about 1083 MCM, brings the total Turkish water demand to 11,913 MCM and 14,079 MCM respectively for the Euphrates.[145]

From the 1950s on, the construction of dams has held great appeal for newly independent developing states. The act of building large dams often symbolized power and capability and helped to legitimize authoritarian regimes throughout the Third World. In almost direct opposition to these attractive large-scale water development projects stood the costly drainage and maintenance works. For decision makers, the management aspects of water and land resources have never been as attractive or (politically) useful as building large dams, especially in exclusionary political systems. Poor water resource management, for example, has remained rampant in Iraq and Syria and its consequences have been exacerbated in recent years. The prolonged drought of 2006–11 drastically affected the poorest segments of the Syrian populace, particularly those living in the northeastern parts of Syria. The Syrian regime's response to this crisis was less than desirable, but nevertheless was dictated by the logic of exclusionary governance structures that incentivized the regime to respond to the needs of its relatively small core of supporters concentrated in the western urban centers and to ignore the needs of the politically and economically unimportant segments of the society. The negative economic shocks from the multi-year crop failures, water shortages, and mismanagement of water resources led to massive immigration from rural areas to the cities. This strained the already overextended limited state capacity to address the problems brought by rapid urbanization, rising unemployment and inflation, and the resultant social unrest.[146] As we saw earlier, there were already signs of serious technological and institutional capacity problems for Syria at the turn of the century. In general, growing economic difficulties along with heightened sectarian and ethnic problems emanating from internal immigration and refugee problems can become uncontrollable in the context of political systems based on oppression and exclusion and can lead to social unrest and civil wars. In this, Syria was tragically no exception.

### *The New Century of Instability*

The terrorist attacks of 11 September 2001 led to an unprecedented response by the US. As a part of the Global War on Terrorism, the US and its coalition partners destroyed the territorial base of al-Qaeda in Taliban controlled areas of Afghanistan. In cooperation with Iraqi Kurdish forces, the US and its coalition partners, the United Kingdom, Australia, South Korea, Italy, and Poland, invaded Iraq in March 2003 officially to disarm Iraq, which was in violation of the UN security council resolution concerning weapons of mass destruction (WMD). President George Bush declared the end of major combat on 1 May 2003 with the termination of the Ba'th party rule and the removal of Saddam Hussein from office. However, the end of major combat has not brought an end to fighting; initial resistance against the invasion took the form of guerrilla warfare against the US forces and an internal civil war among the three major ethnic/religious groups, the Kurds, Shi'i and Sunni Arabs. The US policies and subsequent developments rendered the hope of establishing inclusive governance institutions in Iraq elusive.

To build a unified democratic Iraq, the US created the Coalition Provisional Authority (CPA) and appointed Paul Bremer as its chief executive in May 2003. The first two fateful orders of the CPA, which led to the expulsion of Ba'th Party members from the new Iraqi government and the dissolution of the largely Sunni Iraqi Army, mainly triggered the prolonged instability in the region. Soon thereafter the insurgency started with various militias organized along sectarian lines, which began to attack both the CPA and each other. In June 2004, the Iraqi Interim Government replaced the CPA and in 2005 the new constitution was approved and parliamentary elections took place. The insurgency continued unabated and intensified as more war crimes were made public leading the US to increase the troop number and to commence training the new Iraqi army. By 2007, the US and the coalition partners started to withdraw their forces on an agreed upon timetable. The completion of troop withdrawals in 2011 coincided with the Arab Spring, anti-government protests and demonstrations. Meanwhile, in Iraq, power became increasingly concentrated and exclusionary in the hands of Nuri al-Maliki, who was Prime Minister from 2006 to 2014. The insurgency intensified as Sunnis boycotted the parliament, the Shi'i dominated government, and its oppressive and discriminatory policies. The level of violence further spread with the outbreak of the Syrian civil war in 2011.

In the course of the US-led war against Iraq, military relations between the US and Turkey were strained. Fearing the consequences of a possible Iraq war on the stability of the region, the Turkish parliament vetoed the use of Turkish military bases by the US during the invasion. Turkey's unwillingness to allow the use of Turkish territory as a northern front for intervention into Iraq was a surprising reversal in Turkish policy, since the US had had the privilege of using Turkish bases for the previous fifty years. The failure of the US in getting a UN resolution, in providing reliable evidence for WMDs, and in proving Iraqi ties to al-Qaeda, prompted this decision. However, the concerns over regional stability, the Kurdish problem, and Iraq's territorial integrity were also instrumental in bringing the Turkish veto. As feared by Turkey, the PKK moved its operations to the Kurdish districts of Iraq and refused to renew the five-year ceasefire agreement of 1999 with Turkey, with the covert backing of United States' troops in Iraq. Thus, the authority vacuum in Iraq following the US invasion has led to the re-insurgence of PKK terrorism, which is a main concern for Turkey and a source of its discontent towards the US Iraq policy.

The regime change in Iraq also presented new opportunities for cooperation, however. On 10 July 2008, Turkey and Iraq created the High-Level Strategic Cooperation Council and on 15 October 2009 signed 48 Memoranda of Understanding on issues ranging from political and economic relations, security, trade, energy, and water. With the water protocol, both sides agreed to exchange hydrological and meteorological information and expertise in these fields and also emphasized efficiency in the utilization and management of regional water resources.[147] The sticking point in their relations – the use of Northern Iraq as a PKK base – gradually waned as

Turkey started anew an internal peace process and took steps to make its governing institutions more inclusive. The relations with the Northern Iraqi Kurdish administration improved significantly as Turkey recognized new opportunities for economic relations, especially the sale of oil through Turkish pipelines and lucrative trade relations.[148] In 2010, a Turkish consulate opened in Erbil in addition to those in Mosul and Basra. By 2011, Iraq had become the second largest export market for Turkey while Turkish construction companies have become active in Iraqi reconstruction and development projects. The increasing volume of trade and economic relations points to the foundation of mutually beneficial relations between Turkey and Iraqi Kurds. In addition to this, the stability of Kurdish controlled Northern Iraq along the Turkish border and the possibility of countering the increased influence of Iran in Iraqi Shi'i dominated government in the region, such as Iran's role in keeping Assad regime alive, has provided additional incentives for changes in Turkey's long standing policy of the protection of Iraqi territorial integrity.

At the turn of the century, at least initially, Syria and Turkey had found potential allies in their objection to the Iraq war. It was not hard to foresee the complications of the US policies favoring sectarian and ethnic divisions. In 2004, Syrian President Bashar al-Assad visited Turkey, becoming the first Syrian president in history to visit Ankara. Turkey and Syria signed a free trade agreement and reached a consensus on the joint construction of a dam on the Orontes at the border. Turkey also gave a green light to the Syrian request to pump water from the Tigris. This constituted Turkey's approval of the 2002 bi-lateral agreement between Syria and Iraq that allowed Syria to establish a pumping station on the Syrian side of the river. Turkey's President Sezer also visited Damascus despite the US objections and its policy of putting pressure on Syria. The Global War on Terrorism also put Syria under increased international pressure as it had long been on the list of states supporting terrorism. Iraq's displeasure with Syrian attacks had led to the deterioration of bi-lateral relations between Syria and Iraq. Reminiscent of the 1975 crisis between the two countries, Iraq had become an increasingly vocal critic of Syria's policies of harboring and financing Iraqi Ba'athists, and of allowing terrorist camps in Syria and insurgents to cross the borders.[149] The gradual toughening of the US policy towards Syria since the invasion of Iraq was likely instrumental in the change of Syrian policies, that is, the sudden desire to seek Turkey's alliance. Having resolved the problem of PKK terrorism originating from Syrian territories in 1999, the Syrian rapprochement was a welcome development from the Turkish perspective.

Cooperation in Turkish-Syrian bilateral relations peaked in 2009 with the creation of a Strategic Cooperation Council. During the first meeting of the Council on 15 October 2009, 50 Memoranda of Agreements were signed in a meeting on energy, cooperation, transportation, trade, and security. Four of these agreements were related to water. As mentioned earlier, one of them was about the construction of a joint multi-purpose dam, the Friendship dam, on the Orontes River.[150] Another memorandum formalized the Syrian water withdrawal from the Tigris with an installation of a pumping station. It was agreed that Syria would withdraw 1.25 BCM when the flow of Tigris water was within the average and when time and place allowed it. This represented the first agreement with any quantity provision on the Tigris. The remaining two memoranda were on the efficient utilization of water resources and the pursuit of joint efforts to combat drought and water quality remediation.

These 2009 Agreements on water between Turkey and its lower watercourse states presented an opportunity for the implementation of modern water conservation and management in the Euphrates/Tigris watercourse. The 2000 European Union Water Framework Directive was the blueprint for Turkey's new cooperation initiative on water including establishing environmental quality standards.[151] As part of its European Union accession, Turkey has adopted various EU legislations and standards in the process of undertaking a series of economic and political reforms and aligning with the EU *acquis*. Among these adoptions under the Environment and Climate Change chapter is legislation directly related to environmental protection, water quality, and industrial pollution control and risk management, among other things. The 2009 Agreements on water, which called for cooperation on the efficient use of water resources and for the adoption of common standards for measuring the quality and quantity of water resources in the Euphrates and Tigris, could have been the first real steps towards achieving the long elusive goal of a water rights arrangement. But, the operationalization of these agreements presented immediate challenges due to factors ranging from the technical capacity to the financial means of all the watercourse states. The current decade of the new century (2010–20) has been even more portentous then the previous one engulfing both lower watercourse states in extreme violence making these 2009 Agreements effectively now defunct. Currently (2016), it is far from clear whether the existing national borders will remain intact or if the Euphrates and Tigris watercourse will see the rise of new watercourse states, and thus new players in an already fraught and difficult situation.

### *When Things Fall Apart*

After the end of the Cold War, the spread of the third wave of democratization passed by the authoritarian regimes of the Middle East. Likewise, the US efforts to bring stability and democracy to Iraq with the hope that it would spread across the region failed and led to insurgency.[152] On 18 December 2010, demonstrations and protest erupted for better government in Tunisia and quickly inspired protesters across the Arab world. Within a short time frame, the authoritarian regimes of Ben Ali of Tunisia and Mubarak of Egypt were toppled. The regimes' poor economic performance, among other things, fueled popular demands for democracy and accountability, but these widespread protests did not always end with the protestors' desired outcomes, especially in the countries with the most oppressive regimes. In Syria, the spread of pro-democracy protests elicited the regime's heavy-handed response and culminated in the outbreak of the Syrian civil war in March 2011. At the same time, increasing violence born of unresolved political and sectarian issues has engulfed Iraq.

In short order, the brief rapprochement between Turkey and Syria ended when Turkey's attempt to mediate the Syrian civil war failed as the Assad regime did not follow up on its promises to end the violence and undertake reforms. By the end of June 2011, Turkey became blatant in its criticism of the Assad regime's crackdown of the anti-regime protestors when three thousand refugees showed up at the border. As the Syrian death toll and refugee situation has exponentially worsened, Turkey urged Assad to stop the atrocities and be more inclusive and responsive to the opposition's pro-democracy demands. When such pleas failed to change the regime's brutal response, Turkey called for Assad's removal from power to hasten the resolution of the Syrian civil war.[153] A few days after the imposition of broad trade sanctions by the Arab League,[154] Turkey imposed similar sanctions, such as freezing the Syrian government's asset, banning military sales and blockading weapons deliveries from third countries through Turkey.[155] These sanctions, as the Turkish government emphasized, did not include vital supplies like water and electricity that could harm the Syrian people. Indeed, Turkey has continued to keep its obligations regarding water. A private Turkish company also continued to supply about 20 percent of the electricity consumed in Syria up until October 2012 when the distribution network in Syria was damaged.[156] Notably Turkish food exports on humanitarian grounds have continued throughout the civil war and had returned to the level it was at before the unrest by February 2015.[157]

Currently, the four major players of the Syrian civil war are the Syrian regime, the Kurds (YPG and its allies), the Sunni insurgents of the Islamic State of Iraq and Levant (ISIL), and Syrian rebels who belong to various Islamic factions such as Jabhat al-Nusra and more moderate ones including the Free Syrian Army, the Islamic Front, the Mujahedeen Army, and Asala wa al-Tanmiya Front, some of which formed the Levant Front or al-jabha al-Shamiya in northern Syria on 26 December 2014. The Kurds have an interim government in three autonomous areas, namely Afrin, Jazira, and Kobani and received direct support from the US; under pressure Turkey also helped the Kurds in the battle of Kobani against ISIL. With Iran's blessing, Hezbollah also plays an important supporting role ensuring the survival of the Syrian regime.

There appears to be a tacit cooperation between the Assad regime and the Kurds, who emerged as a force after the withdrawal of Assad's forces from the Kurdish areas. The YPG has been fighting other rebel groups over the control of various border towns and parts of Aleppo. There are also various accounts of the Syrian regime contributing to the rise of Jihadist extremism.[158] The regime was, for example, selective in its attacks on various rebel groups, it released the majority of the ISIL leadership from its prisons in 2011, and facilitated the creation of armed brigades that allowed ISIL to become a force to reckon with in the region.[159] It seems that in the short run the Syrian regime benefited from the deterioration of the security situation as its supporters argued that the ouster of Assad would likely lead to the further spread of chaos and extremism in the region. The deteriorating security situation eventually enabled the Syrian regime to regain some support, as the law and order it represented became increasingly more valuable. Furthermore, strategically the emergence of ISIL as a threat has given the regime breathing space. The US is no longer calling for Assad's ouster from power even though it continues to threaten the use of force against the Syrian regime following the agreement brokered by the US and Russia to destroy all Syrian chemical weapons in line with the United Nations Security Council Resolution 2118, adopted on 27 September 2013.[160] The US continues to provide support for Syrian insurgents but to fight with ISIL not the Syrian regime.[161] There are signs of ongoing cooperation between the Syrian regime and ISIL on power production and its distribution. In fact, the Syrian regime has continued to pay the salaries of the employees at the Tabqa dam and has required the electricity to be sent to regime-controlled areas. A similar situation has also been present at al-Haririye thermoelectric plant. ISIL has military control of the plant but the refined fuel it runs on has been supplied by the Syrian regime.[162] Recent reports further indicate that cooperation between the Syrian regime and ISIL goes beyond power production and includes also the operating and marketing of the oil and gas fields, the majority of which now are located in ISIL controlled areas.[163] This situation undermines the Syrian regimes claims of fighting against ISIL. Though the Syrian regime survives, the United States rejected partnering with the regime against ISIL despite support for the idea from the United Kingdom and France.[164]

In 2014, ISIL seized control of large swaths of Syria and Iraq along the banks of the Euphrates and Tigris including major cities such as Tikrit, Fallujah, Mosul, and parts of Kirkuk.[165] Gaining control of the water supply and the dams along the Euphrates and Tigris seems to be central to ISIL's expansion strategy. There have also been several instances of ISIL's use of water as a weapon. For example, after the 2013 capture of Syria's largest dam on the Euphrates, the Tabqa dam, on 11 August 2014 ISIL militants threatened Turkey for the drastic drop in the Euphrates flow as the water level plummeted in Lake Assad. The real culprit for the lower level was the dramatic increase in electricity supply on ISIL's orders, which instructed that all turbines run continuously at full capacity. By mid-May, Raqqah, the unofficial capital of ISIL, had electricity up to 16 hours a day up from one hour a day when the Free Syrian army controlled the dam. Gaining popular support by providing basic services like electricity and water seems to have played a role in ISIL's decision. Iraq's Fallujah dam is another example. After capturing the dam in April 2014, ISIL initially closes the gates halting the flow and once the reservoir had filled, they let it overflow flooding to the east before finally opening the gates causing major flooding downstream.[166] ISIL's repeated attempts to capture the Haditha dam, which impounds Iraq's second largest reservoir and provides water and power to millions of people, was thwarted by Iraqi forces with the help of a series of air strikes by the US. The Syrian regime and other opposition forces also used similar methods to weaken and punish their perceived enemies. As a result, attacks on the water and power infrastructure have become commonplace throughout the course of the current quagmire.

Since September 2014, the US-led coalition has launched airstrikes against ISIL and al-Nusra front. Daily coalition airstrikes helped Kurdish fighters in Syria to retake Kobani in January 2015 and Iraqi forces to regain Diyala and Tikrit in March 2015. Despites these losses, ISIL has continued to expand, seizing another major Iraqi city, Ramadi, on 19 May 2015. This latest advance raises concrete worries about the future of Iraq. It is no surprise how quickly ISIL captured large swaths of Iraqi lands. Also it is no surprise that many former Ba'ath army officers have joined the ranks of ISIL forces.[167] As we saw earlier, the current Iraqi government has had serious issues in developing formal and informal inclusive governance institutions. In the absence of civil society organizations with their cross cutting ties, ethnic and sectarian forms of identity have become the dominant form of interest representation and the basis for the distribution of benefits. Following inconclusive elections in April 2014, Nuri al-Maliki tried to hold on to power, but under international pressure he stepped down. Haidar al-Abadi, who casts himself as a more moderate and inclusive Shi'i leader than his predecessor, formed the new government on 9 September 2014. Nevertheless, harassment by Iraqi security forces and Shi'i militias has been rising. Shi'i militias have been on a quest for revenge as a response to ISIL violence against the Shi'is preventing the return of people to their homes, destroying property, and carrying out kidnapping and extrajudicial killings of Sunnis in the areas taken back from ISIL.[168] Sectarian violence similar to the civil war that left tens of thousands people dead in 2006 and 2007 remains a serious risk in Iraq, especially as Iraqi Sunnis fearful of both Shi'i militias and brutal ISIL rule flee their homes seeking safety.

As conflict rages across the region with no end in sight, millions of people have become refugees to escape the violence. The main host countries, Turkey, Lebanon, and Jordan, have been overwhelmed as the ongoing crisis poses a detrimental threat to their political and economic stability.[169] According to Turkish official figures, as of November 2014, Turkey has 1,734,448 refugees while the unofficial figure is above 2 million (AFAD) and 85 percent of those live outside the camps. All told, refugees account for close to 2.14 percent of the population. Turkey initially declared 100,000 refugees as a critical threshold but the continued waves of refugees made this unfeasible. The sheer number of refugees puts pressure on social services and infrastructure, strains already tight budgets and the capacities of local administrations creating sociological, economic, political and security problems in almost all parts of Turkey, with the border towns taking the major brunt of it. Rising divorce rates and polygamy levels, the abuse of children and women, the expansion of shanty towns and slums, and uncontrolled urbanization are the most obvious direct negative effects. In economic terms, there are direct and indirect costs. The Turkish government has spent upwards of US$ 4.5 billion while the aid from the UN and EU only amounted to a paltry $246 million between April 2011 and November 2014. Rising rents and prices due to increased demand, rising levels of smuggling and black market activities, rising unemployment levels that topped 10 percent are among the indirect effects. Perhaps the most important challenges come in the form of political and security problems. The refuges have changed the fragile demographic balance in southeast Anatolia. For example, the local minority groups, the Arab Alevis in Hatay or the Turkmens in Kilis feel increasingly at unease with the influx of Sunni Arabs either because their minority status has been undermined or they have become the minority where before they were the majority. The conflict between local populations and refugees has been on the rise due to competition over scarce resources and public services, such as healthcare, which is provided free of charge to registered refugees, and to the re-emergence of eradicated diseases like polio or measles in the region. The local poor feel strong resentments towards Syrians, who receive free benefits and who supposedly are taking their jobs.

Local administration budgets and the infrastructure are built around the needs of local populations; the refugees are putting enormous pressures on the quality of the services as well as on their availability. Indeed the increased polarization has led to outbreaks of violence such as the small-scale skirmishes that took place between locals and refugees in July 2014 in Kahramanmaras and Gaziantep. A further escalation is likely as Syrian refugees have started to organize to provide for their own security and order. As of 19 May 2015, according to UNHCR data,[170] close to 4 million Syrians have fled their country going to Turkey (1,759,846), Lebanon (over 1,183,327), Jordan (627,287), and Iraq (248,367), while 7.6 million Syrians are internally displaced and 4.8 million are in hard to reach areas, leaving 12.2 million people within Syria alone in need of humanitarian assistance. The international community has been extremely slow in resettling and receiving refuges, nor has it been forthcoming with financial contributions to help with the costs of hosting millions refuges. This exacerbates the political polarization further as support for the refugees by local moderates is lost. Local populations' fears about the increased risk of terrorist attacks are real. Among the refugees, there are people who have ties to the Assad regime, ISIL, and the PKK. This increases and creates widespread security risks for Turkey in general and the border region in particular along with the long-term problems associated with poverty, destitution, marginalization and the rise of criminality generally among refugees.

In closing this chapter on the recent history of water and conflicts surrounding the Euphrates and Tigris watercourse, there are a few observations to be made. Under anarchy, the fact that people's inalienable natural rights of life, liberty, and property as identified by Locke in the seventeenth century might only by enjoyed by the strong gives ordinary people incentives to overcome collective action problems and to form institutions to govern themselves bringing order and containing violence. Collective action problems and the problem of violence continue to occupy scholars and it seems they will continue to do so for some time yet as both seem endemic to the human condition. But while the current situation in the region seems bleak, eventually the widespread violence will be subdued and order bringing peace and prosperity will emerge from the chaos. Tilly's now famous dictum that war made states and the state made war underpins the importance of war making in the formation of the modern state, especially its impact on state capacity.[171] Many commentators have drawn parallels between the Thirty Years War and the current Middle Eastern conflict. As Kissinger stresses in his recent book, *World Order*, the peace of Westphalia became possible only after the ravages of the Thirty Years War with the new order emerging after the will to fight was drained from the participants thus reaching an equilibrium when no party can thought of getting a better deal by continuing fighting. It remains to be seen whether the current calamities in the Middle East will lead to the emergence of such peaceful equilibrium. If so, the conflict may provide an opportunity for the rise of states in Iraq and Syria with greater organizational and bureaucratic capacity embedded within a more inclusive institutional set up in the near future.

The emergence of inclusive political and economic institutions is essential for remedying the conditions that have provided fertile ground for the breakdown of order and the emergence of extremist radical groups like ISIL. Reports of localized resistance to ISIL have been on the rise as increasing discontent in the ISIL controlled areas has encouraged organic resistance to oppressive ISIL rule. The coalition forces under US leadership have carried out airstrikes since September 2014 and will continue to do so until the security situation improves. The long-term solution suggests that military force alone will not be sufficient against ISIL. It is not easy to 'degrade' and 'destroy' terrorist organizations born of ideologies of political and economic despair and oppression without dealing first with the underlying impulses.

The mostly authoritarian political leaderships in the region are corrupt and operate under perverse incentive structures. The incentive structure is such that rather than tackling governance problems and addressing the concerns raised during the Arab Spring, the leaders, especially in the most oppressive regimes, like Libya and Syria, have encouraged ethnic and sectarian conflicts leading their people into civil violence in order to stay in power. Any stability in the Euphrates and Tigris watercourse and the sustainable exploitation of its land and water resources will depend on the elimination if not the improvement of the socio-economic and political conditions that led the way to the civil war and subsequent rise of ISIL and other similar non-state actors. The US war in Iraq prepared fertile ground for Islamic extremists around the world to find a place to grow in strength and numbers. The fledging Iraqi state mired with corruption and capacity problems on the one hand, and economic problems exacerbated by the severe droughts from 2006 to 2011 on the other hand, has been an ideal place for widespread discontent to foment and spread from Iraq and into Syria. There the large-scale population dislocations due to the worsening economic conditions in rural areas following the drought intensified urbanization problems and crippled the economy with a lack of electricity and water putting more pressure on the authoritarian Syrian state. Not only did the unemployment rate rapidly increase but inflation also went haywire with housing prices going up significantly. If one thinks of inflation as regressive tax, as it is, the worsening economic marginalization fed into further social marginalization against the dangerous background of diverse sectarian and ethnic cleavages within Syrian society and of the exclusionary political and economic institutions benefiting a small ruling coalition of Assad supporters. The story of Syria and Iraq in the twenty-first century is a cautionary tale about the dangers of exclusionary political and economic institutions not only for Syrians and Iraqis, but for all of us.

Out of the civil and sectarian violence, it can only be hoped that there will come the establishment of more inclusive political and economic institutions in Syria and Iraq that will create more resilient and open societies that can solve their problems peacefully and that will have the capacities to deal with adverse shocks, like water scarcity, droughts, climate change, and economic crises. The rise of open societies will also facilitate the development of a community of watercourse states and lead to the emergence of water rights institutions that are best suited for the sustainable and environmentally sound exploitation of natural resources.

# CONCLUSION

As Jean-Jacques Rousseau's stag hunt game goes, if the hunters coordinate their actions and cooperate they could catch a stag, which could feed all of them and more. If one of the hunters defects and goes after a hare, he could only feed himself and the rest will go hungry. The defector will receive a higher payoff regardless of what the others do, but all the hunters will be better off if they cooperate. In international watercourses if the watercourse states coordinate their actions and cooperate on the basis of the principles of integrated water resource management, which treats the basin as whole and aims to coordinate development and management of water, land, and other resources, they could achieve social equity, economic efficiency, and ecological sustainability. If they pursue unilateral exploitation of the resources in their portion of the watercourse, the upper watercourse states will have the higher payoff especially if the majority of the water originates within its borders, but all the watercourse would be better off if they cooperate. The solution of the collective action dilemma in these types of situations requires high-levels of trust and reciprocity, in other words a strong community among the actors and therefore also implies attendant similarity in formal and informal institutions.

There is no such community of watercourse states in the majority of international watercourses, including, as we have seen, in the Euphrates and Tigris watercourse. The closest the watercourse states came to achieving such a community was in 2009 marking the Turkish AKP government's attempts to reinvigorate its long neglected relations with Middle Eastern states emphasizing their commonality of shared religion. Reminiscent of the failure of the late nineteenth century pan-Islamism of the Sultan Abdulhamid, this recent attempt failed spectacularly in the face of concrete incompatibilities in the logic of political survival dictated by the governing institutional structures of the watercourse states. The AKP government was surprised when President Assad of Syria did not take their good advice of undertaking reform and giving the people voice and instead chose to repress the protests with violence.

When community is not possible, the next best alternative to the integrated water resource management (IWRM) is the delineation of property rights on water specifying ownership, corresponding duties and liabilities among watercourse states. This is also a challenging task. There is no universal first-best property based solution to international watercourse conflicts. The appropriate institutions for water rights are second-best institutions that take into account the context and source-specific circumstances of the contested resource. This requires watercourse states to reach a voluntary self-enforcing, that is, incentive compatible, contract. States could enter into such contracts with each other by establishing property rights institutions to protect their long-term benefits and ensure the sustainability of common water resources. But such an endeavor involves a costly and long bargaining process that often gets mired in failures due to similar problem facing the IWRM schemes. Indeed, the competitive unilateral exploitation of international watercourses regardless of their long-term sustainability has been pretty much the norm in semi-arid and arid regions. This has and will continue to lead to an avoidable tragedy of resource misuse and mismanagement.

Why then do states often fail to establish water rights institutions for governing international watercourses? At the most rudimentary level, there is a reason why such rights have not been specified. Water rights do not emerge in a vacuum. Social, economic, technological, geographic, environmental, and more importantly political factors play an important role in determining the cost of defining and imposing property rights international watercourses. As the history of international relations, which is replete with failed negotiations over the sharing and managing of international water resources attests, such costs have been quite high in the majority of international watercourses. Indeed, after years of negotiations, the three watercourse states of the Euphrates and Tigris still do not have a common standard for measuring quality and quantity of their shared water resources, as their experts have continued to disagree on the data during the Joint Technical Meetings. The failure to reach an agreement on even basic metrics among watercourse states indicates the magnitude of challenges facing watercourse states in their struggle to reconcile their conflicting interests and ensuring in the process of finding common interests a means of using the water efficiently and sustainably. To expand on this further, in the two following sections,

I present first the theoretical conclusions and then the empirical conclusions of this study.

## Theoretical Conclusions

Watercourse states have both common interests in the long-term sustainability of the shared resources and conflicting views in how best to share them and distribute costs among themselves. In light of the wealth-acquiring and wealth-generating capacity of natural resources, avoiding sub-optimal outcomes and achieving Pareto efficient resource allocation present a daunting task for states, especially for those which have been at odds with each other or are involved in a protracted conflict. States that are in conflict over high politics issues are often disinclined to cooperate over low politics issues. The existence of a protracted conflict among states could make the escalation of conflict less likely due to spillover fears, but could also create a status quo bias. Water issues cannot be readily isolated from other issues of ongoing conflict among states. Even if we leave aside the political impediments, *ceteris paribus*, it is not always possible to make one state better off without making the other one worse off, especially in international watercourses when it comes to the division of the resource. Aside from political circumstances, social, economic, technological, geographic, and environmental circumstances all play a role in determining the cost of delineating water rights by creating a gap between the social cost and benefits and the private costs and benefits of comprehensive water rights institutions.

In this study, I set out to trace the parameters of conflicts over water rights in international watercourses. I presented a new analytical framework in which a watercourse state' geographic position in the watercourse, the distribution of relative power capabilities, the institutional features, the transactions costs, and the context of (non)emergence of water rights are the key determinants. Building on the collective action theories of common pool resources, as well as the realist and liberal perspectives of conflict and cooperation in explaining such conflicts, the bargaining framework presented in this book provides a complete model for understanding international water conflicts. As noted earlier, watercourse states have varying degrees of common and conflicting interests with respect to shared water resources and the consequences of non-cooperation, therefore the failure to form comprehensive water rights institutions does not have a uniform impact on them. In fact, although non-cooperation may present socially suboptimal watercourse-wide outcomes and may more likely be Pareto inefficient, some watercourse states could accrue benefits from such non-cooperation and thus might have a strong preference for the continuation of the current status quo.

The impact of competitive unilateral exploitation of water resources varies depending on the characteristics of the resource in question. The general characteristics of common pool resources makes all users suffer equally from the decrease and contamination of the resource regardless of their geographic position in the basin. For example, underground water aquifers are subject to a simultaneous use scenario with a more or less symmetric distribution of detrimental effects on the states. This makes the discrepancy between socially optimal outcomes and privately optimal outcomes closer in the long run. However, this does not suggest that in the short run states would be able to overcome collective action problems and institute a water rights regime ensuring the long-term sustainability of the aquifer, even though the incentives for doing so would be stronger. This is especially so given the technological advances in our understanding of the physical characteristics of underground water resources, the intensity of states' common interests, and the more or less equal suffering that inaction would bring, all of which it would seem would facilitate reaching an agreement since the alternative would be the complete loss of the resource. International surface water resources, such as rivers, on the other hand, flow through different national territories sequentially and thus are not subject to such equally shared detrimental impacts. This sequential use increases the importance of one's geographic position in the watercourse. Accordingly, the asymmetric distribution of the negative effects, as well as the upper watercourse states' capability to decrease the quantity and the quality of water available for downstream use, separate international rivers from other types of common pool resources and necessitate the inclusion of other considerations in the analysis. The distribution of power among watercourse states and a state's geographic position – upper, middle, or lower – are the most important factors that govern the nature of the relationship by creating asymmetric costs, benefits, and bargaining leverage among watercourse states. The delineation of water rights in international watercourses is thus not a common pool resource problem, but a bargaining problem among watercourse states.

I have also offered two analytical steps for considering these problems consisting of the specification of states' interests and the specification of their strategic setting. Understanding how watercourse state's interests are formed is important in explaining the variation in incentives to specify water rights for international watercourses. Rulers have varying incentives to respond to societal interests that are mediated through states' governing institutions. As a result, the institutional features of watercourse states play an important role in the formation and intensity of watercourse state' interests. The more inclusive the governing institutions, the more incentives there are for rulers to undertake infrastructure projects and to provide public goods, such as access to safe drinking water and the development of efficient irrigation networks serving the needs of unorganized diffuse interests, such as farmers. The opposite holds for the exclusive end of the spectrum of governing institutions. The more exclusive the governing institutions the lower the incentives are to provide public goods, which leads to the subsequent widespread inefficient and mismanagement of not just water resources but the entire economy of a country. The second analytical step is the specification of the strategic setting in which the bargaining takes places. The continuously shifting context, especially if the majority of watercourse states do not have institutions that facilitate the credibility of their commitments and the solution of collective action problems, could undermine watercourse states efforts to locate a contract that is acceptable to all. The instability of the Middle Eastern subsystem due partly to frequent foreign intervention increases uncertainty and the transaction costs of gathering information, negotiating, executing the terms of agreement, and so on, and therefore contributes to the conflicting expectation of watercourse states. Thus, the strategic setting in which bargaining takes place is acutely important for the emergence of water rights among watercourse states, since variables such as a state's geographic position, its relative power capabilities, institutional capabilities, and conflict-ridden international relations can easily cause the role of common interests to be superseded by conflicting interests.

There are three possible outcomes in such situations, namely a continuation of the current status quo, an escalation of the conflict, and a negotiated settlement. The desirability of each depends on a raft of potential international and domestic consequences. A symmetrical distribution of power among watercourse states would cause the cost of imposing a negotiated settlement or avoiding one to be very high. In situations of mutually assured harm, states on equal footing are likely to avoid the use of force and to try to resolve their differences through negotiations. An asymmetrical distribution of power on the hand would provide strong watercourse states with the capability to protect their interest better. Strong watercourse states often choose to act unilaterally leaving weaker watercourse states with a *fait accompli*, as we saw, for example, with the policies of Turkey on the Euphrates, Israel on the Jordan, and Egypt on the Nile. The clear asymmetries in power capabilities and the possibilities of spillover act as a deterrent for weaker watercourse states to escalate the conflict. Consequently, the variations in both the configurations of power and geographic positions lead to different types of outcomes in international watercourse disputes.

In this context, a state's institutional features, more specifically the nature of its domestic governance institutions and the extent that they facilitate the mitigation of informational asymmetries play an instrumental role. Democratic states are in general more open and thus successful in revealing their intentions and in posing credible threats. Furthermore, the more inclusive a country's institutions, the better they would be at facing challenges. Inclusive institutions reduce the intensity of a conflict in a number of ways. They might decrease a need to create conflict as a means of taking attention away from domestic policy failures. In heterogeneous societies, they might thwart opportunities for the internal and external manipulation of ethnic, sectarian, or other divisions. Furthermore, the informal institutions of inclusive societies, such as the norms of compromise and high levels of trust, facilitate the resolution of domestic collective action problems and so might also have a positive influence on the resolution of similar problems at the international level.

The escalation of conflicts is obviously the least favorable outcome. States have a general interest in the negotiated settlements of conflicts or the continuation of the status quo due to the high costs and the inherent unpredictability of the (threat of) use of force. The cost of the use of force and the uncertainty surrounding the outcome of wars provide rational states with sufficient incentives to negotiate settlements, and if that is not feasible, with incentives to maintain the status quo. These incentives include, but are not limited to the mitigation of undesired domestic and international consequences. It is customary for states to use diplomatic means prior to the use of force to resolve international issues. Therefore, the study of the context of multilateral negotiations is vital. In addition, anarchy, that is a lack of authority above sovereign states to enforce agreements, presents another challenge that states have to consider in their calculations of the expected costs and benefits of various outcomes.

As a result, watercourse states face two main dilemmas: (1) locating a negotiated settlement of water rights that is acceptable to all, and (2) finding a substitute mechanism for a supra-national authority to enforce agreements in the international system. Among sovereign states the enforcement of agreed upon rules is a first order problem, one that ideally needs to be resolved before proceeding to any other terms of a settlement.

Each state enters into the bargaining process with varied preferences and capabilities to pursue their goals. Interstate bargaining is a process through which states try to reach a settlement that is incentive-compatible and acceptable to all sides and thus intrinsically enforceable. In other words, any final agreement on water rights needs to be self-enforcing, reflecting an equilibrium point from which no state has an incentive to defect. The role of states (in their strategic calculations) is not just limited to convening and reaching an agreement on how to divide a common resource, there is also a strong incentive to invent control mechanisms for overcoming collective action problems and to reduce, if not to eliminate completely, the need for third party enforcement. Thus, the emergence of international water rights institutions ultimately rests on watercourse states' ability to reach voluntarily an incentive-compatible settlement.

## Empirical Conclusions

The prerequisite for the emergence of water rights institutions is the emergence of a consensus about its desirability among the watercourse states. As is the case with the Nile[1] and the Jordan Rivers, with the Euphrates and Tigris, there is no such consensus among the watercourse states. Another crucial yet often overlooked aspect of the literature dealing with international water rights conflicts is that reaching any kind of settlement on water rights requires states to agree on the object of the conflict, the purpose of the negotiations, and the terms of settlement. This has also not been the case in the Euphrates and Tigris watercourse. Turkey, Syria, and Iraq have yet to agree on what the definition of international watercourse is, whether the Euphrates and Tigris watercourse is an international one or constitutes a single watercourse, and whether the subject of the negotiations is only the Euphrates' waters or includes the Tigris and the Orontes waters as well. More importantly, however, Turkey, Syria, and Iraq have yet to agree on the most crucial aspect driving the water rights conflicts: is water scarce in the Euphrates and Tigris watercourse?

Water scarcity has been the primary driving force behind attempts to develop an international legal framework and the struggle to specify water rights by the watercourse states in arid or semi-arid regions. The rulers, even in democracies, almost always respond to clear and present problems rather than less clear and projected ones set to occur some time in the future. As a result, the main driver of water rights conflicts in arid and semi-arid regions of the world is the actual scarcity of water. The Euphrates and Tigris watercourse states have yet to experience the effects of acute water scarcity due to unilateral exploitation of water. The conflict has been driven by a perception of water scarcity at some point in the future when Turkey will have completed GAP and Syria will have completed the Euphrates scheme. There is yet no objective evidence that the lack of a water rights agreement in the Euphrates and Tigris will significantly and negatively affect the welfare of the people in the watercourse.

Turkey has consistently claimed that there is enough water to meet the needs of the lower watercourse states, Syria and Iraq, if they do not waste water and use their resources efficiently. There is no water scarcity problem; there is a water management problem. And there is some truth to this claim. Both lower watercourse states have hugely inefficient water and agricultural management practices that are detrimental the long-term sustainability of the resource and the environment. Indeed, flood irrigation is a common practice that wastes a lot of water and causes soil salinization. These quality problems, however, are not only due to irrigation and agricultural practices, but also due to inadequate wastewater treatment that has led to release of raw sewage and industrial discharge into the rivers. Both lower watercourse states have also been subject to an imbalanced approach to higher level water management issues. As we have seen, the construction of dams held great appeal for newly independent developing states during the second half of the twentieth century. The feat of building large dams often symbolized power and capability and helped to legitimize authoritarian regimes throughout the Third World. Drainage and conservation measures are costly and maintaining and managing water and land resources have not been as attractive for rulers as building projects. This is especially the case in exclusionary political systems like those that have recently ruled both Syria and Iraq. This type of inefficient management of water resources is a symptom of overall poor institutional quality.

In the twenty-first century, agriculture is no longer the basis of wealth and power among nations. Economic development, a structural transformation of economies from one based on the production of primary goods with high volatility and low income potential to one based on the production of industrial and manufactured goods with high income potential, is the key for higher living standards and the elimination of poverty. This requires investment in more dynamic and productive sectors of the economy. In Iraq and Syria, agriculture claims an estimated 80–90 percent of all available fresh water resources, but contributes to only 5–20 percent of the GDP, while employs close to 30 percent of the work force. The reallocation of resources within the economy might not only cure the water scarcity problem but also lead to the elimination of rural poverty and a chance for living standards to improve beyond subsistence for millions of people. In the long run, the industrialization and urbanization of the Euphrates and Tigris watercourse states will lead to less emphasis on agriculture, as in more developed economies where agriculture employs less than 5 percent of the population yet produces more. This will not necessarily lead to a decline in agriculture, but a more efficient and productive agriculture sector. The application of modern technologies to agriculture increase productivity. There is also room for significant improvements in irrigation; new investments are required for irrigation technology, which has improved significantly in recent years. Among the new developments are drip-irrigation, which uses a very small amount of water and is suitable for desert-like soils, and technologies with minimal or no water run off that can alleviate salinity and pollution problems. In addition, the absence of wastewater treatment, for both urban and agricultural areas, reduces the availability of freshwater suitable for domestic and agricultural use. The reuse of treated wastewater obviously will increase the available amount of water. There is also room for improvements in crop patterns: salt and drought resistant crops could be cultivated instead of low value water-intensive crops, like wheat and rice. It is cheaper to import these water intensive crops.

As mentioned, GAP has been the primary reason for worries about impending water scarcity in the Euphrates and Tigris watercourse, especially since Syria's Euphrates Scheme has proven improbable.[2] There are strong attenuating factors, however. As we have seen, Turkey's growing energy needs have been the primary driving force behind GAP. The realization rate of the project shows that almost all dams with hydroelectric power plants have been completed while the rate of completion is only about 22 percent for irrigation projects. The energy investment have more than paid off as the total value of the energy generated in the plants has been higher than the invested amount. The irrigation projects are making slow progress, but are subject to an economic rationality and new legislations adopted as part of aligning Turkey with EU *acquis* on environmental protection, water quality, industrial pollution, and climate. The implementation of new water laws and environmental regulations has put Turkey on the path to adopt the best water practices lessening the worries about quality problems in the Euphrates and Tigris watercourse. As noted, Turkey's stated water demands on both the Euphrates and Tigris for irrigation purposes are much more than what is needed to irrigate the proposed area of land and strongly suggests that it might include the water needed to deal with salinization problems, losses to evaporation, and unforeseen future demands. The actual amount water used when all the irrigation schemes are completed would likely be less than the proposed amount. Furthermore, if the experience of the currently irrigated land is a guide, water use in the irrigated areas will decline over time. The irrigation of the Harran plain initially led to increased water use, but ten years of irrigated agriculture caused a steady decline in evaporation rates and decreased the water use.[3] If a similar pattern of evaporation rates persists, it is predicted that there will be a 40 percent decline in water use in the planned irrigation areas.[4] This has obviously positive implications for both water quantity and quality and sustainable land and water management in the watercourse. GAP project is not just about irrigated agriculture as it was transformed into an integrated sustainable development project that has lead to the development of burgeoning industrial and services sectors. The dam construction in the region has brought investment in the transportation and communication networks. The region has experienced high rates of urbanization around urban growth industrial centers spurred on by the employment and education opportunities. In the long run, if the development trend continues, agriculture in the region will also be much more technologically oriented and efficient thus minimizing water use and alleviating water quality problems. More importantly the region will be economically stronger and able to weather any negative shocks.

A watercourse state's institutions, especially in dealing with resource depletion and degradation in their portion of the watercourse, has a significant effect on the strategies that states adopt internally and externally with respect to international water rights. As we have seen, the crises in the Euphrates and Tigris watercourses have roots in the structural composition of state-society relationship encompassing both political and economic realms. The region of the watercourse constitutes one of the less developed and ethnically/ religiously sensitive parts of Turkey, Syria, and Iraq, a fact that almost automatically politicizes the water rights conflicts. It thus becomes necessary to discern to what extent the water rights conflicts among Turkey, Syria, and Iraq has really been about water rights.

The study of the crises that have broken out over the Euphrates and Tigris have revealed that the water rights crisis, on at least one occasion, was the side-effect of other issues of conflicts among the watercourse states. It also reveals that watercourse states act in their dealings with each other under premises of strategic interaction. The choice of one strategy over others in dealing with the depletion or degradation of water resources is influenced by the watercourse states' expectations about their adversaries' actions and the overall impact of certain policy choices on the economic, political, strategic balances among the watercourse states. In this context, the existing political and ideological conflicts not only prevent watercourse states from reaching an agreement, but it also contributes to engendering a crisis over international watercourses. The crisis of 1975, which brought Iraq and Syria to the brink of war, nicely illustrates the significance of the existing political conflict on negotiations. The previous acrimonious political conflict between the Ba'thist rulers of Syria and Iraq was one of the major reasons for the failure of the negotiations. Both Syria and Iraq were seeking to undermine each other and were rightly suspicious of each other's subversive activities, fearing the other one was plotting to bring their downfall. The tension increased significantly when Iraq nationalized the Iraqi Petroleum Company, rejecting the Syrian demand for an increase in royalties in early 1973, and signed an agreement with Turkey for the construction of an oil pipeline to transport Iraqi oil. Strategically, this was not a welcome development from the Syrian perspective and its response was to instigate Shi'i unrest, affecting the majority of the agricultural sector heavily dependent on the Euphrates' water. A policy of limited crisis with Iraq also served the Syrian Ba'th regime's interests also by providing an opportunity to expel regime dissidents on charges of plotting against the government, and of being sympathetic to the historic leadership of the Ba'th in exile in Iraq. The dwindling amount of the Euphrates' water and conflicting water data constituted a good opportunity for the watercourse states to settle scores. The acrimonious political conflict between the Ba'thist rulers of Syria and Iraq over the leadership of the Middle East was the main reason for the transformation of the dispute over the Euphrates waters into a major issue of contention. The 1975 crisis provided the first example of how water rights issues among states become entangled with other important issues of conflict in bilateral and regional relations and helped the advancement of those domestic and international political interests. If the crisis really was over the dwindling Euphrates' waters, it could have been avoided by just looking at the water data, as we have seen, since the decrease in the water flow could not be explained by the impounding of the lake behind the Tabqa dam in Syria. An examination of the strategic context in which interstate bargaining takes place among the watercourse states therefore provides a better understanding of the breakout of crises over water rights and also the inconclusive nature of such conflicts.

In the Euphrates and Tigris watercourse, the lower watercourse states involvement in other protracted conflicts and the ensuing conflicting interests in these other conflicts have helped to block discussion over the water rights on the Euphrates and Tigris. In addition to this, the upper watercourse state, Turkey, has strong interests in maintaining the status quo. Turkey's position is also facilitated by its strong military and economic capabilities and its relative domestic political stability compared to the lower watercourse states Syria and Iraq. For Turkey, the cost of delay in reaching a settlement on water rights has not been high in comparison to the expected benefits of any future agreement for Turkey as it completes GAP. The cost of delay was relatively higher for the lower watercourse states. As a result, the lower watercourse states have generally been the first to initiate negotiations to settle water issues. In bargaining with a reluctant upper watercourse state, the lower watercourse states have several strategies at their disposal to change their disadvantaged bargaining situations. Among these strategies are creating artificial incentives and issue linkages, taking the issue to international arbitration institutions, and forming a common front against the upper watercourse state.

The history of the Euphrates and Tigris conflict suggests that not only have the negative issue linkage strategies not worked, but have also undermined the watercourse states' chances of reaching a voluntary contract and the emergence of a community of watercourse states. Throughout the period under consideration, Syria routinely supported clandestine organizations in both Turkey and Iraq for various purposes. As we have seen, Syrian efforts to link its support for clandestine organizations to the water issue have failed. Syria underestimated Turkey's resolve on separating water issues from the other issues of conflict in Turkish-Syrian bilateral relations. Turkey eventually forced Syria, by threatening to use military force, to sign an agreement that stipulated the termination of Syrian support for the Kurdish Separatist movement in October 1998, rather than settling the water rights issue with Syria. This study strongly suggests that the best strategy for reaching a voluntary contract that specifies water rights is not to use negative issue linkages, but positive issue linkages, like oil, trade, economic and political cooperation. Iraq, for example, succeeded in securing Turkish concessions on the Euphrates' water and collaboration against the Kurdish threat in exchange for oil in 1975. As economic interests have typically driven Turkey's policies in the region, close economic and commercial ties are likely to produce positive outcomes.

Nor has the internationalizing of the problem produced the intended outcomes for the lower watercourse states. The Arab League, for example, was as ineffective as Syria in attempting to link the Euphrates and Tigris conflict to the conflict over the Golan Heights. At the first sign of a link between the Euphrates and Tigris conflict and Syrian-Israeli conflict over water resources, Turkey offered to sell water from its Ceyhan and Seyhan watercourses, and already started to sell Manavgat waters to Israel. Only recently, during the last large dam project, the Ilisu dam, has international pressure had somewhat limited success as the project lost its funding on different occasions. However, lower watercourse states had very little to do with this international reaction as it originated in the burgeoning transnational environmentalist movements against dam building and the marketization of water. The controversy reflected changing perception of dams in the face of a growing environmental consciousness. The lower watercourse states, especially Iraq, which is also planning new dams, will also be facing similar pressures as they undertake such projects, especially with their very poor record of maintaining such large infrastructures, as the ongoing fears about the fragile status the Mosul dam demonstrate. Oil revenues could, of course, reduce Iraqi dependence on international financing. The loss of international funding, however, could be a double-edged sword if the countries are capable of funding such projects, as it could lead to the loss of important leverage that could potentially ensure environmentally sound sustainable development practices in developing countries.

The overall impact of the large-scale developments of water resources throughout the twentieth century has been a mixed one. On the positive side, there has been an increase in food supply, the provision of cheap and clean energy, and the prevention of floods and overall contributions to economic development. On the negative side, there are environmental problems, such as increased salinity, water-logging, loss of sedimentation, loss of water to evaporation, and losses of habitats and biodiversity. Easing the transfer and use of new technologies that minimize the negative impacts of such development projects on the environment holds great promise for equitable solutions to environmental problems. There has been a global market failure in conserving the world's remaining biodiversity and the protection of the Mesopotamian marshlands is no exception. Nature's services are not factored in calculating the cost of producing agricultural and related goods. Granted there is no easy way to put a price these services now, this is likely going to change in the coming years as we become more informed about the impact of development on natural resources and global environmental change. Market mechanisms are currently weak and we have only just started to address the global market failure for environmental protection and the creation of water markets. The understanding of water as a gift of nature or god has always been problematic, as it has led to the treatment of water not as a valuable gift to be carefully husbanded, but rather something 'free' and disposable, leading to much waste and paving the way for the unsustainable consumption practices that endanger the future of fresh water resources.

It can be safely predicted that at the current levels of instability in the Middle East with the ongoing war in Syria and Iraq, the outcome of which is uncertain not only in terms of how or if state borders will be redrawn, but also whether any new states will be introduced to the Euphrates and Tigris watercourse, the chances of an emergence of water rights regime in the near future is low. As we saw earlier, due to sequential access, appropriation, and usage, international watercourses are impure common pool resources with strong private good characteristics. The most likely outcome in the mid- to long-term is going to be the formalization of the current de facto regime on the Euphrates. This would create a less desirable private property regime with each watercourse state responsible for the management of the water within its own borders rather than a common property regime that would create a supra-national structure with watercourse states governing the entire watercourse as co-owners. As it has already been adopted by Turkey, the polluter pays principle could guide quality concerns. The formalization of the flow of 500 cubic meters per second in a percentage form on the Euphrates is less than the two-thirds of flow demanded by Iraq and Syria, but it is likely to be an acceptable amount under the notion of *equitable and fair use*. The World Bank, which is committed to the protection of *acquired rights* in its funding decisions for the dams, funded the Karakaya dam on the basis of the view that the Turkish guarantee of 450 cubic meters per second on the Euphrates was appropriate and sufficient enough to prevent *appreciable* or *significant harm*. The current international law on non-navigational uses of international watercourses gives priority to equitable and fair use over any other principles of international law that watercourse states claim in advancing their interests. The amount of water consumed through inefficient water use and management practices, especially with their adverse effects on environment, can no longer be the basis of appreciable or significant harm claims.

One result of this study is that the outcome of bargaining over water rights that falls short of cooperation is less puzzling. The rules of the game that the Euphrates and Tigris watercourse states have played have not been conducive to the emergence of such cooperation. No cooperation, however, does not mean that states will wage war over scarce water resources. Conflicts over water resources are intrinsically different then conflicts over oil resources. Water neither constitutes a natural resource that could have enormous impact on the relative power capabilities of the watercourse states, nor does it justify the use of force. As we have seen not only are the underlying causes of the various crises over the Euphrates and Tigris watercourse related to other international conflicts that the watercourse states are involved in, but also water scarcity that is due to a upper watercourse state's exploitation is not an acute problem. Even if it becomes an issue in the long run, the use of force is less likely to be employed as a method to settle water rights conflicts in the Euphrates and Tigris watercourse. The properties of the type of contract that is needed for the emergence of water rights requires the voluntary cooperation of watercourse states. Furthermore, technological developments in dry-land farming methods, irrigation techniques, drought resistant crops, and desalination could significantly reduce overall water consumption. In comparison to the cost of war, the cost of the better management of waters is very low and happily it is also better for the long-term sustainability of the resources given the looming threat from climate change. The efficient management of resources, however, is closely tied to the quality of the governing institutions. Amartya Sen's reasoning for the disappearance of famines[5] applies here as well since efficient water and land resource management could be achieved if there is an effort to do so, and the institutional features of democracies, like electoral accountability, a free press, and transparency, force rulers to exert such efforts. It takes time for inclusive institutions to set in and to deepen as the initial prevalent informal institutions, i.e., norms and rules, may not always be conducive. Only such institutions create an incentive structure favorable for political and economic development and building resilient societies that are able to adapt to change.

Changes in the global climate and the increasing occurrences of multi-year droughts in the late twentieth and early twenty-first centuries have put increased pressures on governments. The end of the Cold War did not bode well for the exclusionary governments of Middle Eastern states dependent on their outside patrons for support. As people have protested the quality of government and have demanded better, freer lives for themselves, the victor of the Cold War, the US, has come under intense pressure to cut its support for oppressive regimes, while Russia has lost most of its clout along with the objective basis of its power, namely its economic and financial resources. Following upon changes in the global economy and the global financial crisis of 2007, the pervasive poor economic management of a country's resources has increased the risk of internal conflict. Ethnic and sectarian conflicts are not the cause of the civil wars raging the two lower watercourse states of the Euphrates and Tigris watercourse, but they are symptomatic of the prevalent exclusionary institutions that govern politics and economics in these countries. The emergence of inclusive institutions ultimately rests on the warring elites' settlement on the democratic rules of the game. The inclusive nature of democratic institutions facilitates the peaceful resolution of conflicts in general and strengthens a society's capacity to solve difficult collective action problems while addressing negative shocks originating from both endogenous and exogenous sources. Should it happen, the establishment of new democratic states with inclusionary governing institutions in the lower reaches of the Euphrates and Tigris watercourse may create a large enough shift that it can make the emergence of common property water rights institutions possible at long last.

# NOTES

## Introduction

1. United Nations Development Programme, *Human Development Report 1994* (New York: Oxford University Press, 1994), p. 23. Andrew Mack, ed., *Human Security Report* (New York: Oxford University Press, 2005), p. viii.
2. Kofi A. Annan, *We the People: The Role of the United Nations in the 21st Century. New Century New Challenges* (New York: United Nations, 2000), p. 44.
3. *A National Security Strategy of Engagement and Enlargement* (Washington: The White House, 1996).
4. *The National Security Strategy of the United States of America* (Washington: The White House, 2006), p. 52.
5. *UNEP News Release*, 5 August 2002. Sustainable Development Security Imperative: Says Top US Government Official.
6. According to the International Organization Immigration (IOM) October 2009 Monthly Report, the 2007–9 drought forced 20,000 people to move in search of more sustainable access to drinking water and livelihoods. The drought also reduced the crop coverage about forty percent of the cropland and decimated the livestock. See UN Inter-Agency Information and Analysis Unit, June 2012. 'Climate Change in Iraq.'
7. See Paul K. Huth, *Standing Your Ground: Territorial Disputes and International Relations* (Michigan: University of Michigan Press, 2009) and Paul K. Huth and Todd L. Allee, *The Democratic Peace and Territorial Conflict in the Twentieth Century* (New York: Cambridge University Press, 2003); and for territorial disputes as cause of armed conflicts see Kalevi J. Holsti, *Peace and War: Armed Conflicts and International Order, 1648–1989* (New York: Cambridge University Press, 2001); and Richard N. Rosecrance, *The Rise of the Trading State: Commerce and Conquest in the Modern World* (New York: Basic Books, 1986).
8. The UCDP/Prio conflict data indicate that more than half of the conflicts that took place between 1946 and 2013 were about territory. See http://www.pcr.uu.se/research/ucdp/datasets/ucdp_prio_armed_conflict_dataset/ (accessed on 20 March 2015). Also see Lotta Themnér and Peter Wallensteen, 'Armed Conflicts 1946–2013,' *Journal of Peace Research* 51.4 (2014), pp. 541–54.
9. Skirmishes between fishing vessels and coastal states occasionally make headlines: the Cod Wars, the Turbot Wars, and so on.

10. See World Resources Institute (WRI), Pilot Analysis of Global Ecosystems (PAGE): Freshwater Systems 2000, available at http://www.wri.org/wr2000/freshwater_page.html; World Health Organization (WHO), Global Water Supply and Sanitation Assessment 2000 Report, available at http://www.who.int/water_sanitation_health/Globassessment/GlobalTOC.htm; United Nations Environment Programme (UNEP), Global Environmental Outlook 2000, available at http://www.unep.org/Geo2000.
11. Only less than 0.01 percent of the world's water resources are available for human use out of the total 2 million cubic kilometers of water in the world. This amount is equal to approximately 2,300 cubic meters per capita. We should also keep in mind that this is an average and per capita water availability grossly varies throughout the world. If a country has less than 1000 cubic meters of water per capita, it is considered water scarce. See Steven C. Lonergan, 'Water and Conflict: Rhetoric and Reality,' in Paul F. Diehl and Peter Nils Gleditsch, eds, *Environmental Conflict* (Boulder: Westview Press, 2001), p. 110.
12. For detailed discussion of the problems facing common pool resources see Garrett Hardin, 'The Tragedy of Commons,' *Science* 162 (1968), pp. 1243–8; Robert Keohane and Elinor Ostrom, eds, *Local Commons and Global Interdependence: Heterogeneity and Cooperation in Two Domains* (Thousand Oaks: Sage, 1995); Mancur Olson, *The Logic of Collective Action* (Cambridge: Harvard University Press, 1965); Oran R. Young, George J. Demko, and Kilaoarti Ramakrishna, eds, *Global Environmental Change and International Governance* (Hanover: University Press of New England, 1996); Elinor Ostrom, *Governing the Common Pool Resources* (Cambridge: Cambridge University Press, 1990); Elinor Ostrom, Roy Gardner, and James Walker, 'Covenants with and without a Sword: A Self Governance is Possible,' *American Political Science Review* 86 (1992), pp. 404–17; *Rules, Games, Common Pool Resources* (Ann Arbor: University of Michigan Press, 1994); and Elinor Ostrom, Joanna Burger, Christopher B. Field, Richard B. Norgaard, and David Policansky, 'Revisiting the Commons: Local Lessons, Global Challenges,' *Science* 284 (April 1999), pp. 278–89.
13. For a discussion of relative gains see Stephen D. Krasner, ed., *International Regimes* (Ithaca: Cornell University Press, 1983); David A. Baldwin, ed., *Neorealism and Neoliberalism: The Contemporary Debate* (New York: Columbia University Press, 1993); and Robert Powell, *In the Shadow of Power: States and Strategies in International Politics* (Princeton: Princeton University Press, 1999).
14. For detailed discussions of the problems facing common pool resources see Garrett Hardin, 'The Tragedy of Commons,' *Science* 162 (1968), pp. 1243–8; Robert Keohane and Elinor Ostrom, eds, *Local Commons and Global Interdependence: Heterogeneity and Cooperation in Two Domains* (Thousand Oaks: Sage Publication, 1995); Mancur Olson, *The Logic of Collective Action* (Cambridge: Harvard University Press, 1965); Oran R. Young, George J. Demko, and Kilaoarti Ramakrishna, eds, *Global Environmental Change and International Governance* (Hanover: University Press of New England, 1996); Elinor Ostrom, *Governing the Common Pool Resources* (Cambridge: Cambridge University Press, 1990); Elinor Ostrom, Roy Gardner, and James Walker, 'Covenants with and without a Sword: A Self Governance is Possible,' *American Political Science Review* 86 (1992), pp. 404–17; *Rules, Games, Common Pool Resources* (Ann Arbor: University of Michigan Press, 1994); and Elinor Ostrom, Joanna Burger, Christopher B. Field, Richard B. Norgaard, and David Policansky, 'Revisiting the Commons: Local Lessons, Global Challenges,' *Science* 284 (April 1999), pp. 278–89.
15. The distinction between rules in use and rules in form is useful. Rules in use is how people understand and practice the rules, which can differ from the rules in form or the legal

rules. Rules in use could serve the function of property rights in the absence of clearly defined property rights.

16. For earlier studies of the complex structure of the decision making process and strategic interaction see Robert Jervis, *Perception and Misperception in International Politics* (Princeton: Princeton University Press, 1976), Duncan Snidal, 'The Game Theory of International Politics,' in Kenneth N. Oye, ed., *Cooperation under Anarchy* (Princeton: Princeton University Press, 1986), and Emerson M.S. Niou, Peter C. Ordeshook, and Gregory F. Rose, *The Balance of Power Stability in International Systems* (Cambridge: Cambridge University Press, 1989).
17. Monitoring and enforcing compliance with agreed upon rules have been underlined by the studies on common pool resources as being the most challenging dilemma of governing common resources. See Garrett Hardin, 'The Tragedy of Commons;' Robert Keohane and Elinor Ostrom, eds, *Local Commons and Global Interdependence: Heterogeneity and Cooperation in Two Domains*; Mancur Olson, *The Logic of Collective Action*; Oran R. Young, George J. Demko, and Kilaoarti Ramakrishna, eds, *Global Environmental Change and International Governance*; Elinor Ostrom, Roy Gardner, and James Walker, *Rules, Games, Common Pool Resources*.
18. To date, this watercourse has received little attention. John F. Kolars and William A. Mitchell's *The Euphrates River* (Carbondale: University of Illinois Press, 1991) is the only book dedicated solely to the Euphrates/Tigris conflict.
19. The data are from the Cost of War Project. According to their report released on the 10th anniversary of the war, the war has killed at least 190,000 people, including military, contractors, and civilians and will cost the United States US$ 2.2 trillion including the future war costs of veteran care through 2054, exceeding significantly the initial 2002 estimates by the US Office of Management and Budget of US$ 50 to US$ 60 billion. http://www.costsofwar.org/ (accessed on 30 July 2014).
20. Common pool resources refer to natural resource systems that are large enough to make costly the exclusion of potential beneficiaries from obtaining benefits from its use if there is a rivalry in consumption. In common pool resources situations everybody suffers from the overexploitation of common resources, which usually leads to destruction of common resources unless users come together and regulate the consumption. Clearly, Turkey's suffering due to the lack of an agreement on water rights is minimal or not deep enough.
21. The literature on bargaining negotiations, for example, between trade unions and employers revolves around the question of why employee representatives and employers cannot reach an agreement before costly delay, or more concisely, why it is that strikes occur despite the fact that it is costly for both sides of the conflict.

## Chapter 1 The Nature of the Problem

1. Hume [1739–40] 1978, bk. 3, part 2, sect. 8, p. 538. E-book. http://www.gutenberg.org/files/4705/4705-h/4705-h.htm.
2. Burundi, China, and Turkey voted against the adoption of the convention, and Andorra, Argentina, Azerbaijan, Belgium, Bolivia, Bulgaria, Colombia, Cuba, Ecuador, Egypt, Ethiopia, France, Ghana, Guatemala, India, Israel, Mali, Monaco, Mongolia, Pakistan, Panama, Paraguay, Peru, Rwanda, Spain, Tanzania, and Uzbekistan abstained. United Nations member states were invited to ratify this convention before 20 May 2000. It entered into force on 17 August 2014 when it received thirty-five state deposits in the form of either ratification, acceptance, approval, or accession.

3. The treaty was a result of the efforts of the International Law Commission that started in 1970 to codify customary principles of international law and procedural requirements for notification and consultation among watercourse states concerning the use and development of international watercourses.
4. I recognize that even this choice may not be value-free as it seems to endorse the 1997 law and its main tenet that international rivers should be treated as a whole. Even so, it provides a clear criterion for selecting the subjects for study that belong to a specific type of watercourse, for example, international rivers. This definition is also commendable for its simplicity.
5. In the US, we often pay for some treating and delivery of water, but not for water itself.
6. Elinor Ostrom, *Governing the Common Pool Resources* (Cambridge: Cambridge University Press, 1990), p. 51.
7. Aristotle, *Politics* (New York: Cambridge University Press, 1988).
8. Thomas Hobbes, *Leviathan* (Baltimore: Penguin, [1651] 1972), pp. 185–6.
9. J. J. Rousseau, *Discourse on Inequality* (New York: Penguin Books, 1984), p. 38.
10. In game theory, the dominant strategy is a strategy that yields the best outcome for an individual regardless of what anyone else does. Anatol Rapoport, 'Prisoner's dilemma,' In *The New Palgrave Dictionary of Economics*, edited by J. Eatwell, M. Milgate and P. Newman (London: Macmillan, 1987), pp. 973–6.
11. The main assumptions of the prisoner's dilemma game are (1) complete information, (2) the lack of communication among actors, which is forbidden, and (3) that it is a one shot game. Under these assumptions the only rational response is to defect (Robert Jervis, 'Cooperation under the Security Dilemma,' *World Politics* 30 (2) (January 1978), p. 171).
12. *Pareto optimum* refers to an equilibrium in which there is no possibility of making someone better off without making at least one individual worse off through the allocation of resources in the economy (Thrainn Eggertsson, *Economic Behavior and Institutions* (Cambridge: Cambridge University Press, 1990), p. 19). *Pareto inferior*, therefore, refers to the misallocation of resources.
13. Collective action problems can assume four different strategic structures: prisoner's dilemma, chicken, assurance, and inaction. In the chicken structure, given the choice between two actions, individual prefers the one that is opposite of what most others are doing. If everybody contributes, for example, then you will choose to free ride. This will neither have an impact on another's pay off nor on the provision of the collective action. In collective inaction, the socially optimal outcome is achieved if some members do not participate or take action, like fishing or grazing the commons. Total payoff is maximized when overuse/overexploitation of the commons is avoided. See, Avinash Dixit, S. Skeath, and D. Reiley, *Games of Strategy* (New York: Norton, 1999), pp. 417–22.
14. Adam Smith, *An Inquiry into the Nature and Cause of the Wealth of Nations* (Oxford: Oxford University Press [1776], 1976), bk. 4, ch. 2, p. 456.
15. Ibid., bk. 4, ch. 2.3, p. 456.
16. See Friedrich A. Hayek, *Road to Serfdom* (Chicago: University of Chicago Press, 1944).
17. Friedrich A. Hayek, 'The Use of Knowledge in Society,' *American Economic Review* 35 (1945: 4): 519–30. Although Hayek was not received well initially, his ideas and work became more influential towards the end of the twentieth century. 'The Use of Knowledge in Society' was among the top twenty articles published in the *American Economic Review* during the journal's first hundred years for making the case for the importance of a price system in achieving coordination and efficiency in resource use.

18. We have known, for example, how to fight malaria for decades—spraying walls with a chemical (pyrethrum)—but the problem still persists. See William A. Easterly, *Tyranny of Experts* (New York: Basic Books, 2014).
19. Friedrich A. Hayek, 'The Use of Knowledge in Society,' pp. 521–2.
20. Ibid., p. 527.
21. In the theory of spontaneous order, institutions are comparable to languages, money (prices), common law, and similar institutions, in that they are product of individuals' interactions over long periods of time, and that they evolve through trial and error structuring social interactions. Both Smith and Hayek drew parallels between linguistic and economic systems since both dealt with how people cooperate and coordinate. Hayek thought 'the ability of small children to use language in accordance with the rules of grammar and of idiom of which they are wholly unaware' was the most striking example of this phenomenon of people following rules without explicitly knowing them. Institutions, although they are products of individual's actions, are not products of rational design by individuals. Hume, Smith, and Hayek were all skeptical of central planners' abilities to design institutions to achieve socially optimal outcomes. 'Perception, and Intelligibility,' *Proceedings of the British Academy* (1962) 48, reprinted in *Studies in Philosophy, Politics, and Economics*, (London: Routledge & Kegan Paul, 1967), pp. 43–65, p. 43.
22. The US Acid rain program, launched in 1995, was the first cap-and-trade program; now over 50 states have a similar program either implemented or in the process of being implemented. Cap and Trade Around the Globe. Available at http://www.epa.gov/captrade/international.html (accessed on 16 May 2015).
23. *The Economist*, 'The Invisible Green Hand', 4 July 2002. Available at http://www.economist.com/node/1200205 (accessed on 16 May 2015).
24. Water rights trading schemes are similar to cap and trade programs. There is a cap on the quantity of water that is instituted to ensure sustainability and the usage rights are then traded in the market to achieve the allocation of the scarce resource to its best use. On tradable water rights see Paul Holden and Mateen Thobani, 'Tradable Water Rights: a Property Rights Approach to Resolving Water Shortages and Promoting Investment,' *Policy Research Working Paper* 1727 (1996). World Bank, Latin America and the Caribbean Technical Department. Washington, DC: World Bank; B. R. Bruns, C. Ringler, and R. Meinzen-Dick, *Water Rights Reform: Lessons for Institutional Design* (Washington, DC: International Food Policy Research Institute, 2005); Peter Debaere, et al., 'Water Markets as a Response to Scarcity,' *Water Policy* 16 (2014), pp. 625–49.
25. So far only Australia has implemented a successful cap and trade-type water rights trading program, which was developed over a 30-year period following the severe drought of 1982–3. For a recent article on this program and the challenges it faced following a ten year long drought in the 2000s, see Andrew Maddocks, 'Australia's Water Markets Succeeding, Yet Severe Challenges Loom,' *Circle of Blue*, February 20, 2013. Available at http://www.circleofblue.org/waternews/2013/world/australias-water-markets-succeeding-yet-severe-challenges-loom/.
26. For an account of how structural reform programs pushed by the International Monetary Fund and the World Bank led to disastrous outcomes in Eastern Europe, Latin America, and Africa, see William Easterly, *White Man's Burden: Why the West's Efforts to Aid the Rest Have Done So Much Ill and So Little Good* (New York: Penguin, 2007). Following in the footsteps of Hume, Smith, and Hayek, Easterly also draws our attention to the need for detailed knowledge of local conditions for market reforms and the ill consequences of a top down approach to impose markets from above, such as undermining a nascent informal system.

27. A popular Turkish saying gives the gist of what *imece* means: 'bir elin nesi var iki elin sesi var, ne ekersen onu bicersin, suruden ayrilani kurt kapar, azi karar cogu zarar,' which roughly translates as 'two heads are better than one, you harvest what you sow, the wolf eats the sheep separated from the flock, too much of a good thing is bad, enough is better than a lot in consumption.'
28. Garrett Hardin, 'The Tragedy of Commons,' *Science* 162 (1968), pp. 1243–8.
29. Ibid., p. 1244.
30. For a discussion of hegemonic stability theory, see Charles P. Kindleberger, *The World in Depression, 1929–1939* (Berkeley: University of California Press, 1973); Robert Keohane, 'The Theory of Hegemonic Stability and Changes in International Economic Regimes, 1967–1977,' in Ole R. Holsti, Randolph M. Siverson and Alexander George, eds, *Changes in the International System* (Boulder: Westview Press, 1980); Robert Keohane, *After Hegemony: Cooperation and Discord in the World Political Economy* (Princeton: Princeton University Press, 1984); Duncan Snidal, 'Limits of Hegemonic Stability Theory,' *International Organization* 39 (Autumn 1985), pp. 579–614.
31. In this respect, the story of Bali is striking. The government, with the help of World Bank experts, introduced the green revolution without taking into account the role of the water temples that had managed the water tables for over a thousand years. A few years after the introduction of the new system, water shortages appeared along with pests and diseases ruining crops. As it turned out, local knowledge was critical for sustainable resource management, which consisted of individual users' knowledge and practice, including a system of irrigation canals and shrines built over time, and religious beliefs that strongly guided the behavior and interaction within the community. Following Lansing's study the water temples critical role was recognized and they soon returned to their original role of managing the water tables. See J. Stephen Lansing, *Priests and Programmers: Technologies of Power in the Engineered Landscape of Bali* (Princeton: Princeton University Press, 1991).
32. R. C. O. Mathews, 'The Economics of Institutions and the Sources of Growth,' *Economic Journal* 96 (1986), pp. 903–10, p. 906.
33. Kenneth J. Arrow, 'The Organization of Economic Activity: Issues Pertinent to the Choice of Market versus Non-market Allocation,' in *The Analysis of and Evaluation of Public Expenditure: The PPB System*. Joint Economic Committee, 91st Congress, 1st Session, Vol.1. (Washington: US Government Printing Office, 1969), pp. 59–73, p. 48
34. Oliver E. Williamson, *The Economic Institutions of Capitalism: Firms, Markets, and Relational Contracting* (New York: Free Press, 1985), p. 19.
35. Yoram Barzel, *Economic Analysis of Property Rights* (Cambridge: Cambridge University Press, 1997), p. 4.
36. For a discussion of the effects of transaction costs on the emergence of institutions see Ray Challen, *Institutions, Transaction Costs and Environmental Policy: Institutional Reform for Water Resources* (Massachusetts: Edward Elgar Publishing, 2000); Katja Weber, *Hierarchy amidst Anarchy: Transaction Costs and Institutional Choice* (Albany: State University of New York, 2000).
37. Erik G. Furubotn and Rudolf Richter, *Institutions and Economic Theory: The Contribution of the New Institutional Economics* (Ann Arbor: The University of Michigan Press, 1997), p. 40.
38. Eggertsson, *Economic Behavior and Institutions*, p. 14.
39. Ronald H. Coase, 'The Nature of the Firm,' *Economica* 16 (1937), pp. 386–405, and 'The Problem of Social Cost,' *Journal of Law and Economics* 3 (1960), pp. 1–44.
40. Ibid., p. 390.

41. B. Weingast and J.W. Marshall, 'The Industrial Organization of Congress; or, Why Legislatures, Like Firms, Are Not Organized as Markets,' *Journal of Political Economy* 96 (1988), pp. 132–63.
42. See on the importance of informational considerations in the emergence international institutions Stephan Krasner, *International Regimes* (Ithaca: Cornell University Press, 1983); and Robert Keohane, *After Hegemony: Cooperation and Discord in the World Political Economy* (Princeton: Princeton University Press, 1984).
43. See Williamson, *The Economic Institutions of Capitalism* and *Economic Organization: Firms, Markets and Policy Control* (Brighton: Wheatsheaf, 1986), p. 177.
44. In *The Economic Institutions of Capitalism*, Williamson differentiates between *ex ante* and *ex post facto* transaction costs: *Ex ante* transaction costs refer to the costs of drafting, negotiating, and safeguarding the agreement, and *ex post facto* transaction costs refer to the bargaining of the set up and running costs of governing structures. He argues that it is easier to justify recurrent transactions with the creation of a specialized institutional framework, since the set up costs of a highly specific structural apparatus often cannot be recovered for occasional transactions.
45. Unlike people, it is often very difficult to shame states into action/inaction. The strong moral basis of informal rules is not easily transferable to the community of states.
46. Williamson, *The Economic Institutions of Capitalism*, pp. 48–9.
47. Robert Axelrod, *The Evolution of Cooperation* (New York: Basic Books, 1984).
48. See Katja Weber, *Hierarchy Amidst Anarchy.*
49. See Kenneth N. Oye, ed., *Cooperation under Anarchy* (Princeton: Princeton University Press, 1986). There might be situations in which large number of actors might facilitate cooperation. For a discussion of this issue see Krasner, *International Regimes*; Lisa Martin, *Coercive Cooperation: Explaining Multilateral Economic Sanctions* (Princeton: Princeton University Press, 1992).
50. In some cases, where there is no water scarcity, there is no need to determine property rights.
51. Ronald Coase, *The Firm, the Market, and the Law* (Chicago: University of Chicago Press, 1988), pp. 14–15.
52. It may appear confusing, but I define institutions broadly to include both formal and informal rules guiding a pattern of action among states; property rights therefore are also institutions. We need institutions, but institutions, such as markets, firms, governments, are more or less failures as Coase observed (1960). The primary role of institutional arrangements is to minimize transaction costs, especially at the international level. For example, in designing property rights institutions, the main concern aside from reducing transaction costs and achieving more or less optimal, efficient, and sustainable use of scarce water resources is whether it is self-enforcing. Institutional arrangements that take into account the other features of the institutional context and the binding constraints on states would be more likely to be self-enforcing and successful. There is really no one set of water rights arrangements that is applicable to all international watercourses. Each international watercourse is different and states face different challenges. I extrapolate here from Dixit's argument for the suitability of self-enforcing institutional arrangements in the early stages of economic development of developing countries. The weak institutional structure that characterizes the early stages of economic development has strong parallels with the international system. See Avinash Dixit, *Lawlessness and Economics: Alternative Modes of Governance* (Princeton: Princeton University Press, 2003).

53. Contemporary literature on the origins of property rights includes Harold Demsetz, 'Towards a Theory of Property Rights,' *Journal of Political Economy* 57 (1967), pp. 347–59; Robert Nozick, *Anarchy, State and Utopia* (New York: Basic Books, 1974); James Buchanan, *The Limits to Liberty* (Chicago: University of Chicago Press, 1975); John R. Umbeck, *A Theory of Property Rights* (Ames: Iowa State University Press, 1981); Ken Binmore, *Game Theory and the Social Contract Vol. I: Playing Fair* (Cambridge: MIT Press, 1994); and *Game Theory and The Social Contract, Vol. II: Just Fair* (Cambridge: MIT Press, 1998).
54. Thomas Hobbes, *Leviathan* 1.14–15, 2.29 (Baltimore: Penguin Books [1691], 1972).
55. Ostrom, *Governing the Common Pool Resources*, 1990, pp. 99–100.
56. As Coase (1960, p.44) observed unregulated private control does not exist in the world under any system of law: 'The rights of a land-owner are not limited [. . .] A system in which the rights of the individual were unlimited would be one in which there were no rights to acquire.'
57. For detailed discussions of four general types of property regimes, namely state property, private property, common property, and non-property regimes, see Dam Bromley, *Environment and Economy: Property Rights and Public Policy* (Oxford: Basil Blackwell, 1991); Daniel Cole, *Pollution and Property: Comparing Ownership Institutions for Environmental Protection* (Cambridge: Cambridge University Press, 2002); Carl J. Dahlman, *The Open-Field System and Beyond: Property Rights Analysis of an Economic Institution* (Cambridge: Cambridge University Press, 1980); and Harold Demsetz, *Ownership, Control and the Firm, Vol. I: The Organization of Economic Activity* (Oxford: Basil Blackwell, 1988).
58. In this context, it means a simple resource allocation among the watercourse states based on some formula: County X gets X percent, country Y get Y percent of the shared water.
59. There are partial agreements among some of the watercourse states, such as those between Jordan and Israel on the Jordan Watercourse; Egypt and Sudan on the Nile River; and Syria and Iraq on the Euphrates. However these agreements often just relate to the division of the resource and do not include other watercourse states, like Syria, Lebanon, and the Palestinian Authority on the Jordan; all the upper watercourse states of the Nile, Ethiopia, Congo, Rwanda, Burundi, Uganda, Kenya, and Tanzania; and Turkey on the Euphrates. These partial bilateral agreements create a de facto situation and still leave the final settlement of water rights unresolved in their respective watercourses. It should be also noted that these agreements are subject to critical challenges.
60. In 1951 and 1953, Israel prevented Syria's diversion schemes on Lake Huleh by using military force. In another case, Iraq threatened to bomb Syria's Tabqa dam on several occasions in the mid-1970s.
61. The importance of clearly defined property rights for economic development is now better understood. For the role of property rights and institutions see, Daron Acemoglu and James Robinson, *Why Nations Fail: The Origins of Power, Prosperity, and Poverty* (New York: Random House, 2013); Timothy Besley and Maitreesh Ghatak, 'Property Rights and Economic Development,' in Dani Rodrik and Mark Rosenzweig, eds, *Handbook of Development Economics*, Vol. 5 (The Netherlands: Elsevier, 2010); Douglass C. North, John J. Wallis, and Barry Weingast, *Violence and Social Order: A Conceptual Framework for Interpreting Recorded Human History* (Cambridge: Cambridge University Press, 2009).
62. International law cannot be applied to a state if a state is consistently and continuously opposed to the law throughout its codification process.
63. Scholars with a strong environmentalist streak, like Shiva, argue that water is a common resource because it is the ecological basis of all life and because its sustainability and

equitable allocation depend on cooperation among community members. Shiva criticizes the current push for the privatization of water resources, which according to her, runs against human history since water resources have been managed as common resources across diverse cultures and throughout time. See Vandana Shiva, *Water Wars: Privatization, Pollution, and Profit* (Cambridge: South End Press, 2002), pp. 24, 35.

64. Syria has strongly opposes to the concept of 'water pricing' and calls for its replacement with 'cost recovery' in which citizens will only pay for the services. During the Second World Water Forum discussions in 2000, the Syrian head of the international water bureau in the Syrian Ministry of Irrigation, Masri, reiterated the Syrian position stating that Syria is absolutely against the privatization of water, since water belongs everybody—a concept that is rooted in the rulings of Islam (*Jordan Times*, 22 March 2000).
65. According to some water is inherently different from other resources since it cannot be substituted and this makes it un-tradable. We should approach this line of argumentation with reservation. Market solutions to water scarcity problems are not free from fallacies and drawbacks, but the argument that water cannot be substituted, and therefore it cannot be traded as a commodity, is also fallacious.
66. For data and reports on state failure see the State Failure Task Force, which consists of Jack A. Goldstone, Ted Robert Gurr, Barbara Harff, Marc A. Levy, Monty G. Marshall, Robert H. Bates, David L. Epstein, Colin H. Kahl, Pamela T. Surko, John C. Ulfelder, Jr., and Alan N. Unger, in consultation with Matthew Christenson, Geoffrey D. Dabelko, Daniel C. Esty, and Thomas M. Parris. The Task Force defines a failed state as a state that is incapable of sustaining itself as a member of the international community. The report broadens the concept of state failure to include a wider range of civil conflicts, political crises and massive violations of human rights and outlines four kinds of state failure: revolutionary wars, ethnic wars, mass killings, and adverse or disruptive regime change.
67. Walt W. Rostow, *The Stages of Economic Growth: A Non-Communist Manifesto* (Cambridge: Cambridge University Press, 1960), pp. 4–16.
68. This is not the case with single commodity dependence, such as oil. Concepts like Dutch disease and the resource curse have developed to explain the failure of states in such cases. On account of their characteristics of separateness, oil and water creates different economic, political, and, social opportunities for states. See Hazem Beblawi and Giacomo Luciani, eds, *The Rentier State* (London: Croom Helm, 1987); Alan Richards and John Waterbury, *A Politic Economy of the Middle East* (Boulder: Westview Press, 1996); Kiren Aziz Chaoudry, *The Price of Wealth: Economies and Institutions in the Middle East* (Ithaca: Cornell University Press, 1997), Terry Lynn Karl, *The Paradox of Plenty: Oil Booms and Petro-States* (Berkeley: University of California Press, 1997), and Clement M. Henry and Robert Springborg, *The Politics of Economic Development in the Middle East and North Africa* (Cambridge: Cambridge University Press, 2002). For a succinct literature review, see Michael Ross, 'The Political Economy of the Curse,' *World Politics* 51 (January 1999), pp. 297–322.

## Chapter 2 Realist Perspectives

1. Thomas Hobbes, *De Cive* (Oxford: Clarendon Press, [1588–1679] 1983), p. 9.
2. Waltz argues that in an anarchic international system, a state of war could have existed even if states seek only to ensure their safety. See Kenneth N. Waltz, 'The Origins of War in Neorealist Theory,' in Robert I. Rotberg and Theodore K. Rabb, eds, *The Origin and Prevention of Major Wars* (Cambridge: Cambridge University Press, 1989), p. 44.

3. Anarchy refers to lack of a central authority to monitor and enforce the rule of law in the international system.
4. See Nazli Choucri and Robert C. North, *Nations in Conflict: National Growth and International Violence* (San Fransisco: Freeman, 1975); 'Lateral Pressure in International Relations: Concept and Theory' in Manus I. Midlarsky ed., *Handbook of War Studies* (Ann Arbor: University of Michigan Press, 1989), pp. 289–326; Peter H. Gleick, 'Water and Conflict: Fresh Water Resources and International Security,' *International Security* 18 (1993), pp. 79–112; *Water in Crisis: A Guide to the World's Fresh Water Resources* (New York: Oxford University Press, 1993); *The World's Water 1998–1999* (Washington: Island Press, 1998); Thomas F. Homer-Dixon, 'On the Threshold: Environmental Changes as Causes of Acute Conflict,' *International Security* 16 (1991), pp. 76–116; 'Environmental Scarcities and Violent Conflict: Evidence from Cases,' *International Security* 19 (1994), pp. 5–40; *Environment, Scarcity, and Violence* (Princeton: Princeton University Press, 1999); Thomas F. Homer-Dixon, Jeffrey H. Boutwell, and George W. Rathjens, 'Environmental Scarcity and Violent Conflict,' *Scientific American* 268 (1993), pp. 38–45, p. 45. For a critique of Homer-Dixon, see Marc A. Levy, 'Is the Environment a National Security Issue?' *International Security* 20 (1995), pp. 35–62; and Paul F. Diehl and Nils P. Gleditsch, *Environmental Conflict* (Boulder: Westview Press, 2001).
5. Robert Gilpin, *War and Change in World Politics* (Cambridge: Cambridge University Press, 1981), p. 112.
6. Paul M. Kennedy, *The Rise and Fall of Great Powers: Economic Change and Military Conflict from 1500 to the Present* (New York: Random House, 1987), p. xxii
7. Fareed Zakaria, *From Wealth to Power: The Unusual Origins of America's World Role* (Princeton: Princeton University Press, 1998), p. 3.
8. Charles Tilly, 'Reflections on the History of European State-Making,' in Charles Tilly, ed., *The Formation of National States in Western Europe* (Princeton: Princeton University Press, 1975), p. 42.
9. These studies focus on long-term changes in hegemonic powers' leadership capabilities and subsequent restructuring of international system to adjust these changes and the problems associated with the adjustment process. One can trace the origin of these studies to Thucydides' *History of the Peloponnesian War*. See Robert B. Strassler, ed., *The Landmark of Thucydides: A Comprehensive Guide to the Peloponnesian War* (New York: Free Press, 1996); Edward H. Carr, *The Twenty Years Crisis, 1919–1939: An Introduction to the Study of International Relations* (New York: Harper & Row, 1964); William R. Thompson, *On Global War: Historical Structural Approaches to World Politics* (Columbia, SC: University of South Carolina Press, 1988); Robert Gilpin, *War and Change in World Politics* (Cambridge: Cambridge University Press, 1981).
10. Quoted in Gilpin, *War and Change in World Politics*; John M. Keynes, *The Economic Consequences of the Peace* (New York: Harcourt, Brace, Jovanovich, 1920).
11. Strassler, *The Landmark of Thucydides*, p. 352.
12. See Jack Snyder, *Myths of Empire: Domestic Politics and International Ambition* (Ithaca: Cornell University Press, 1991) and Robert Jervis and Jack Snyder, eds, *Dominoes and Bandwagons: Strategic Beliefs and Great Power Competition in the Eurasian Rimland* (Oxford: Oxford University Press, 1991).
13. States also seek to influence the behavior of other states and to control or at least to exercise influence over the world economy. Gilpin, *War and Change in World Politics*, pp. 23–4.
14. For example, according to hydraulic imperative theory, access to water resources was a major motivation behind the Israeli conquest of the Golan Heights the West Bank, and

the 1978 and 1982 Israeli invasions of Lebanon, as well as its reluctance to forgo these lands. For detailed arguments on this issue see Alwyn R. Rouyer, *Turning Water into Politics: The Water Issue in the Palestinian Israeli Conflict* (London: Macmillan, 2000); Hussein A. Amery, *Hydropolitics Along the Jordan River: Scarce Water and its Impact on the Arab-Israeli Conflict* (Tokyo: United Nations University Press, 1995); and 'A Theory of Water Diversion from Lebanon,' in Hussein A. Amery and Aron T. Wolf, *Water in the Middle East: A Geography of Peace* (Austin: University of Texas Press, 2000).

15. See Peter H. Gleick, 'Water and Conflict: Fresh Water Resources and International Security,' *International Security* 18 (Summer 1993), pp. 79–112; 'Water, War and Peace in the Middle East,' *Environment* 36 (April 1994), pp. 6–15 and pp. 35–42; and Peter H. Gleick, ed., *Water in Crisis: A Guide to the World's Fresh Water Resources* (Oxford University Press: New York, 1993).
16. Homer-Dixon, 'On the Threshold: Environmental Changes as Causes of Acute Conflict,' *International Security* 16 (Fall 1994), pp. 76–116.
17. Take, for example, Japan: if the per capita availability of resources is the determining factor, we should then expect to see civil strife there.
18. Wenche Hauge and Tanja Ellingsen, 'Beyond Environmental Scarcity: Causal Pathways to Conflict,' *Journal of Peace Research* 35 (May 1998), pp. 299–317. Clionadh Raleigh and Henrik Urdal, 'Climate Change, Environmental Degradation, and Armed Conflict,' *Political Geography* 26.6 (2007), pp. 674–94.
19. For example, it is cited to support the causal link between scarcity and conflicts by several prominent studies: Thomas Homer-Dixon, *Environment, Scarcity and Violence* (Princeton: Princeton University Press, 1999) and Colin Kahl, *States, Scarcity, and Civil Strife in the Developing World* (Princeton: Princeton University Press, 2006), p. 28.
20. See Indra de Soysa, 'Ecoviolence: Shrinking Pie, or Honey Pot,' *Global Environmental Politics* 2 (November 2002), pp. 1–34. Using World Bank data on the total per capita stock of natural capital, de Soysa concluded that resource scarcity has little if any relationship to armed conflict.
21. See Ole Magnus Theisen, 'Blood and Soil? Resource Scarcity and Internal Armed Conflict,' *Journal of Peace Research* 5 (November 2008), pp. 801–18.
22. Raleigh and Urdal found that both land degradation and water scarcity increase the risk of civil conflict. See Clionadh Raleigh and Henrik Urdal, 'Climate Change, Environmental Degradation, and Armed Conflict,' *Political Geography* 26.6 (2007), pp. 674–94.
23. See Vally Koubi, Gabriele Spilker, Tobias Bohmelt, Thomas Bernauer, 'Do Natural Resources Matter for Interstate and Intrastate Armed Conflict? *Journal of Peace Research* 51.2 (2014), pp. 227–43; Jaroslav Tir and Douglas Stinnett, 'Weathering Climate Change: Can Institutions Mitigate International Water Conflict?' *Journal of Peace Research* 49.1 (2012): 211–25; Theodora-Ismene Gizelis and Amanda E. Wooden, 'Water Resources, Institutions, and Intrastate Conflict,' *Political Geography* 29.8 (2010): 444–53; Daniel C. Esty, et al., *State Failure Task Force Report: Phase II Findings*. (McLean, VA: Science Applications International, for State Failure Task Force, 1998); Nils Petrer Gleditsch, 'Armed Conflict and the Environment: A Critique of the Literature,' *Journal of Peace Research* 35.3 (1998), pp. 363–80; Nils Petter Gleditsch, et al., 'Conflicts Over Shared Rivers: Resource Scarcity or Fuzzy Boundaries?' *Political Geography* 25 No. 4 (2006), pp. 361–82. In my PhD thesis, 'A Bargaining Framework for Explaining International Water Rights Conflicts: The Case of the Euphrates and Tigris', The University of Texas at Austin, 2006, I also found no statistically significant link between water scarcity and international conflict, though water scarcity had a negative co-efficient

using International Conflict data. The data used in large-N studies are national aggregates, and there is no easy way of capturing regional scarcity. To my knowledge only Tir and Stinnet's 2012 study found water scarcity to increase the risk of military conflict, but that risk is offset by formal agreements. Their measure of water scarcity is also problematic, since they also use aggregate data and measure water availability using the renewable per capita from the FAO Aquastat database. See Jaroslav Tir and Douglas Stinnett, 'Weathering climate change: Can institutions mitigate international water conflict?', *Journal of Peace Research* 49.1 (2012), pp. 211–25.

24. A further indication of the problems with the selection bias and endogeneity due mostly to omitted variables.
25. One of the main assumptions of realist theories is that states operate in an anarchic international system in which 'self-help' is the operational code.
26. Territorial issues between watercourse states may also render water rights issues insolvable as we have seen in the Orontes conflict. Syria's non-recognition of Alexandretta as Turkish territory leads to the non-recognition of Turkey as a lower watercourse states in the Orontes.
27. Balancing refers to allying with weaker states in the face of a threat from a strong state; bandwagoning refers to joining in an alliance with a stronger state. On alliances see, Stephen M. Walt, *The Origin of Alliances* (Ithaca: Cornell University Press, 1987); Kenneth N. Waltz, *Theory of International Politics* (New York: Random House, 1979); Randall L. Schweller, 'Bandwagoning for Profit: Bringing the Revisionist State Back In,' *International Security* 19 (Summer 1994), pp. 72–107; 'Neorealism's Status Quo Bias: What Security Dilemma?' *Security Studies* 5 (Spring 1996), pp. 90–121; 'New Realist Research on Alliances: Refining and Not Refuting, Waltz's Balancing Proposition,' *The American Political Science Review* 91 (December 1997), pp. 927–30; and *Deadly Imbalances: Tripolarity and Hitler's Strategy of World Conquest* (New York: Columbia University Press, 1998).
28. Waltz, *Theory of International Politics*.
29. Examples of recent defensive realist scholarship include Thomas J. Christensen and Jack Snyder, 'Chain Gangs and Passed Bucks: Predicting Alliance Patterns in Multipolarity,' *International Organization* 44 (Spring 1990), pp. 137–68; Stephen van Evera, 'The Cult of the Offensive and the Origins of the First World War,' *International Security* 9 (Summer 1984), pp. 58–108; 'Offense, Defense, and the Causes of War,' *International Security* 22 (Spring 1998), pp. 5–43; *Causes of War: Power and the Roots of Conflict* (Ithaca: Cornell University Press, 1999); Barry R. Posen, *The Sources of Military Doctrine: France, Britain, and Germany between the World Wars* (Ithaca: Cornell University Press, 1984).
30. See John H. Herz, *International Politics in the Atomic Age* (New York: Columbia University Press, 1959); and 'Idealist Internationalism and the Security Dilemma,' *World Politics* 2 (January 1950), pp. 157–80.
31. Robert Jervis defines 'security dilemma' as 'a situation in which the means by which a state tries to increase its security decreases the security of others.' See Robert Jervis, 'Cooperation under the Security Dilemma,' *World Politics* 30 (January 1978), pp. 167–214; and also John H. Herz, 'Idealist Internationalism and the Security Dilemma.'
32. Legro and Moravcsik, 'Is Anybody Still a Realist,' *International Security* 24 (Fall 1996), pp. 5–55, p. 17. Interestingly, Legro and Moravcsik also argue that issue linkages are not possible, which leaves us with threat of use of force/use of force and side payments as the only available means to re/distribute resources. Considering the fact that the distinction

between side payments and issue linkages is a thin one, this point needs to be further clarified and supported by evidence.

33. Randall L. Schweller, 'Neorealism's Status quo Bias: What Security Dilemma?,' *Security Studies* 5 (3), pp. 90–121.
34. Schweller argues that Walt confuses bandwagoning with strategic surrender when he defines bandwagoning in order to make it fit to his balance-of-threat framework [Randall L. Schweller, 'New Realist Research on Alliances: Refining and Not Refuting, Waltz's Balancing Proposition,' *The American Political Science Review*, 91 (4), p. 928]. Referring to Paul Kecskemeti's 1958 book, *Strategic Surrender: The Politics of Victory and Defeat* (Stanford: Stanford University Press, 1958), he notes:

    > Walt's bandwagoning is a preventive form of strategic surrender. The prospective looser agrees not to initiate hostilities and to transfer its residual military capability to the prospective winner in exchange for immunity of life, the avoidance losses it would incur in a certain military rout, and (if the loser retains some bargaining assets) the possibility of political concessions, e.g., the survival of the loser's authority structure. Sometimes the weaker side capitulates rather than fights in order to conserve its energy for a future battle under more favorable conditions. By giving in without a fight, it gains a breathing spell, during which it expects the balance of power to shift against the more powerful aggressor.

35. Schweller, 'New Realist Research on Alliances,' p. 928. This article is a response to John A. Vasquez critical article 'The Realist Paradigm and Degenerative versus Progressive Research Programs: An Appraisal of Neotraditional Research on Waltz's Balancing Proposition,' *The American Political Science Review* 91 (December 1997), pp. 899–912.
36. Inevitably, Schweller also deviates from core realist assumptions when he attributes different characteristics to states, such as wolves and jackals, which are intrinsically revisionist and risk takers, and lambs and lions, which intrinsically favor the status quo. See Randall L. Schweller, *Deadly Imbalances: Tripolarity and Hitler's Strategy of World Conquest*, New York: Columbia University Press, pp. 84–9. According to Legro and Moravscik, Scheweller reverses realism's causal arrow and ends up offering 'a compelling account of how governments adjust their power to their preferences.' See Legro and Moravscik, 'Is Anybody Still a Realist,' p. 30.
37. Schweller, 'Bandwagoning for Profit,' pp. 255–7.
38. See Joyce R. Starr, 'Water Wars,' *Foreign Policy* 82 (1991), pp. 17–36; John Bulloch and Adel Darwish, *Water Wars: Coming Conflict in the Middle East* (London: Victor Gollancz, 1993); Marc de Villiers, *Water Wars: Is the World's Water Running Out?* (Weidenfeld & Nicolson, 1999); Green Cross International and AWIRU, *Water Wars: Enduring Myth or Impending Reality? The Africa Dialogue Monograph Series No. 2.* (KwaikZulu-Natal: Creda Communications, 2000. Available at World Wide Web http://www.accord.org.za/publications); John Anthony Allan for a critique of conflict-driven approaches and his innovative explanation for the lack of war *Virtually No Water: The Middle East in 1997* (London: EMAP Business International Ltd., 1997); '"Virtual Water:" A Long Term Solution for Water Short Middle Eastern Economies?' *SOAS Occasional Papers No. 3*. Available at World Wide Web: http://www.soas.ac.uk/Geography/WaterIssues/Papers. Note that 'virtual water' refers to the amount of water required to produce a certain good. In agriculture, it is used to express a product in the amount of water required for its production. The production of grains, for example, usually requires 2 to 3 cubic meters/kilogram water depending on the efficiency of production. Thus, according to Allan, the trading of grains involves the trading of virtual water.
39. Robert A. Dahl, *On Democracy* (New Haven: Yale University Press, 1998).

40. Zeev Maoz and Bruce M. Russett, 'Normative and Structural Causes of Democratic Peace,' *American Political Science Review* 87 (1993), pp. 624–38; Zeev Maoz and Nasrin Abdolali, 'Polity Types and International Conflict,' *Journal of Conflict Resolution* 33 (1989), pp. 3–35; Stuart Bremer, 'Dangerous Dyads: Conditions Affecting the Likelihood of Interstate War, 1816–1965,' *Journal of Conflict Resolution* 36 (June 1992), pp. 309–41.
41. Edward D. Mansfield and Jack Snyder, 'Democratization and the Danger of War,' *International Security* 20 (Summer 1995), pp. 5–38; 'Democratic Transitions, Institutional Strength, and War,' *International Organization* 56 (Spring 2002), pp. 297–337.
42. Hein E. Goemans, *War and Punishment: The Causes of War Termination and the First World War* (Princeton: Princeton University Press, 2000), pp. 47–71. For the impact of domestic regime type on foreign policy see Snyder, *Myths of Empire: Domestic Politics and International Ambition*; Alan C. Stam, *Win, Lose, or Draw: Domestic Politics and the Crucible of War* (Ann Arbor: University of Michigan Press, 1996); George W. Downs and David Rocke, 'Conflict, Agency, and Gambling for Resurrection: The Principal-Agent Problem Goes to War,' *American Journal of Political Science* 38 (May 1994), pp. 362–80; for the impact of foreign policy failures on political survival of varying regime types see Bruce Bueno de Mesquite and David Lalman, 'Domestic Opposition and Foreign War,' *American Political Science Review* 84 (September 1990): 747–66; Bruce Bueno de Mesquite, Randolph M. Siverson, and Gary Wolfer, 'War and the Fate of the Regimes: A Comparative Analysis,' *American Political Science Review* 86 (September 1992), pp. 638–46; Bruce Bueno de Mesquite, Randolph M. Siverson, 'War and the Survival of Political Leaders: A Comparative Analysis of Regime Types and Accountability,' *American Political Science Review* 89 (December 1995), pp. 841–55; Frederick W. Mayer, 'Managing Domestic Differences in International Negotiations: The Strategic Use of Internal Side Payments,' *International Organization* 46 (Autumn 1992), pp. 793–818.
43. The demands for political liberalization by Syria's professional unions of lawyers, engineers, physicians led to the dissolution of the unions and imprisonment of their leaders two years earlier. See Volker Perthes, 1995, *The Political Economy of Syria under Asad*. London: I.B.Tauris, p. 137.
44. See for example, Colin P. Kelley, et al., 'Climate Change in the Fertile Crescent and Implications of the Recent Syrian Drought,' *Proceedings of the National Academy of Sciences of the United States of America* Vol. 112 No. 11 (2015), pp. 3241–6; Peter Gleick, 'Water, Drought, Climate Change, and Conflict in Syria,' *Weather, Climate, and Society* 6 (2014), pp. 331–40.

## Chapter 3 Liberal Perspectives

1. For example, in their appeal to Spartans, as Thucydides presented it, the Corinthians underlined the importance of differences in national characters and institutions on the formulation and conduct of foreign policies. Robert B. Strassler, ed., 1996, *The Landmark of Thucydides: A Comprehensive Guide to the Peloponnesian War*, New York: Free Press, pp. 38–41.
2. Hanson points out that most of the Greek city-states were democracies in the Classical period and they were in a constant state of war with each other. See Victor Hanson, *Carnage and Culture: Landmark Battles in the Rise of Western Power* (New York: Anchor, 2002), pp. 453–4.
3. Hippocrates, *On Airs, Waters, and Places* (http://classics.mit.edu/Hippocrates/airwatpl.mb.txt), part 16 (accessed on 16 May 2015); Aristotle, *Politics* (New York: Cambridge University Press, 1988), 1327 b 24 ff.

4. Charles de Montesquieu, *The Spirit of Laws* (Cambridge University Press [1748], 1989), pp. 8–9.
5. There is little question that water played a crucial role in the emergence of the first civilizations appearing in Mesopotamia (and the Indus and the Nile valleys). Karl Wittfogel [*Oriental Despotism: A Comparative Study of Total Power* (New Haven: Yale University Press, 1956)] reminds us of the critical role of water in the development of these early civilizations, which he styles 'hydraulic societies,' and in the emergence of despotic states. He argued that the first large-scale irrigation projects were followed by despotic states, since the construction and maintenance of irrigation works required the establishment of bureaucratic organizations, which in turn increased the power of the central state. See also Eyal Benvenisti, 'Collective Action in the Utilization of Shared Freshwater: The Challenges of International Water Resources Law,' *American Journal of International Law 90* (1996), pp. 384–415. Benvenisti notes that in all great ancient societies, Sumer and Assyria in Mesopotamia, Pharaonic Egypt, the Inca Empire of Peru, and China and India, the taming of rivers was the catalyst of their evolution. The social implications of large-scale hydraulic works seem to reinforce the political outcomes of centralization and the emergence of authoritarian political structures. However, the perception of water as a catalyst for the advancement of civilizations has not gone uncontested. Jared Diamond, for example, objects to the correlation between irrigation and the formation of states and suggests that population size was the most important predictor of societal complexity, centralization and stratification. See Jared Diamond, *Guns, Germs, and Steel: The Fates of Human Societies* (New York: Norton, 1997), p. 284; H. Rabie, 'Some Technical Aspect of Egyptian Agriculture in Medieval Egypt,' in A. L. Udovitch, *The Islamic Middle East, 700–1900: Studies in Economic and Social History* (Princeton: Princeton University Press, 1981), p. 239.
6. Montesquieu, *The Spirit of Laws*, p. 338.
7. On the civilizing influences of trade see Albert Hirschman, *Passions and Interests* (Princeton: Princeton University Press, 1977).
8. Audience cost is crucial for making commitments credible. If a ruler renege on his/her commitments, s/he pays a price, hence the audience cost.
9. All these propositions are highly contentious. See for example Christopher Layne, 'Kant or Cant: The Myth of the Democratic Peace,' *International Security* 19 (1994), pp. 5–49; James L. Ray, *Democracy and International Conflict: An Evolution of the Democratic Peace Proposition* (Columbia, SC: University of South Carolina Press, 1995).
10. Similar expectations are widespread even now. Most recently, in reaction to the Russian annexation of Crimea, US Secretary of State John Kerry condemned Russia's 'incredible act of aggression' stating that 'You just don't in the twenty-first century behave in nineteenth century fashion by invading another country on a completely trumped up pre-text.' CBS TV Show, *Face the Nation*, 2 March 2014.
11. For a literature review on the incompatibility of democracy and war see Albert Hirschman, 'Rival Interpretations of Market Society: Civilizing, Destructive, or Feeble?' *Journal of Economic Literature* 20 (December 1982), pp. 1463–84.
12. See Zeev Maoz and Nasrin Abdolali, 'Polity Types and International Conflict,' *Journal of Conflict Resolution* 33 (1989), pp. 3–35; Zeev Maoz and Bruce M. Russett, 'Normative and Structural Causes of Democratic Peace,' *American Political Science Review*, 87 (1993), pp. 624–38; John Owen, 'How Liberalism Produces Democratic Peace,' *International Security* 19 (1992), pp. 87–125; Stuart Bremer, 'Dangerous Dyads: Conditions Affecting the Likelihood of Interstate War, 1816–1965,' *Journal of Conflict Resolution 36* (June 1992), pp. 309–41; Bruce Bueno De Mesquita, and David Lalman, *War and Reason:*

*Domestic and International Imperatives* (New Haven: Yale University Press, 1992); Dan Reiter and Allan C. Stam, 'Democracy, War Initiation, and Victory,' *American Political Science Review* 92 (1998), pp. 377–90 and also *Democracies at War* (Princeton: Princeton University Press, 2002).

13. Michael W. Doyle, 'Kant, Liberal Legacies, and Foreign Affairs,' Parts 2, *Philosophy and Public Affairs* 12 (1983), pp. 323–53 (Part 2 reprinted in Robert J. Art and Robert Jervis eds, *International Politics: Enduring Concepts and Contemporary Issues*) (New York: Harper Collins, 1996, 4th edn), pp. 95–107, p. 106.
14. For the importance of domestic structures see Robert D. Putnam, 'Diplomacy and Domestic Politics: The Logic of Two-Level Games,' *International Organization* 42 (Summer 1988), pp. 448–50; Robert D. Putnam, eds, *Double-Edged Diplomacy: International Bargaining and Domestic Politics* (Berkeley: University of California Press, 1993).
15. For institutional strand of the theory see Kant, 'Perpetual Peace: A Philosophical Sketch', in Hans Reiss eds., *Kant: Political Writings* (New York: Cambridge University Press, 1991), pp. 93–130. Doyle, 'Kant, Liberal Legacies, and Foreign Affairs,' Parts 1 and 2, Philosophy and Public Affairs 12 (1983), pp. 205–35 and 12 (1983), pp. 323–53; and 'Liberalism and World Politics,' *American Political Science Review* 80 (1986), pp. 1151–70; and Bueno de Mesquita and Lalman, War and Reason; for the normative strand see Martha Finnemore, *National Interest in International Society* (Ithaca: Cornell University Press, 1996).
16. See Douglass C. North, John J. Wallis, Barry Weingast, *Violence and Social Order: A Conceptual Framework for Interpreting Recorded Human History* (Cambridge: Cambridge University Press, 2009) and Douglass C. North, John J. Wallis, and Steven B. Webb, eds, *In the Shadow of Violence: The Problem of Development for Limited Access Order Societies* (Cambridge: Cambridge University Press, 2013); Daron Acemoglu and James Robinson, *Why Nations Fails Fail: The Origins of Power, Prosperity, and Poverty* (New York: Random House, 2013).
17. The first is the foraging or primitive order and is characterized by small social groups characteristic of hunter-gatherer societies.
18. Daron Acemoglu and James Robinson, *Why Nations Fail: The Origins of Power, Prosperity, and Poverty* (New York: Random House, 2013).
19. Colin Kahl, *States, Scarcity, and Civil Strife in the Developing World* (Princeton: Princeton University Press, 2006).
20. The inclusivity of state institutions, which is more likely a characteristic of democratic states, refers to the degree to which key social groups are institutionally empowered to participate in, and influence, decision making by state elites. Institutional inclusivity reduces the probability of conflict (Kahl, *States, Scarcity, and Civil Strife in the Developing World*, 2006: pp. 54–5).
21. Groupness refers to the degree to which clusters of individuals depend on distinct identity-groups (ethno-cultural, kin-, tribe-, religious-, or class-based) for physical, economic, and psychic security, as opposed to a number of overlapping and cross-cutting identity-groups (Kahl, *States, Scarcity, and Civil Strife in the Developing World*, 2006: pp. 52–4).
22. Neo-Malthusians often predicts that the mixture of population growth, environmental degradation, and poor distribution of natural resources results in deprivation among the poorest elements of society increasing the probability of violence (Kahl, *States, Scarcity, and Civil Strife in the Developing World*, 2006: p. 11). The poor are often too poor to engage in political action, like protests, or violence. It is costly to engage in activities that involve violence especially in authoritarian institutional setting. If one can no longer feed a

population because of a prolonged drought, it is far easier to move to urban areas than engage in insurgency against the government.

23. The Syrian civil war seems to provide confirming evidence for the state exploitation hypothesis.
24. Kekcskemeti suggests otherwise that democracies are particularly prone to crusades. See Paul Kecskemeti, *Strategic Surrender: The Politics of Victory and Defeat*, Stanford: California University Press, 1958. I argue that the nature of governing institutions holds the key here. Democracies with exclusionary institutions are not necessarily going to adopt peaceful resolutions to conflicts. The changes to formal institutions can be implemented very quickly, but it takes time for informal institutions, like prevalent norms of the society to develop and democracy to take roots in a country. Formal institutions cannot operate in a vacuum and this is one of the reasons why formal institutions do not always carry over. Institutions are embedded in society.
25. Inclusive institutions are concomitant with a democratic type of governance, while exclusive institutions, which concentrate power in the hands of a few without any checks and balances on power, are not.
26. For example, Fisher suggested that the cost of settling the Israeli-Palestinian water conflict might be cheaper than the cost of a single jet fighter. Reference to this was made during the hearing before the Committee on International Relations, House of Representatives, *Water Scarcity in the Middle East; Regional Cooperation as a Mechanism toward Peace, 108 Congress Session*, 5 May 2004.
27. Regime type may not be the real culprit, but the more inclusive institutional structure of these countries makes them more successful and easily adaptable in general. Since there is a clear congruence between democratic countries and inclusive institutions and authoritarian countries and exclusive institutions, I shall continue to use democracy interchangeably with open inclusive institutions. I know of no authoritarian country with inclusive political and economic institutions. The more inclusive a country's institutions, the better it is in solving its problems through peaceful means.
28. Vertical accountability refers to a type of accountability imposed upon the state by citizens through free, fair, and regular elections. Horizontal accountability, on the other hand, refers to a type of accountability imposed upon the state by some agencies of government, such as the judiciary, the legislature, auditor generals, anti-corruption bodies, electoral and human rights commissions, ombudsmen, and so on.
29. Credible commitments represent a much more difficult problem for authoritarian regimes to solve as their commitments by definition are less credible given the strong incentives for arbitrariness and there being no checks on power. The problem of regime stability also makes it difficult or even impossible for autocrats to make credible commitments. See Mancur Olson, 'Dictatorship, Democracy, and Development,' *American Political Science Review* 87 (1993): pp. 569–76.
30. Przeworski and Limongi argue that political institutions, especially property rights and credible commitments, matter for growth, but thinking in terms of regimes does not seem to capture the relevant differences. See Adam Przeworski and F. Limongi, 'Political Regimes and Economic Growth,' *Journal of Economic Perspectives* 7.3 (1993): pp. 51–69.
31. Mancur Olson, 'Dictatorship, Democracy, and Development,' *American Political Science Review* 87 (1993): pp. 569–76.
32. Weiss and Jacobson found that democracies are more likely to comply with environmental agreements because they respect the rule of law. See Edith B. Weiss and Harold

K. Jacobsen. 'Getting Countries to Comply with International Agreements,' *Environment* 41 (1999) pp. 16–23.

33. Bueno de Mesquita et al.'s selectorate theory provides one of the best explanations of how incentive structures are created by different institutional settings. The size of the winning coalition (the minimal set of individuals in the selectorate whose support an incumbent needs to remain in office) relative to the size of the selectorate (the part of the population that is eligible to vote) is the key for understanding government policies. This ratio is high in democracies forcing leaders to win the support of a majority of the population to remain in office, while it is small for authoritarian regimes where the authoritarian rulers can retain office by keeping the support of a very small number of individuals. *Ceteris paribus*, democratic leaders are incentivized to provide more public goods and to adopt policies beneficial to the majority of citizens than their authoritarian counterparts in order to remain in office. See Bruce Bueno de Mesquita, Alastair Smith, Randolph M. Siverson, and James D. Morrow, *The Logic of Political Survival* (Cambridge: MIT Press, 2003); and Bruce Bueno de Mesquita and Alastair Smith, *The Dictator's Handbook: Why Bad Behavior is Almost Always Good Politics* (New York: Public Affairs, 2011).
34. Rousseau et al. find that democracies are more pacific in general. See David Rousseau, Christopher Gelpi, Dan Reiter, and Paul K. Huth, 'Assessing the Dyadic Nature of the Democratic Peace,' *American Political Science Review* 90 (1996), pp. 512–44. James L. Ray, on the other hand, argues that democracies are more peaceful in general in *Democracies and International Conflict: An Evaluation of the Democratic Peace Proposition* (Columbia, SC: University of South Carolina Press, 1995).
35. Here a relevant case worth citing is the War of 1812, in which the US President James Madison was essentially pushed into starting the war against his better judgment by pressure from Congress and the general public.
36. Mogens H. Hansen, *The Athenian Democracy in the Age of Demosthenes* (Cambridge: Blackwell, 1991), pp. 264–65.
37. In the United Kingdom, the executive has the sole power to make wars and treaties.
38. According to Owen this was the underlying reason behind the hijacking of governments by illiberals in democratic states leading them to engage in conflicts with other liberal democracies. See John M. Owen, 'How Liberalism Produces Democratic Peace,' p. 149.
39. Following Burton and Higley, I define elites as the several (thousand) persons who hold top positions in large or otherwise powerful organizations and movements and those who participate in or directly influence political decision making. See Michael G. Burton and John Higley, 'Invitation to Elite Theory: The Basic Contentions Reconsidered,' in G.W. Domhoff and T. R. Dye, eds, *Power Elites and Organizations* (Newbury Park: Sage, 1987).
40. The validity of the propositions that democracies are more peaceful towards each other than towards non-democracies, as well as the harmony of interests between the democratic states, is dubious. There is no reason for a democratic public be less apprehensive of war if the opposing state is non-democracy. Some democratic peace scholars also argue that regardless of an adversary's regime type democracies are more peaceful. See Brett A. Leeds and David Davis, 'Beneath the Surface: Regime Type and International Interactions 1953–1978,' *Journal of Peace Research* 36 (1999), pp. 5–21; 'Domestic Political Vulnerability and International Disputes,' *Journal of Conflict Resolution* 41 (December 1997), pp. 814–34.
41. See Kenneth A. Schultz, 'Do Democratic Institutions Constrain or Inform? Contrasting Two Institutional Perspectives on Democracy and War,' *International Organization* 53

(Spring 1999), pp. 233–66; 'Domestic Opposition and Signaling in International Crises,' *American Political Science Review* 92 (December 1998), pp. 829–44; and for more detail, *Democracy and Coercive Diplomacy* (London: Cambridge University Press, 2001).

42. Doyle, 'Kant, Liberal Legacies, and Foreign Affairs,' pp. 95–107.
43. The text of the Kellogg-Briand Pact is available as part of the Yale Law School, The Avalon Project, Documents in Law, History and Diplomacy online at http://avalon.law.yale.edu/20th_century/kbpact.asp (accessed on 7 December 2015).
44. See Stephen D. Krasner, 'State Power and The Structure of International Trade,' *World Politics* 28 (1976), pp. 317–47; and his critique by Robert O. Keohane, 'Problematic Lucidity: Stephen Krasner's 'State Power and the Structure of International Trade,' *World Politics* 50 (1997), pp. 150–70.
45. See Katherine Barbieri, 'Economic Interdependence: A Path to Peace or Source of International Conflict,' *Journal of Peace Research* 33 (1996), pp. 29–49; and Michael S. de Viries, 'Interdependence, Cooperation, and Conflict: An Empirical Analysis,' *Journal of Peace Research* 27 (1990), pp. 429–44.
46. Barbieri and Levy's study on the short- and long-term impact of war on trade in seven dyads since 1870 did not find significant impact on trading relationships in most cases. See Katherine Barbieri and Jack S. Levy, 'Sleeping with Enemy: The Impact of War on Trade,' *Journal of Peace Research* 36 (1999), pp. 463–79.
47. Such as Michael W. Doyle, *Ways of War and Peace: Realism, Liberalism, and Socialism* (New York, Norton, 1997); John R. Oneal and Bruce M. Russett, 'The Classical Liberals were Right: Democracy, Interdependence, and Conflict, 1950–1985,' *International Studies Quarterly* 41 (March 1997), pp. 267–94.
48. See the critical analysis of classical liberal thinking of this era by Edward H. Carr, *The Twenty Years Crisis, 1919–1939: An Introduction to the Study of International Relations* (New York: Harper & Row, 1964).
49. Ricardo's famous example is cloth-producing England and wine-producing Portugal. He suggested that if both countries specialize in making what they are most efficient at producing, and produce it at a lower opportunity costs, both countries and the world would gain from this division of labor. The opportunity cost of a product is determined by the amount a competitor product needs to be given up in order to produce one more unit of the product. This is also what separates Ricardo's theory of comparative advantage from absolute advantage. England has a comparative advantage in cloth production, because of the amount of wine England has to give up to produce another unit of cloth is less than the amount of wine that Portugal has to give up to in order to produce another unit of cloth. See David Ricardo, *On the Principles of Political Economy and Taxation* (Amherst: Prometheus Books [1817], 1996).
50. See for an analysis of the distributional consequences of trade policy and political conflict, Michael J. Hiscox, *International Trade and Political Conflict: Commerce, Coalitions, and Mobility* (Princeton: Princeton University Press, 2002).
51. Timothy J. McKeown, 'Hegemonic Stability Theory and 19th Century Tariff Levels in Europe,' *International Organization* 37.1 (1983), pp. 73–91.
52. Stephan D. Krasner, 'State Power and the Structure of International Trade.'
53. See Edward D. Mansfield, *Power, Trade, and War* (Princeton: Princeton University Press, 1994).
54. Joanne Gowa and Edward D. Mansfield, 'Power Politics and International Trade,' *American Political Science Review* 87 (1993), pp. 408–20, p. 408.
55. When information asymmetries are high, the increased cost of exchange creates a need for institutions to reduce uncertainty and stabilize expectations.

56. Keohane, *After Hegemony.*
57. Barbara Koremenos, Charles Lipson, and Duncan Snidal, 'The Rational Design of International Institutions,' *International Organization* 55 (2001), pp. 761–800.
58. Keohane, *After Hegemony,* pp. 83–95.
59. See Ernst B. Haas, 'Do Regimes Matter? Epistemic Communities and Mediterranean Pollution Control,' *International Organization* 43 (1998), pp. 377–403.
60. Ibid., p. 384.
61. Charles Lipson, 'International Cooperation in Economic and Security Affairs,' *World Politics* 37 (October 1984), pp. 1–23, p. 12.
62. See Joseph M. Grieco, 'Anarchy and the Limits of Cooperation: A Realist Critique of the Newest Liberal Institutionalism,' *International Organization* 42 (Summer 1988), pp. 485–507; 'Understanding the Problem of International Cooperation: The Limits of Neo-Liberal Institutionalism and the Future of Realist Theory,' in David A. Baldwin ed., *Neorealism and Neoliberalism* (New York: Columbia University Press, 1993); and also John J. Mearsheimer, 'The False Premise of International Institutions,' *International Security* 19 (Winter 1994/95), pp. 5–49; 'A Realist Reply,' *International Security* 20 (Summer 1995), pp. 82–93.
63. Keohane, 'Institutional Theory and Realist Challenge,' in Baldwin ed., *Neorealism and Neoliberalism,* p. 283.
64. See Stephen D. Krasner, 'Structural Causes and Regime Consequences: Regimes as Intervening Variables,' in Stephen D. Krasner ed., *International Regimes*; Robert Keohane, 'The Theory of Hegemonic Stability and Changes in International Economic Regimes, 1967–1977,' in Ole R. Holsti, Randolph M. Siverson, and Alexander George eds, *Changes in the International System* (Boulder: Westview Press, 1980); and Duncan Snidal, 'Limits of Hegemonic Stability Theory,' *International Organization* 39 (1985), pp. 579–614.
65. Keohane, *After Hegemony.*
66. See also Olson, *The Logic of Collective Action.* He illustrates how the differences in individual preferences and necessities lead individuals to produce collective goods in spite of free riders.
67. Elinor Ostrom, *Governing the Common Pool Resources* (Cambridge: Cambridge University Press, 1990).
68. By examining several long-standing common pool resources regimes, including Swiss grazing meadows, Japanese forests, and Spanish irrigation systems, Ostrom underlined the importance of clearly defined boundaries, congruence between appropriation and provision rules and local conditions, democratic decision making, monitoring is done by the users or people who are accountable to the users, graduated sanctions against violators, access to low-cost local arenas to resolve conflicts, the recognition of the rights of the users to organize by external government authorities, and nested enterprises for common pool resources that are parts of larger systems. See Ostrom, *Governing the Common Pool Resources*, p. 90.
69. Ostrom, *Governing the Common Pool Resources*, pp. 99–100.
70. The assumptions of the prisoner's dilemma game are complete information, the lack of communication between the players, and the one-shot game. See Robert Jervis, 'Cooperation under the Security Dilemma,' *World Politics*, 30 (January 1978), p. 171.
71. Here again I use the broad definition of institutions as formal and informal rules that governs the relationship among states.

72. In some cases, the settlement of private property rights by definition is impossible. How can one determine private property rights in ocean fisheries, for example?
73. The impact of transnational epistemic communities on peaceful resolutions of conflicts is therefore discounted if the situation involves mixed regime types. The international context in which these contingent commitments take place is also discounted. Mutual interests among states what often makes international cooperation possible.
74. For instance, the Joint Technical Committee facilitated the 1989 Treaty between Syria and Iraq concerning the apportionment of the Euphrates waters.
75. Kindleberger linked the Great Depression to the absence of a lender of last resort in the international financial system and laying the foundation of this theory in *The World in Depression, 1929–1939* (Berkeley: University of California Press, 1973). Later on, Keohane labeled it Hegemonic Stability Theory in 'The Theory of Hegemonic Stability and Changes in International Economic Regimes, 1967–1977.'
76. See Barry Eichengreen, *Globalizing Capital: A History of the International Monetary System* (Princeton: Princeton University Press, 1996). For discussion of malign and benign variants of Hegemonic Stability Theory see Snidal's 'Limits of Hegemonic Stability Theory,' pp. 579–614.
77. The earliest extant arbitration over water rights comes from the period of the *Pax Romana*. See J. S. Richardson, 'The Tabula Contrebiensis: Roman Law in Spain in the Early First Century BC,' *Journal of Roman Studies* 73 (1983), pp. 33–41.
78. The United States' interest in the Jordan watercourse is linked to Israel. Since the establishment of the state of Israel, often by conditioning its aid to Israel and Jordan for water related projects, the United States has played a role in the Jordan watercourse. See Miriam Lowi, *Water and Power: The Politics of a Scarce Resource in the Jordan River Basin* (Cambridge: Cambridge University Press, 1993), and Sharif S. Elmusa, *Water Conflict: Economics, Politics, Law and Palestinian-Israeli Water Resources* (Washington: Institute for Palestinian Studies, 1997). The effect of the United States even in the Jordan watercourse is limited considering the fact that Arab states, with the exception of Jordan, have long refused the United States' plans for various reasons. For instance, the Johnston Plan of 1955 was rejected by Arab states due to the fact that acceptance meant a tacit recognition of Israel. See on this subject, Jad Isaac and Leonardo Hosh, 'Roots of the Water Conflict in the Middle East,' a paper presented at the Conference on The Middle East Water Crisis: Creative Perspectives and Solutions, 7–9 May 1992, University of Waterloo, Canada.
79. The Egyptian dominance of the Nile watercourse suffers from similar predicaments. To date, Egypt, a lower watercourse state, has secured the continuous flow of the Nile. This can be explained by Egypt's hegemonic position due to its being the most economically developed watercourse state on the Nile, but also to the under-development of the upper watercourse states. Even Sudan, which is entitled to 18.5 billion cubic meters by the 1959 Treaty, has not been able to use its full share. See John Waterbury, *Hyrdopolitics of the Nile Valley* (New York: Syracuse University Press, 1979), p. 72. According to the 1959 Treaty, Egypt is entitled to 55.5 billion cubic meters of water, which is more than 86 percent of the Nile waters. There is no guarantee that the upper watercourse states will ever have the economic resources necessary to develop and utilize the Nile. Besides, the 1959 Treaty has already been challenged by Ethiopia, which holds the headwaters of the Blue Nile and contributes 60 percent of the total flow, and also contributes to the Sawba and Atbara, the tributaries of the White Nile, with a total contribution of about 86 percent of the Nile. In the long-run, Egypt and

Sudan cannot disregard water rights of the upper watercourse states challenging the existing treaties. The Egyptian efforts to persuade the upper watercourse states to recognize its share of the Nile waters and its failure to date to do so is an indication of Egypt's weaknesses as a hegemonic state in imposing water rights in the Nile watercourse. For a discussion of the Nile water rights conflict, see John Waterbury, *The Nile Basin: National Determinants of Collective Action* (New Haven: Yale University Press, 2002).

80. Haas's spillover effects, which refer to the expectations that the positive effects of cooperation on one issue area among conflicting parties will extend to other issue areas leading to a peaceful relationship among them through the broadening of potential side payments and thus facilitating agreement, does not seem to be in effect here. See Ernest B. Haas, 'Why Collaborate? Issue Linkages and International Regimes,' *World Politics* 32 (1980), pp. 357–405.
81. Mansfield and Snyder, 'Democratization and the Danger of War,' pp. 5–38; 'Democratic Transitions, Institutional Strength, and War,' pp. 297–337.
82. Keohane, *After Hegemony,* p. 107.
83. See Tony Allan, *The Middle East Water Question* (London: I.B.Tauris, 2000), p. 259.

## Chapter 4 A Bargaining Framework for International Water Rights

1. David Fromkin, *A Peace to End All Peace, The Fall of the Ottoman Empire and the Creation of the Modern Middle East* (New York: Avon Books, 1989), p. 190.
2. See, for example, Anatol Rapoport, *Strategy and Conscience* (New York: Shocken Books, 1964); John G. Cross, *The Economics of Bargaining* (New York: Basic Books, 1969), p. 7.
3. Oran R. Young, 'Strategic Interaction and Bargaining,' in Oran R. Young ed., *Bargaining: Formal Theories of Negotiation* (Urbana: University of Illinois Press, 1975), p. 5.
4. Thomas C. Schelling, 1966, *Arms and Influence*. New Haven: Yale University Press. See also Carl von Clausewitz, *On War* (Princeton: Princeton University Press, 1976). For Clausewitz war is a continuation of pre-war negotiations and it happens as a result of choice. For a similar contemporary conceptualization of war, see R. Harrison Wagner, 2000, 'Bargaining and War,' *American Journal of Political Science*, 44 (3), pp. 469–84.
5. Schelling, *Arms and Influence*, p. 142. Schelling notes the existence of limited wars as a clear indication of this.
6. It is, for example, more difficult for exclusionary states to make credible commitments and the use of force could make their threats more credible.
7. Schelling, *Arms and Influence*, p. v.
8. The only example of this in recent history is the Syrian attempt to divert the headwaters of the Jordan River in retaliation to Israeli water diversion via the National Water Carrier in 1964 and the subsequent Israeli air strikes to stop the diversion works a few years preceding to the Third Arab-Israeli War of June 1967. Even then, it seems water was just an ancillary factor to the real drivers of the Arab-Israeli conflict. If we think of in counterfactual terms, the Third Arab-Israeli war would have occurred regardless of Syrians attempt to divert the headwaters of Jordan River, since the

Arab-Israeli conflict has caused at least five major wars since the second half of the twentieth century.

9. Here the agreement/cooperation outcome in bargaining negotiations refers to the agreement over the distribution of water rights among the states. It does not necessarily incorporate the establishment of basin-wide institutions to develop water and land resources of the international watercourse.
10. To name a few: Egypt versus Ethiopia, Turkey versus Syria and Iraq, Israel versus Jordan, India versus Pakistan, the US versus Mexico.
11. There is the possibility of nuclear war, for example, between India and Pakistan.
12. Young, 'Strategic Interaction and Bargaining,' p. 6.
13. Robert Jervis, 1976, *Perception and Misperception in International Politics*, Princeton: Princeton University Press, p. 32.
14. Duncan Snidal, 'The Game Theory of International Politics,' in Kenneth N. Oye, ed., *Cooperation under Anarchy*, Princeton: Princeton University Press, p. 39.
15. See Kalyan Chatterjee, 'Disagreement in Bargaining: Models with Incomplete Information,' in Alvin E. Roth ed., *Game-Theoretic Models of Bargaining* (New York: Cambridge University Press, 1985).
16. If, for example, a watercourse state expects a river to dry out due to climate change, it could prefer not to have formal commitments.
17. The classical principal-agent problem, which refers to situations in which the interests of rulers are inconsistent with the interests of the general public of their country, rears its head here.
18. I define 'power' as military capabilities, which is of course is related to the economic and political capabilities of a state.
19. A good example of the tendency of states to be opportunistic in misrepresenting private information is the Syrian-Egyptian alliance to recover the Arab territories that were lost to Israel in 1967. During the war preparation negotiations between Syria and Egypt, the differences in war aims did not become clear, which gravely impaired the chances of realizing war aims during the October war of 1973. After the war, it became clear that the Egyptians in providing false war plans deliberately led the Syrians into believing that the Egyptian offensive would be wider in scope (see Patrick Seale, *Assad of Syria: The Struggle for the Middle East* (Berkeley: California University Press, 1988), pp. 185–201. Jordan also kept secret from Syria its negotiations with Israel concerning the Jordan River's water.
20. Here cooperation is defined narrowly as an agreement outcome/negotiated settlement over the distribution of water rights among the watercourse states. It does not necessarily contain the establishment of watercourse-wide institutions to develop and exploit the resources of the watercourse.
21. According to Fearon, commitment problems and the issue of indivisibilities are the other two reasons why states may be unable to locate a peaceful settlement that both would prefer. See James D. Fearon, 'Rationalist Explanations for War,' *International Organization* 49 (1995), pp. 379–414.
22. The existence of private information also limits a hegemonic state's ability to affect the outcome of the conflicts. There is no reason to expect a hegemonic state to have access to private information or to be able to verify information provided by the parties. See John Kennan and Robert Wilson, 'Bargaining with Private Information,' *Journal of Economic Literature* 31 (1993), pp. 45–104, p. 98.
23. Kennan and Wilson, 'Bargaining with Private Information,' p. 48.

24. Fearon, 'Rationalist Explanations for War,' pp. 379–414; and 'Bargaining, Enforcement, and International Cooperation,' *International Organization* 52 (1998), pp. 269–306.
25. Syria underestimated Turkey's displeasure of its safeguarding and support for the Kurdistan Workers' Party (PKK), which led to a crisis in 1999. The crisis started when Turkey moved its military troops to the Syrian border, and demanded Syrian compliance with its terms regarding the PKK. The crisis ended with Syrian acquiescence.
26. Robert Keohane, *After Hegemony: Cooperation and Discord in the World Political Economy*, Princeton: Princeton University Press, 1984; Ray Challen, 2000, *Institutions, Transaction Costs and Environmental Policy: Institutional Reform for Water Resources*, Massachusetts: Edward Elgar; Katja Weber, *Hierarchy amidst Anarchy: Transaction Costs and Institutional Choice*, Albany: State University of New York, 2000; and Ronald Coase, *The Firm, the Market, and the Law*, Chicago: University of Chicago Press, 1988, pp. 386–405.
27. Issue linkages refer to situations in which a state's policy in one issue area is contingent upon another state's policy in another issue. For discussion of issue linkages and side payments see Ernest B. Haas, 'Why Collaborate? Issue Linkages and International Regimes,' *World Politics* 32 (1980), pp. 357–405.
28. See for detailed discussion of the Nile waters John Waterbury, *The Nile Basin: National Determinants of Collective Action* (New Haven: Yale University Press, 2002).
29. For detailed analysis of the conflict over Jordan watercourse see Miriam Lowi, *Water and Power: The Politics of a Scarce Resource in the Jordan River Basin* (Cambridge: Cambridge University Press, 1993), and Sharif S. Elmusa, *Water Conflict: Economics, Politics, Law and Palestinian-Israeli Water Resources* (Washington: Institute for Palestinian Studies, 1997).
30. For a discussion of iteration and tit-for-tat and other strategies see Robert Axelrod, *The Evolution of Cooperation*, New York: Basic Books, 1985; Jervis, 'Cooperation under the Security Dilemma,' pp. 167–214. For the discussion of issue linkages and side payments sew Haas, 'Why Collaborate? Issue Linkages and International Regimes,' pp. 357–405.
31. Issue linkages refer to situations in which a state's policy in one issue area is contingent upon other state's policy in another issue.
32. International Freshwater Treaties Database. Available at http://www.transboundarywaters.orst.edu/database/interfreshtreatdata.html (accessed on 27 April 2015).
33. See most recent review of the transboundary freshwater treaties, M. Giordano, et al., 'A Review of the Evolution and State of Transboundary Freshwater Treaties,' *International Environmental Agreements* (2014), pp. 245–64.

## Chapter 5 Bargaining for Water Rights in the Euphrates and Tigris Watercourse

1. The name Mesopotamia is a Greek translation of the Old Persian *Miyanrudan*, which means 'the Land between the Rivers;' *Beth-Nahrin*, 'House of Two Rivers,' is the Aramaic name of the area. To the west flows the Euphrates, the name of which comes to us from Greek. It is *Pu-rat-tu* in ancient Assyrian, *Ufrat* in Old Persian, *Prâth/Frot* in Aramaic, *Al-Furat* in Arabic, *Fırat* in Turkish. To the east flows the Tigris. The name *Tigr* is Old Persian and means 'the fast one.' It is called *Deqlath* in Syrian Aramaic, *Dijla* in Arabic, and *Dicle* in Turkish.
2. George A. Barton, 'Inscription of Entemena 7,' in *The Royal Inscriptions of Sumer and Akkad* (New Haven: Yale University 1929), pp. 61, 63, and 65. [Reprinted in D. Brendan Nagle and Stanley M. Burstein, *The Ancient World: Readings in Social and Cultural History* (Englewood: Prentice Hall, 1995), pp. 30–31.]

3. Thomas Naff and R.C. Matson, *Water in the Middle East: Conflict or Cooperation* (Boulder: Westview Press, 1984), p. 89.
4. T.C. Foreign Ministry, *Water Issues between Turkey, Syria and Iraq* (Ankara: Foreign Ministry of Turkey, 1996), p. 8. Dante Caponera, 'The Legal and Institutional Concepts of Cooperation,' paper submitted to the International Conference on Transboundary Waters in the Middle East: Prospects for Regional Cooperation, 2–3 September 1991, Bilkent University, Ankara, p. 2.
5. Samir Salha, *Turkiye, Suriye ve Lübnan Iliskilerinde Asi Nehri Sorunu* (Ankara: Hacettepe Üniversitesi Dıs Politika Enstitüsü, 1995), p. 15.
6. Naff and Matson, *Water in the Middle East*, p. 122.
7. Ibid., p. 120.
8. Ray Krishna, 'International Watercourses: World Bank Experience and Policy' paper presented at the Conference on Water in the Middle East, School of Oriental and Asian Studies, 19–20 November, 1992, pp. 6–8.
9. Gün Kut, 'Burning Waters: the Hydropolitics of the Euphrates Tigris,' *New Perspectives on Turkey* Fall 1993, pp. 1–18, p. 4.
10. Naff and Matson, *Water in the Middle East*, p. 119.
11. *The Middle East,* 'Dam It. It's Our Water,' December 1993, pp. 32–3.
12. T.C. Foreign Ministry, *Water Issues between Turkey, Syria, Iraq*, p. 8.
13. The water quality problems are not specific to the Orontes. Until recently, Syria did not have any effective wastewater treatment facilities and untreated wastewater, originating from industrial, domestics, and agriculture, had been disposed into rivers and the sea. The most recent (2008) UNFAO AQUASTAT for Syria also points to the lack of water management capacity and resulting pollution and significant increase in waterborne diseases. http://www.fao.org/nr/water/aquastat/countries_regions/syr/index.stm (accessed on 2 May 2015).
14. The 2013 UN Economic and Social Commission for Western Asia report, *Inventory of Shared Water Resources in Western Asia*, pp. 232–6.
15. In 1936, the Turkish government filed a complaint about the mistreatment of the Turks in the governorate of Alexandretta with the League of Nations. Meanwhile, the governorate had gained autonomy in 1937 through an arrangement brokered by the League of Nations. Riots erupted between Turks and Arabs precipitating the creation of the 'Republic of Hatay' under joint French and Turkish military control. The election for the parliamentary seats resulted in the election of Tayfur Sokmen, who was also a member of Turkish Parliament. In 1939, majority Turkish members of parliament voted for unification with Turkey and subsequently the former governorate became a Turkish province. Alexandretta joined Turkey in 1939. The unification decision was not welcomed by Syria and after Syria gained its independence from France in 1946, it has become one of the significant sources of resentment between the two states. It was still shown as a part of Syria on official Syrian maps, except for one occasion in order to assure Turkey's participation in the Mediterranean Games of 1987.
16. It was signed on 1 June 2004 and entered into force on 1 March 2006. Turkey and Syria officially recognized each other borders, though there is an interesting clause in the agreement indicating this to be the case 'for the purposes of this agreement only' just before the definition of Turkey and Syria. See the text of the Agreement on Reciprocal Promotion and Protection of Investment http://investmentpolicyhub.unctad.org/Download/TreatyFile/2335 (accessed on 2 May 2015).

17. It was signed on 22 December 2004 and entered into force on 1 January 2007. The text of the Treaty is available at http://investmentpolicyhub.unctad.org/Download/TreatyFile/2702 (accessed on 2 May 2015).
18. *Middle East Economic Digest*, 28 July 1972.
19. *Keesing's Contemporary Archives*, September 1994.
20. Salha, *Turkiye, Suriye ve Lübnan Iliskilerinde Asi Nehri Sorunu*, p. 27.
21. He also responded the question about Syria's intentions with regards to its neighbors as follows: 'Do you believe Syria is a threat to Turkey? Who would think we are threatening Turkey while we are trying to improve our relations with you and at a time when we want to see you on our side against Israel. We never want tension in our relations.' *Milliyet*, 6 June 1986.
22. Naff and Matson, *Water in the Middle East: Conflict or Cooperation*, p. 122.
23. On 6 February 2011, the work on the Friendship dam started only to be halted a few months later due to the ongoing instability in Syria.
24. See John F. Kolars, 'Hydro-imperative of Turkey's Search for Energy,' *Journal of Middle Eastern Studies* 40 (1), p. 55 and Peter Beaumont, 'The Euphrates River,' *Environmental Conservation* 5 (1978), pp. 35–43.
25. See John F. Kolars and William A Mitchell, *The Euphrates River and Southeast Anatolia Development Project*, Carbondale: Southern Illinois University Press, 1991.
26. The Southeastern Anatolia Project (GAP) intends to harness the potential of the Euphrates and Tigris rivers and their tributaries by building 22 high dams and 19 hydropower plants generating 27 billion kWh of electricity a year and irrigating 1.7 million hectares of farm land.
27. Further bureaucratic restructuring occurred in 1989 in accordance with the changing face of GAP from a water and land development project into an integrated development project. The Southeastern Anatolia Regional Development Administration (GAP-RDA) was formed along with GAP Higher Board, which is comprised of the state minister in charge of GAP, the state minister in charge of the State Planning Organizations, and the minister of Public Works and Settlement. GAP Regional Development Administration (GAP-RDA) plans and implements projects in accordance with GAP Higher Board decisions. For the brief history of GAP, see T.C. GAP Regional Development Administration, *The Brief History of GAP*, available at http://www.gap.gov.tr/site-icerik/gap_in_tarihcesi.aspx (accessed on 2 May 2015).
28. Data are from the Turkish Statistical Institute (TURKSTAT), Energy Statistics website available at http://www.tuik.gov.tr., http://www.tuik.gov.tr/PreTablo.do?alt_id=1029 (accessed on 2 May 2015).
29. Kut, 'Burning Waters,' p. 4.
30. *Turkish Daily News*, 6 May 1996.
31. Hasam Chalabi and Tarek Majzoub, 'Turkey, the Waters of the Euphrates, and Public International Law,' in John A. Allan and Chibli Mallat, eds, *Water and the Middle East: Legal, Political and Commercial Implications* (London: I.B.Tauris, 1995), pp. 189–239; *Middle East Economic Digest*, 30 May 1975.
32. Naff and Matson, *Water in the Middle East*, pp. 90–5.
33. See Hillel, *Rivers of Eden. The Struggle for Water and the Quest for Peace in the Middle East* (New York: Oxford University Press, 1994); Philip Robins, *Turkey and the Middle East* (London: Pinter, 1991).
34. All direct quotations are from *Keesing's Contemporary Archives*, 18–24 August 1975 unless noted otherwise.

35. Syria accused Turkey of severely reducing the river flow during the 1973–4 winter and sometimes cutting the flow of the Euphrates entirely.
36. Ziya Bari, 1977, 'Syrian-Iraqi Dispute over the Euphrates Waters,' *International Studies* 16 (April-June), p. 243.
37. Ibid.
38. Kolars and Mitchell, *The Euphrates River and Southeast Anatolia Development Project*, pp. 89–97.
39. Patrick Seale, *Assad of Syria: The Struggle for the Middle East* (Berkeley: California University Press, 1988), pp. 262–3.
40. The dispute goes back to the bloody split of the Ba'th party in 1966 when Michel 'Aflaq was defeated and was expelled from Syria. The Iraqi Ba'th party, which came to power on 17 July 1968, supported 'Aflak and Iraq became a safe haven for the Syrian exiles, the old guard Ba'thist, and the opponents of Damascus, such as the former head of the Syrian State, Amin al-Hafiz. Therefore, they were not overjoyed when they heard the news about the coup in Baghdad. See Seale, *Assad of Syria*, p. 147.
41. Bari, 'Syrian-Iraqi Dispute over the Euphrates Waters,' pp. 241–2.
42. Iraq was not planning a war against Israel; the first and foremost goal was to achieve strategic superiority against Israel by focusing on economic, technological, and military development. This was what was explained to the domestic audience.
43. Seale, *Assad of Syria*, p. 262
44. Hillel, *Rivers of Eden: The Struggle for Water and the Quest for Peace in the Middle East*, p. 108 and Bari, 'Syrian-Iraqi Dispute over the Euphrates Waters,' pp. 243–4.
45. Eberhard Kienle, *Ba'ath V Ba'ath: The Conflict Between Syria and Iraq 1968–1989* (London: I.B.Tauris, 1990), pp. 96–100.
46. In retrospect, this number was not feasible: the Euphrates Basin project was likely launched without sufficient economic and technical feasibility studies being done and suffered from bureaucratic incompetence. Indeed, no substantial expansion of irrigated lands occurred until the early 1990s. See Annika Rabo, *Change on the Euphrates: Villagers, Townsman, and Employees in Northeast Syria* (Stockholm: University of Stockholm, 1986), p. 134; Volker Perthes, *The Political Economy of Syria under Assad* (London: I.B.Tauris, 1995), pp. 44–45, 63–64, p. 78.
47. Philip Robins, *Turkey and the Middle East*. London: Pinter, 1991.
48. Christine M. Hems, *Iraq: Eastern Flank of the Arab World* (Washington, D.C.: Brookings Institution, 1984), p. 46; and Hanna Batatu, 'Iraq's underground Shi'a movements,' *Middle East Journal* 35 (Autumn 1981), pp. 589–90.
49. Nazih N. Ayubi, *Over-stating the Arab State: Politics and Society in the Middle East* (London: I.B.Tauris, 1995), pp. 112, 113, 261.
50. Iraq and Syria have played host to each other's exiles, who were opposed to reconciliation for the fear of being sacrificed to it. See Seale, *Assad of Syria*, p. 354.
51. Kienle, *Ba'ath Versus Ba'ath: The Conflict Between Syria and Iraq 1968–1989*, p. 96–100; Naff and Matson, *Water in the Middle East*, p. 95.
52. After the October war, the United States Secretary of State Kissinger's main concern was preventing Iraq from helping Syria to resume hostilities between the Arab states and Israel. In collaboration with Iran and Israel the United States armed and financed the Iraqi Kurds. The ensuing Kurdish revolt weakened Iraq and prevented it from aiding Syria. See Seale, *Assad of Syria*, p. 242–3.

53. Henry Kissinger, *White House Years* (Boston: Little, Brown, 1979), p. 1265 cited in Michael M. Gunter, 'The Foreign Policy of Kurds,' *Journal of South Asian and Middle Eastern Studies* 20 (1997), pp. 1–19.
54. Gunter, 'The Foreign Policies of Kurds,' p. 2.
55. Kienle, *Ba'ath V Ba'ath: The Conflict Between Syria and Iraq 1968–1989*, pp. 96–100.
56. Fida Nasrallah, 'Middle Eastern Waters: The Hydraulic Imperative,' *Middle East International*, 27 April 1990.
57. Seale, *Assad of Syria*, p. 355.
58. Kamuran Gürün, *Rowing against the Current: An Ambassador's Memoirs* (Istanbul: Milliyet Yayınları, 1994), pp. 240–72.
59. As of 2014, 19 dam and 13 HEP projects with 5,539 MW installed capacity and 20.6 billion kilowatt-hours of electricity were completed. This corresponds to 74 percent of the planned energy projects. Turkey produced 23.1 billion kilowatt-hours and GAP provided 49.3 percent of the total with 11.4 billion KWh. While 22.9 percent of the irrigation projects are completed irrigating 411,508 ha land. GAP Action Plan 2014–2018, December 2014. T.C. GAP Regional Development Administration. *GAP Action Plan*. Available at http://www.gap.gov.tr/dosya_ekleri/pdf/GAP_EYLEM_PLANI.pdf.
60. The construction work began on 26 July 2011 and is expected to be completed on 9 September 2016. The original planned completion date was 31 January 2017.
61. It is to be completed by the end of 2015.
62. Ziya Özis, South East Anatolia Project in Turkey, 'International Symposium on Water Resources in the Middle East: Policy and Institutional Aspects', 24–27 October 1993, University of Illinois at Urbana-Champaign, Urbana-Illinois, USA, p. 280.
63. In fact, as a downstream state to the Meric River, Turkey bought water from Bulgaria on several occasions. See Annika Kramer and Alina Schellig, 'Meric River Basin: Transboundary Water Cooperation,' in Aysegul Kibaroglu, Annika Kramer, and Waltina Scheumann, eds, *Turkey's Water Policy: National Framework and International Cooperation* (New York: Springer, 2011), pp. 229–51.
64. See Peter Beaumont, 'Transboundary Water Disputes in the Middle East,' paper presented at the International Conference on Transboundary Waters in the Middle East: Prospects for Regional Cooperation, 2–3 September 1991, Bilkent University, Ankara.
65. This was due to the disappointing performance of the Tabqa dam.
66. The Syrian government reduced this figure to 370,000 ha due to the problems with salinization and the high gypsum content of the soil.
67. According to data provided by Ministry of Irrigation in the Syrian Arab Republic, 2012 to ESCWA-BGR. There is a discrepancy between the 2000 and 2010 irrigation figures. The latter figure is significantly below the estimated 325,000 ha recorded in 2000. In addition to 206,987 ha, 59,550 ha was irrigated by the Khabour and Jagh Jagh rivers. Syria built three dams as a part of Khabour River project starting in the 1960s. The downwardly revised figure may be a result of improved relations between Turkey-Syria and thus a removal of incentives for misrepresenting data. See the report by United Nations Economic and Social Commission For Western Asia, *Inventory for Shared Water Resources in Western Asia*, 2013. Available at http://www.escwa.un.org/information/pubaction.asp?PubID=1362.
68. Robins, *Turkey and the Middle East*, p. 89.
69. T.C. Foreign Ministry, *Water Issues between Turkey, Syria and Iraq*, p. 12.
70. Miriam Lowi, 'Rivers of Conflict, Rivers of Peace,' *Journal of International Affairs* 49 (1995), pp. 123–44, p. 122.

71. Kut, 'Burning Waters: the Hydropolitics of the Euphrates Tigris,' pp. 1–18, p. 9; Natasha Beschorner, *Water and Instability in the Middle East* (London: Adelphi Papers 273), p. 40; Ilter Turan and Gün Kut, 'Political and Ideological Constraints on Intra-basin Cooperation on Transboundary Waters,' *Natural Resource Forum* 3 (1997), pp. 139–45, p. 145.
72. T. C. Foreign Ministry, *Water Issues between Turkey, Syria and Iraq*, pp. 21–3.
73. One might ask why Turkey did not agree to the Syrian and Iraqi water demands of 700 cubic meters per second, roughly two-thirds of the Euphrates flow, if Syria would suffer from salinization problems and would not be able to use the Euphrates water due to lack of resources and capabilities. This was because the problem was not whether Syria or Iraq could use the water or not, but that Turkey would be obligated to provide 700 cubic meters per second at the Turkish-Syrian border. Given the uncertainty about future demands and capacity of the Euphrates and Tigris, Turkey, as an upper watercourse state where almost 89 percent of Euphrates flow and 51 percent of Tigris flow originate within its borders, has strong incentives to be cautious.
74. From the very beginning of the Euphrates Scheme, Syria had salinity problems; it is technically difficult to irrigate semi-desert regions. To give an example: in the Deir-ez-Zohr area less than 20 percent of the land was undamaged by salinity problem. The cost of repairing canals and draining salty soil was uncalculated and had to be given a priority slowing down the process of reclamation. See Rabo, *Change on the Euphrates*, pp. 25–37.
75. T.C. Ministry of Foreign Affairs. Water Issues. Available at http://www.mfa.gov.tr/sub.en.mfa?7148b38a-0862-4a27-a006-2ca989a22629 (accessed 2 May 2015).
76. Eyal Benvenisti, 'Collective Action in the Utilization of Shared Freshwater: The Challenges of International Water Resource Law,' *American Journal of International Law* 90 (1996), pp. 384–415.
77. A closer look into the acquired rights claim reveals its problematic nature especially for Syria. Syria and Turkey simultaneously started develop their portion of the Euphrates, which means Syria could not claim to have a prior established use before the Tabqa dam. As for Iraq, it is also not obvious which date should be the cut off point for determining its acquired rights to water.
78. http://www.mfa.gov.tr/grupa/ad/adg/adgb/Chap1c.HTM.
79. Kienle, *Ba'ath V Ba'ath: The Conflict Between Syria and Iraq 1968–1989*, p. 194.
80. *T.C. Resmi Gazete*. 10 December 1987, no: 19660, p. 6.
81. *Keesing's Contemporary Archives*, November 1989.
82. *Keesing's Contemporary Archives*, June 1989 and September 1990.
83. Cited in Bölükbası, 'Turkey Challenges Iraq and Syria: the Euphrates Dispute,' p. 23.
84. *Keesing's Contemporary Archives*, October 1989 and January 1990.
85. According to some sources, during this time, four hundred articles were published by the Arab press depicting Turkey negatively, which led Turkey to send a delegation to Arab states in order to explain its position. See Robins, *Turkey and the Middle East*.
86. Süha Bölükbasi, 'Turkey Challenges Iraq and Syria: The Euphrates Dispute,' *Journal of South Asian and Middle Eastern Studies* (1993) 16 (4), p. 23, Robins, *Turkey and the Middle East*, pp. 90–4.
87. *Keesing's Contemporary Archives*, November 1990.
88. Nasrallah, 'Middle Eastern Waters: The Hydraulic Imperative.'
89. Robins, *Turkey and the Middle East*, pp. 91–2.
90. T.C. Foreign Ministry, *Water Issues between Turkey, Syria, Iraq*, p. 11; Robins, *Turkey and the Middle East*, p. 92; and Bölükbası, 'Turkey Challenge Iraq and Syria: The Euphrates Dispute,' p. 25.

91. Beschorner, *Water and Instability in the Middle East*, p. 41.
92. Bölükbası, 'Turkey Challenge Iraq and Syria: The Euphrates Dispute,' p. 25.
93. Robins, *Turkey and the Middle East*, p. 93.
94. Bölükbası, 'Turkey Challenge Iraq and Syria: The Euphrates Dispute,' p. 24.
95. Ibid., p. 25.
96. In some sources, Iraq, at the beginning of 1990, was one of the most powerful states in the Middle East surpassing Turkey. After the Iran-Iraq war, Iraq still kept its huge army and military spending budget intact disconcerting its neighbors. In the early 1990s, Iraq was almost ready to add biological weapons to its weapons of mass destruction arsenal. By January 1991, it was within a few years of producing a nuclear weapon. Iraq began its nuclear program shortly after the Ba'thist came to power in 1968 and it became a possibility when Iraq bought the Osirak reactor from France in 1976. The reactor was destroyed by an Israeli air strike in 1981. Iraqi nuclear weapons research program had gained impetus during the late Iran-Iraq war over Saddam's concerns about Iran's nuclear program. See US Government, *Comprehensive Report of the Special Advisor to Director of Central Intelligence on Iraq's Weapons of Mass Destruction*, September 2004. Available at https://www.cia.gov/cia/reports/iraq_wmd_2004/.
97. Ismail Soysal, 'Seventy Years of Turkish-Arab Relations and an Analysis of Turkish-Iraqi Relations (1920–1990),' *Studies on Turkish-Arab Relations, Special Issue on Turkey and the Gulf Crisis, Annual* 6 (Istanbul: Foundation for the Study of Turkish-Arab Relations [TAIV], 1991), p. 70; and Robins, *Turkey and the Middle East*, pp. 110–11.
98. Kemal Kirisçi, 'Post Cold War Turkish Security and the Middle East,' paper submitted at the Conference on Israel and Turkey: Current Politics and Foreign Policy,' 14–5 January 1997, Bar-Ilan University, Israel, p. 16.
99. 1997 saw the beginning of an increase in direct contribution to the project by international organizations. The US, Canada, Israel, France and other European countries, the World Bank, other international organizations, and some foreign funds and credit institutions provided financial contributions for GAP. Turkey was able to secure donated financing equivalent to approximately US$ 2.9 billion from the foreign finance institutions, such as the US Trade and Development Agency (US TDA), the US National Health Institute (US NHI), the Canadian International Development Agency (CIDA), the French Government, the United Nations Children's Fund (UNICEF), NAAN and NETAFIM (Israeli Companies), S. Smith & Sons Ltd. and Wingfield Micro Irrigation (Australia), and the World Bank (IBRD).
100. IWRA is a non-profit organization engaged in interdisciplinary studies on water related issues on scientific grounds and is financed by members' dues and partly sponsored by Southern Illinois University at Carbondale, which provides office space.
101. For detailed information about the United States' arm sales and transfers and military aid to Turkey see Federation of American Scientists, The Arms Sales Monitoring Project Data on US Military Aid and Arms Sales to Turkey available at http://www.fas.org/asmp/profiles/turkey_weapons.htm.
102. According to an official Iraqi estimate, repairing the damage to Iraqi infrastructure inflicted during the war would take an estimated US$ 200 billion.
103. Ayubi, *Overstating the Arab State*, p. 113.
104. On 17 April 1992, Turkey and Syria signed the protocols in Damascus.
105. *Keesing's Contemporary Archives*, April 1992.
106. Ibid., August 1992.
107. Ibid., December 1992.

108. Ibid., December 1992.
109. *Turkish Probe*, 26 January 1993, p. 3.
110. *Keesing's Contemporary Archives*, April 1993.
111. Ibid., November 1994.
112. Alan George, 'Syria and Iraq Threaten Anti-European Action' *The Middle East* 255 (April 1996), p. 21.
113. Ibid., p. 21.
114. This amount was substantially less than the amount gained from the annual volume of trade between 1985 and 1990, which was about US$ 4 billion.
115. *Al-Watan al-Arabi*, May 1996; *The Middle East*, July–August 1996, p. 14.
116. *The Middle East*, June 1996, p. 13.
117. See Mahmut B. Aykan, 'The Turkish-Syrian Crisis of October 1998,' *Middle East Policy* (1999) 6 (2);' Süha Bölükbası, 'Ankara, Damascus, Baghdad, and the Regionalization of Turkey's Kurdish Problem,' *Journal of South Asian and Middle Eastern Studies* (1991) 14 (4), and 'Turkey Challenges Iraq and Syria: The Euphrates Dispute.'
118. Syrian success in this regard would be Turkey's commitment to more than 500 cubic meters per second, closer to the 700 cubic meters per second as requested by both Syria and Iraq. The Syrian policy of supporting terrorism to strengthen its bargaining position was not successful as there was no evidence of change in Turkey's position on the Euphrates. Negative issue linkages rarely, if ever, produce positive outcomes in international relations. To the contrary they are highly counterproductive and cultivate distrust among states, and thus undermine any possibility of cooperation.
119. The drought added to an already serious power shortage in Turkey largely due to the country's growing energy needs and its failure to make adequate investments in the energy sector. Turkey, which consumed 120 billion kWh of electricity each year, faced a shortage of some 10 billion kWh by the end of 2000 according to the Energy Ministry, which predicted that Turkey's electricity demands would climb to 290 billion kWh in 2010 and to 547 billion kWh in 2020, requiring an average investment of up to US$ 4.5 billion every year (Anadolu Agency, *News in English*, 2 March 1999).
120. *BBC News*, 4 June 2002.
121. From its beginnings, the Tabqa dam has had problems due to faulty; its power plant has consistently operated below capacity at somewhere between 30 percent and 65 percent.
122. Available at http://www.unep.org/dams/WCD/report/WCD_DAMS%20report.pdf.
123. Among these NGOs are Friends of the Earth, International Rivers Network, The Kurdish Human Rights Project, and the British think tank Cornerhouse.
124. Skanska of Sweden, ABB and Sulzer Hydro of Switzerland, Impreglio of Italy, Balfour Beatty of the UK and three Turkish companies, Nurol, Kiska, and Tekfen.
125. Paul Brown, 'Ilisu dam in jeopardy as Balfour drops out,' *Guardian*, 13 November 2001. Available at http://www.theguardian.com/uk/2001/nov/14/politics.politicalnews (accessed on 16 May 2015).
126. Following the dissolution of the WCD, the UNEP established the Dams and Development Project in November 2001 as 'a neutral entity to take forward the consideration of the WCD recommendations into local contexts through promoting inclusive multi-stakeholder dialogue and, widely disseminating the WCD materials.' Available at http://www.unep.org/dams/About_DDP/. The World Bank has resumed funding for water infrastructure projects, including dams.

127. For an analysis of these movements, see Ken Conca, *Governing Water: Contentious Transnational Politics and Global Institution Building* (MIT Press, 2006), pp. 167–214.
128. A data compiled by Peter Gleick indicates that 19,441 dams were built since the 1950s. The breakdown is as follows: 2,735, in the 1950s; 4,788, in the 1960s; 5,418, in the 1970s; 4,431, in the 1980s; and 2,069, in the 1990s. By the end of the century almost all the good sites for dams had been dammed. Data are available at http://worldwater.org/water-data/ (accessed on 16 May 2015).
129. The west seems to be more concerned over the impact of economic development on natural resources and environmental change.
130. See Edward B. Barbier, *Natural Resources and Economic Development* (New York: Cambridge University Press, 2005), p. 46.
131. Israel drained the Huleh lake and marshes in the 1950s, which at the time was perceived as one of the greatest engineering feats converting swampland, a breeding ground for malaria carrying mosquitos, into productive agricultural land. See Joel Greenberg, 'Israel Drained Wetland, Reversing Pioneer' Feat, *New York Times*, 9 December 1993. Available at http://www.nytimes.com/1993/12/05/world/israel-restoring-drained-wetland-reversing-pioneers-feat.html (accessed on 16 May 2015).
132. For the assessment of the project, see J. Tsipris and M. Meron, 'Climatic and Hydrological Aspects of the Hula Restoration,' *Wetlands Ecology and Management* 6 (1998), pp. 91–101.
133. The United Nations Environmental Programme, *The Mesopotamian Marshlands: Demise of an Ecosystem* (UNEP, DEWA, GRID, 2001). http://www.grid.unep.ch/activities/sustainable/tigris/mesopotamia.pdf (accessed on 16 May 2015).
134. Also, in addition to more frequent prolonged droughts, the climate change projections for the Euphrates and Tigris foresee a significant decrease in snow coverage in the upper watercourse and annual surface runoff for the periods 2041–2070 and 2071–2099. However, for Iraq the annual surface water volume is projected to increase for both periods. Iranian projects and diversion on various tributaries of the Tigris, such as the Karun, Wand, and Karkh rivers, threaten the water availability in Iraq and marshes and has become a source of tension between the two states since 2009. It is not clear if the restoration of the Mesopotamian marshlands would be feasible in the long run without making changes to the allocation of water among various sectors and increasing the efficiency in water usage. See for climate change projections in the Euphrates and Tigris watercourse, Deniz Bozkurt and Ömer Lutfi Sen, 'Climate Change Impacts in the Euphrates–Tigris Basin Based on Different Model and Scenario Simulations,' *Journal of Hydrology* 480 (2013), pp. 149–61.
135. See for example the 2013 United Nations Economic and Social Commission for Western Asia report, *Inventory of Shared Water Resources in Western Asia*, available at http://www.escwa.un.org/information/pubaction.asp?PubID51362 (accessed on 16 May 2015), p. 72.
136. T.C., State Planning Organization, *GAP Master Plan Final Report*, Volume 4 (1989), p. E20.
137. The Cizre dam project is a multi-purpose one with an installed capacity of 240 MW.
138. Some scholars put the Turkish contribution of the Tigris flow at 44 percent, including the Greater Zap in the figure, or 31.9 percent or 16,800 BCM without it with 52,665 BCM as the total flow. See Peter Beaumont, 'Restructuring of Water Usage in the Tigris-Euphrates Basin: The Impact of Modern Water Management Policies,' *Yale School of Forestry and Environmental Studies Bulletin*, 103 (1998), pp. 168–86.
139. In the future, this could likely be one of the missed opportunities especially for the lower watercourse states.

140. Following the 2011–14 drought, which reduced hydroelectric production and forced California to burn natural gas, leading to an 8 percent increase in emissions of carbon dioxide and other pollutants from California power plants and costing about US$ 1.4 billion. See the Mach 2015 report by the Pacific Institute, Peter Gleick, 'Impact of California's Ongoing Drought: Hydroelectricity Generation' (California: Pacific Institute, 2015), pp. 7–8.
141. Construction work on the first wastewater treatment plant, the Sanlıurfa plant, started in 1982. See T.C., State Planning Organization, *GAP Master Plan Final Report*, pp. D37–D38.
142. The environmental Kuznets curve suggest a U-shaped relationship between the environment and development that as per capita income increases, environmental degradation rises initially but then eventually declines.
143. On 19 September 2009 Turkey agreed to release more water for about a month to Iraq.
144. Chlorine was one of the banned substances throughout the period.
145. See Peter Beaumont, 'Restructuring of Water Usage in the Tigris-Euphrates Basin: The Impact of Modern Water Management Policies,' pp. 168–86, p. 178.
146. See Food and Agriculture Organization 2012 report, Syrian Arab Republic Joint Rapid Food Security Needs Assessment. Avialable at http://www.fao.org/giews/english/otherpub/JRFSNA_Syrian2012.pdf.
147. Republic of Turkey, Ministry of Foreign Affairs. http://www.mfa.gov.tr/relations-between-turkey-and-iraq.en.mfa.
148. On 19 September 2010, the agreement on transporting oil form Kirkuk through Ceyhan pipelines was extended for another 15 years. Trade relations improved to the extent that the Iraqi crisis was instrumental in Moody's decision to downgrade Turkey's credit rating on 30 June 2014. By 2013, Iraq had become Turkey's second largest export market and it accounted for US$ 12 billion or 8 percent of total exports. This represented a six-fold increase from 2004 and the majority of this trade has been driven by the Iraqi Kurdish market.
149. This was the case especially after the bombings targeting Ministries of Foreign Affairs and Finance in Baghdad on 19 August 2009. A few days later, a diplomatic crisis ensued as Syria and Iraq recalled envoys. Syria denied its involvement in the attacks while Iraq demanded the handover of the suspected terrorists and expulsion of terrorist organization that used Syria as a base to attack Iraq. Turkish Foreign Minister Davutoglu visited Iraq and Syria in a diplomatic attempt to alleviate the rising tensions.
150. The cost was going to be shared by the countries and the dam was planned to produce energy and irrigate 20,000 ha in Turkey and 15,000 ha in Syria with a storage capacity of 110 MCM, of which 40 MCM was planned to use for flood prevention. *Sabah*, 1 September 2009. Available at http://www.sabah.com.tr/siyaset/2009/09/01/bagdat_ve_sama_arabulucu_ziyareti (accessed on 16 May 2015).
151. The directive introduces water pricing as a mean to achieve sustainability in water resources and calls the price to be reflective of the true costs of supplying water and waste water treatment. The European Union Water Framework, available at http://ec.europa.eu/environment/water/water-framework/info/intro_en.htm (accessed on 16 May 2015).
152. In the period 2001 through 2014, the US government spent US$ 4.4 trillion on Iraq and Afghanistan. The Costs of War Project Data, Watson Institute for International and Public Affairs, Brown University, available at http://costsofwar.org/article/economic-cost-summary (accessed on 16 May 2015).
153. Sebnem Arsu, 'Turkish Premier Urges Assad to Quit in Syria,' *New York Times*, 22 November 2011. Available at http://www.nytimes.com/2011/11/23/world/middleeast/turkish-leader-says-syrian-president-should-quit.html?_r=0 (accessed on 16 May 2015).

154. Neil MacFarquhar and Nada Bakr, 'Isolating Syria, Arab League Imposes Broad Sanctions,' *New York Times*, 27 November 2011. Available at http://www.nytimes.com/2011/11/28/world/middleeast/arab-league-prepares-to-vote-on-syrian-sanctions.html (accessed on 16 May 2015).
155. Dan Bilefsky and Anthony Shadid, 'Turkey Moves to Intensify Sanctions Against Syria,' *New York Times*, 30 November 2011. Available at http://www.nytimes.com/2011/12/01/world/middleeast/turkey-intensifies-sanctions-against-syrian-regime.html (accessed on 16 May 2015).
156. The official explanation of the policy was to help Syrian people. *Milliyet*, 10 October 2012. Available at http://www.milliyet.com.tr/suriye-salteri-indirdi/ekonomi/ekonomidetay/12.10.2012/1610519/default.htm (accessed on 16 May 2015).
157. According to the figures of T.C. Ministry of Customs and Trade, in 2010 Turkey's exports to Syria amounted to US$ 1.844 billion, which dropped to 498 million dollars before reaching 1.24 billion in 2013 and 1.803 in 2014. Turkish imports went down from US$ 452 million in 2010 to US$ 152 million in 2014. *Sabah*, Turkiye'nin Suriye'ye Ihracatinda Eski Gunlere Donuldu, 25 February 2015. Available at http://www.sabah.com.tr/ekonomi/2015/02/25/turkiyenin-suriyeye-ihracatinda-eski-gunlere-donuldu (accessed on 16 May 2015).
158. Simon Speakman Cordall, 'How Syria's Assad Helped Forge ISIS,' *Newsweek*, 21 June 2014. Available at http://www.newsweek.com/how-syrias-assad-helped-forge-isis-255631 (accessed on 16 May 2015).
159. *Al-Jazeera*, 'Assad's Fatal Strategic Mistakes,' 29 March 2014. Available at http://www.aljazeera.com/indepth/opinion/2014/03/al-assad-fatal-strategic-mistak-201432910353132476.html (accessed on 16 May 2015). This article states that reports from Syria indicate that the Assad regime has been cooperating with ISIL by allowing it access into some towns and not bombing areas under its control and by buying oil from the ISIL run oil wells in the north.
160. There have been several reports indicating problems with Syria's compliance. *Al-Jazeera*, 'Report Reaffirms Syria Chemical Weapons Use,' 7 January 2015. Available at http://www.aljazeera.com/news/middleeast/2015/01/report-reaffirms-syria-chemical-weapon-use-201516223545804947.html (accessed on 16 May 2015); *CNN*, Kerry Condemns Alleged Syrian Chemical Weapons Use, 19 March 2015. Available at http://www.cnn.com/2015/03/19/politics/syria-chemical-weapons-john-kerry/ (accessed on 16 May 2015).
161. Anna Barnard and Somini Sengupta, 'US Signals Shift on How to End Syrian Civil War,' *New York Times*, 20 January 2014. Available at http://www.nytimes.com/2015/01/20/world/middleeast/us-support-for-syria-peace-plans-demonstrates-shift-in-priorities.html?_r=0 (accessed on 16 May 2015).
162. *Al-Jazeera*, 'Water Wars Threatens Syria Lifeline: Water Supplies have Dropped in Key Areas Due to Sharp Increase in Production at the Rebel Controlled Euphrates Dam.' 7 July 2014. Available at http://www.aljazeera.com/news/middleeast/2014/07/water-war-syria-euphrates-2014757640320663.html (accessed on 16 May 2015).
163. *American Center for Democracy*, Syria-ISIS 'Pragmatic Cooperation,' The Meir Amit Intelligence and Terrorism Information Center, 7 April 2015. Available at http://acdemocracy.org/syria-isis-pragmatic-cooperation/ (accessed on 16 May 2015), and Jeffrey White, 'Syrian Regime Military Operations Against ISIS', 13 March 2013. The Washington Institute for Near East Policy. Available at http://www.washingtoninstitute.

org/policy-analysis/view/syrian-regime-military-operations-against-isis (accessed on 16 May 2015).

164. On 7 March 2015, the European Union added Syrian businessman, George Haswani, to the sanctions list for working as an intermediary between Deash and the Syrian Regime. *Reuters*, 8 March 2015. 'EU Accuses Syrian Man of Buying IS Oil for Govt.' Available at http://www.reuters.com/article/2015/03/08/us-syria-crisis-eu-idUSKBN0M40EQ 20150308 (accessed on 16 May 2015).
165. On 29 June 2014, ISIL declared the territory under their control as a sovereign state and a new Caliphate with Abu Bakr al Baghdadi as the Caliph.
166. See Fred Pearce, 'Mideast Water Wars: In Iraq, a Battle for Control of Water,' 25 August 2014, *Yale Environment 360*. Available at http://e360.yale.edu/feature/mideast_water_wars _in_iraq_a_battle_for_control_of_water/2796/ (accessed on 16 May 2015).
167. *Washington Post*, 4 April 2015, 'The Hidden Hand behind the Islamic State Militants? Saddam Hussein's.' Available at http://www.washingtonpost.com/world/middle_east/ the-hidden-hand-behind-the-islamic-state-militants-saddam-husseins/2015/04/04/ aa97676c-cc32-11e4-8730-4f473416e759_story.html (accessed on 16 May 2015).
168. *Human Rights Watch,* 'Iraq: Militias Escalate Abuses, Possibly War Crimes,' 15 February 2015. Available at http://www.hrw.org/news/2015/02/15/iraq-militias-escalate-abuses-possibly-war-crimes (accessed on 16 May 2015).
169. *Amnesty International*, 'Left Out in the Cold: Syrian Refugees Abandoned by the International Community,' December 2014. Available at http://www.amnesty.eu/content/ assets/Reports/Left_Out_in_the_Cold_Syrian_Refugees_Abandoned_by_the_Internati onal_Community_final_formatted_version.pdf (accessed on 16 May 2015).
170. United Nations Refuge Agency. *Stories from Syrian Refugees. Discovering the Human Faces of a Tragedy.* Available at http://data.unhcr.org/syrianrefugees/syria.php (accessed on 16 May 2015).
171. Charles Tilly, 'Reflections on the History of European State Making,' in Charles Tilly ed., *The Formation of National States in Western Europe* (Princeton: Princeton University Press, 1975), p. 42.

## Conclusion

1. See John Waterbury, *The Nile Basin: National Determinants of Collective Action* (New Haven: Yale University Press, 2002), p. 166.
2. In the course of the current civil war, it has become obvious that the Euphrates basin is not considered an essential area for the Syrian regime.
3. Dogan Altinbilek and Cecilia Tortajada, 'The Atatürk Dam in the Context of the Southeastern Anatolia (GAP) Project,' in C. Tortajada et al. eds, *Impacts of Large Dams: A Global Assessment* (Berlin: Springer, 2012), pp. 171–99; M. Irfan Yesilnacar and Sinan Uyanik, 'Investigation of Water Quality of the World's Largest Irrigation Tunnel System: The Sanliurfa Tunnels in Turkey,' *Fresenius Environmental Bulletin* 14.4 (2005), pp. 300–6.
4. Mutlu Özdogan, Curtis E. Woodcock, Guido D. Salvucci, and Huseyin Demir. 2006. 'Changes in Summer Irrigated Crop Area and Water Use in Southeastern Turkey: Implications for Current and Future Water Resources,' *Water Resources Management* 20 (2006), pp. 467–88.
5. Amartya Sen, *Development as Freedom* (New York: Anchor, 1999).

# BIBLIOGRAPHY


Acemoglu, D., and James Robinson. 2013. *Why Nations Fail: The Origins of Power, Prosperity, and Poverty*. New York: Random House.

*Al-Jazeera*, 'Assad's Fatal Strategic Mistakes,' 29 March 2014. Available at http://www.aljazeera.com/indepth/opinion/2014/03/al-assad-fatal-strategic-mistak-201432910353132476.html (accessed on 16 May 2015).

———, 'Report Reaffirms Syria Chemical Weapons Use,' 7 January 2015. Available at http://www.aljazeera.com/news/middleeast/2015/01/report-reaffirms-syria-chemical-weapon-use-201516223545804947.html (accessed on 16 May 2015).

———, 'Water Wars Threaten Syria Lifeline: Water Supplies have Dropped in Key Areas Due to Sharp Increase in Production at the Rebel Controlled Euphrates dam,' 7 July 2014. Available at http://www.aljazeera.com/news/middleeast/2014/07/water-war-syria-euphrates-2014757640320663.html (accessed on 16 May 2015).

Allan, J. Anthony. 1997. '"Virtual Water": A Long Term Solution for Water Short Middle Eastern Economies?' *SOAS Occasional Papers* No. 3. http://www.soas.ac.uk/Geography/WaterIssues/Papers.

———. 1997. *Virtually No Water: The Middle East in 1997*. London: EMAP Business International Ltd.

———. 1999. 'The Nile Basin: Evolving Approaches to Nile Waters Management.' *SOAS Occasional Papers* No. 20.

———. 2000. *The Middle East Water Question*. London: I.B.Tauris.

Altinbilek, Dogan, and Cecilia Tortajada. 2012. 'The Atatürk Dam in the Context of the Southeastern Anatolia (GAP) Project.' In C. Tortajada et al. eds., *Impacts of Large Dams: A Global Assessment*. Berlin: Springer Verlag.

*American Center for Democracy*. 'Syria-ISIS "Pragmatic Cooperation."' The Meir Amit Intelligence and Terrorism Information Center, 7 April 2015. Available at http://acdemocracy.org/syria-isis-pragmatic-cooperation/ (accessed on 16 May 2015).

Amery, Hussein A. 1995. *Hydropolitics Along the Jordan River: Scarce Water and its Impact on the Arab-Israeli Conflict*. Tokyo: United Nations University Press.

———. 2000. 'A Theory of Water Diversion from Lebanon.' In Hussein A. Amery and Aron T. Wolf, eds. *Water in the Middle East: A Geography of Peace*. Austin: University of Texas Press.

*Amnesty International*. 'Left Out in the Cold: Syrian Refugees Abandoned by the International Community.' December 2014.

*Anadolu Agency, News in English*, 2 March 1999.

Annan, Kofi A. 2000. *We the People: The Role of the United Nations in the 21st Century, New Century New Challenges*. New York: United Nations.

Aristotle. 1988. [Stephen Everson, ed.] *The Politics*. New York: Cambridge University Press.

Arrow, Kenneth J. 1969. 'The Organization of Economic Activity: Issues Pertinent to the Choice of Market versus Non-Market Allocation. In United States Congress.' *The Analysis and Evaluation of Public Expenditures: The PBB-System, Joint Economic Committee*, 91st Congress, 1st session, vol. 1. Washington: Government Printing Office.

Arsu, Sebnem. 'Turkish Premier Urges Assad to Quit in Syria,' *New York Times*, 22 November 2011. Available at http://www.nytimes.com/2011/11/23/world/middleeast/turkish-leader-says-syrian-president-should-quit.html?_r=0 (accessed on 16 May 2015).

Axelrod, Robert. 1984. *The Evolution of Cooperation*. New York: Basic Books.

Aykan, Mahmut B. 1999. 'The Turkish-Syrian Crisis of October 1998.' *Middle East Policy* 6 (2): 174–78.

Ayubi, Nazih N. 1995. *Overstating the Arab State: Politics and Society in the Middle East*. London: I.B.Tauris.

Baldwin, David A., ed., 1993. *Neorealism and Neoliberalism: The Contemporary Debate*. New York: Columbia University Press.

Barbier, Edward B. 2005. *Natural Resources and Economic Development*. New York: Cambridge University Press.

Barbieri, Katherine. 1996. 'Economic Interdependence: A Path to Peace or Source of International Conflict.' *Journal of Peace Research* 33 (1): 29–49.

Barbieri, Katherine, and Jack S. Levy, 1999. 'Sleeping with the Enemy: The Impact of War on Trade.' *Journal of Peace Research* 36 (4): 463–79.

Bari, Ziya. 1977. 'Syrian-Iraqi Dispute over the Euphrates Waters.' *International Studies* 16 (April-June): 227–44.

Barnard, Anna, and Somini Sengupta. 'US Signals Shift on How to End Syrian Civil War,' *New York Times*, 20 January 2014. Available at http://www.nytimes.com/2015/01/20/world/middleeast/us-support-for-syria-peace-plans-demonstrates-shift-in-priorities.html?_r=0 (accessed on 16 May 2015).

Barton, George A. 1929. 'Inscription of Entemena 7.' In *The Royal Inscriptions of Sumer and Akkad*. New Haven: Yale University. [Reprinted in D. Brendan Nagle and Stanley M. Burstein, eds. 1995. *The Ancient World: Readings in Social and Cultural History*. Englewood: Prentice Hall Press.]

Barzel, Yoram. 1997. *Economic Analysis of Property Rights*. Cambridge: Cambridge University Press.

Batatu, Hanna. 1981. 'Iraq's underground Shi'a movements.' *Middle East Journal* 35 (4): 589–90.

Bates, Robert H. 2008. *When Things Fell Apart: State Failure in Late Century Africa*. Cambridge: Cambridge University Press.

*BBC News*, 4 June 2002.

*BBC Monitoring Middle East*, 13 October 2006.

Beaumont, Peter. 1978. 'The Euphrates River: An International Problem of Water Resources Development.' *Environmental Conservation* 5 (1): 35–43.

———. 1991. 'Transboundary Water Disputes in the Middle East.' Paper presented at the International Conference on Transboundary Waters in the Middle East: Prospects for Regional Cooperation, September 2–3, 1991, Bilkent University, Ankara.

———. 1998. 'Restructuring of Water Usage in the Tigris-Euphrates Basin: The Impact of Modern Water Management Policies.' *Yale School of Forestry and Environmental Studies Bulletin* 103: 168–86.

Beblawi, Hazem, and Giacomo Luciani, eds. 1987. *The Rentier State*. London: Croom Helm.

Benvenisti, Eyal. 1996. 'Collective Action in the Utilization of Shared Freshwater: The Challenges of International Water Resources Law.' *American Journal of International Law* 90 (3): 384–415.

Beschorner, Natasha. 1992. *Water and Instability in the Middle East*. London: Adelphi Papers 273.

Besley, Timothy, and Maitreesh Ghatak. 2010. 'Property Rights and Economic Development.' In Dani Rodrik and Mark Rosenzweig, eds, *Handbook of Development Economics*, Vol. 5. The Netherlands: Elsevier.

Bilefsky, Dan, and Anthony Shadid, 'Turkey Moves to Intensify Sanctions Against Syria,' *New York Times*, 30 November 2011. Available at http://www.nytimes.com/2011/12/01/world/middleeast/turkey-intensifies-sanctions-against-syrian-regime.html (accessed on 16 May 2015).

Bilen, Özden. 2000. *Turkey and the Water Issues in the Middle East*. Ankara: GAP-RDA.

Binmore, Ken. 1994. *Game Theory and the Social Contract, Volume I: Playing Fair*. Cambridge: MIT Press.

———. 1998. *Game Theory and the Social Contract, Volume II: Just Fair*. Cambridge: MIT Press.

Blatter, Joachim, and Helen Ingram. 2001. *Reflections on Water: New Approaches to Transboundary Conflicts and Cooperation*. Cambridge: MIT Press.

Bozkurt, Deniz, and Ömer Lutfi Sen. 2013. 'Climate Change Impacts in the Euphrates – Tigris Basin Based on Different Model and Scenario Simulations.' *Journal of Hydrology* 480: 149–61.

Bölükbası, Süha. 1991. 'Ankara, Damascus, Baghdad, and the Regionalization of Turkey's Kurdish Problem.' *Journal of South Asian and Middle Eastern Studies* 14 (4): 15–36.

———. 1993. 'Turkey Challenges Iraq and Syria: The Euphrates Dispute.' *Journal of South Asian and Middle Eastern Studies* 16 (4): 9–33.

Brecher, Michael, and Jonathan Wilkenfeld. 2000. *A Study of Crisis*. Ann Arbor: University of Michigan Press.

Bremer, Stuart. 1992. 'Dangerous Dyads: Conditions Affecting the Likelihood of Interstate War, 1816–1965.' *Journal of Conflict Resolution* 36 (2): 309–41.

Bromley, Daniel W. 1991. *Environment and Economy: Property Rights and Public Policy*. Oxford: Basil Blackwell.

Brown, Paul. 'Ilisu Dam in Jeopardy as Balfour Drops Out,' *Guardian*, 13 November 2001. http://www.theguardian.com/uk/2001/nov/14/politics.politicalnews (accessed on 16 May 2015).

Bruns, B. R., C. Ringler, and R. Meinzen-Dick. 2005. *Water Rights Reform: Lessons for Institutional Design*. Washington, DC: International Food Policy Research Institute.

Buchanan, James. 1975. *The Limits to Liberty*. Chicago: University of Chicago Press.

Bueno de Mesquita, Bruce, and David Lalman. 1990. 'Domestic Opposition and Foreign War.' *American Political Science Review* 84 (3): 747–66.

——— 1992. *War and Reason: Domestic and International Imperatives*. New Haven: Yale University Press.

Bueno de Mesquita, Bruce, and Randolph M. Siverson. 1995. 'War and the Survival of Political Leaders: A Comparative Analysis of Regime Types and Accountability.' *American Political Science Review* 89 (4) pp. 841–55.

Bueno de Mesquita, Bruce, and Alastair Smith. 2011. *The Dictator's Handbook: Why Bad Behavior is Almost Always Good Politics*. New York: Public Affairs.

Bueno de Mesquita, Bruce, Randolph M. Siverson, and Gary Wolfer. 1992. 'War and the Fate of the Regimes: A Comparative Analysis.' *American Political Science Review* 86 (3): 638–646.

Bueno de Mesquita, Bruce, Alastair Smith, Randolph M. Siverson, and James D. Morrow. 2003. *The Logic of Political Survival*. Cambridge: MIT Press.

Bulloch, John, and Adel Darwish. 1993. *Water Wars: Coming Conflict in the Middle East*. London: Victor Gollancz.

Burton, Michael G., and John Higley. 1987. 'Invitation to Elite Theory: The Basic Contentions Reconsidered.' In G. W. Domhoff and T. R. Dye, eds, *Power Elites and Organizations*. Newbury Park: Sage.

Caponera, Dante. 1991. 'The Legal and Institutional Concepts of Cooperation.' Paper presented at the International Conference on Transboundary Waters in the Middle East: Prospects for Regional Cooperation, 2–3 September 1991, Bilkent University, Ankara.

Carment, David. 2003. 'Assessing State Failure: Implications for Theory and Policy.' *Third World Quarterly* 24 (3): 407–27.

Carr, Edward H. 1964. *The Twenty Years Crisis, 1919–1939: An Introduction to the Study of International Relations.* New York: Harper & Row.

Chalabi, Hasam, and Tarek Majzoub. 1995. 'Turkey, the Waters of the Euphrates, and Public International Law.' In John A. Allan and Chibli Mallat, eds, *Water and the Middle East: Legal, Political and Commercial Implications.* London: I.B.Tauris.

Challen, Ray. 2000. *Institutions, Transaction Costs and Environmental Policy: Institutional Reform for Water Resources.* Massachusetts: Edward Elgar.

Chatterjee, Kalyan. 1985. 'Disagreement in Bargaining: Models with Incomplete Information.' In Alvin E. Roth, ed., *Game-theoretic Models of Bargaining.* New York: Cambridge University Press.

Chaoudry, Kiren Aziz. 1997. *The Price of Wealth: Economies and Institutions in the Middle East.* Ithaca: Cornell University Press.

Choucri, Nazli, and Robert C. North. 1975. *Nations in Conflict: National Growth and International Violence.* San Francisco: W. H. Freeman.

———. 1989. 'Lateral Pressure in International Relations: Concept and Theory.' In Manus I. Midlarsky, ed., *Handbook of War Studies*. Ann Arbor: University of Michigan Press.

Christensen, Thomas J., and Jack Snyder. 1990. 'Chain Gangs and Passed Bucks: Predicting Alliance Patterns in Multipolarity.' *International Organization* 44 (3): 137–68.

*Circle of Blue*, 20 February 2013. Maddocks, Andrew. 'Australia's Water Markets Succeeding, Yet Severe Challenges Loom.' Available at http://www.circleofblue.org/waternews/2013/world/australias-water-markets-succeeding-yet-severe-challenges-loom/.

Clark, Peter. 2003. 'The Iraqi Marshlands: A Prewar Perspective, Crimes of War Project.' 7 March 2003, Available at http://www.crimesofwar.org/ special/Iraq/news-marshArabs.html.

Clausewitz, Carl von. 1976. *On War.* Princeton: Princeton University Press.

*CNN*, 'Kerry Condemns Alleged Syrian Chemical Weapons Use,' 19 March 2015. Available at http://www.cnn.com/2015/03/19/politics/syria-chemical-weapons-john-kerry/ (accessed on 16 May 2015).

Coase, Ronald H. 1937. 'The Nature of the Firm.' *Economica* 16 (4): 386–405.

———. 1960. 'The Problem of Social Cost.' *Journal of Law and Economics* 3 (1): 1–44.

Cole, Daniel. 2002. *Pollution and Property: Comparing Ownership Institutions for Environmental Protection.* Cambridge: Cambridge University Press.

Collier, David, and Steven Levitsky. 1997. 'Democracy with Adjectives: A Conceptual Innovation in Comparative Research.' *World Politics* 49 (3): 430–51.

Conca, Ken. 2006. *Governing Water: Contentious Transnational Politics and Global Institution Building*. Cambridge: MIT Press.

Cordall, Simon S. 2014. 'How Syria's Assad Helped Forge ISIS,' *Newsweek*, 21 June 2014. Available at http://www.newsweek.com/how-syrias-assad-helped-forge-isis-255631 (accessed on 16 May 2015).

The Costs of War Project Data, Watson Institute for International and Public Affairs, Brown University. Available at http://www.costsofwar.org/article/economi-cost-summary (accessed on 16 May 2015).

Cross, John G. 1969. *The Economics of Bargaining.* New York: Basic Books.

Dahl, Robert A. 1998. *On Democracy.* New Haven: Yale University Press.

Dahlman, Carl. J. 1980. *The Open-Field System and Beyond: Property Rights Analysis of an Economic Institution*. Cambridge: Cambridge University Press.

de Soysa, Indra. 2002. 'Ecoviolence: Shrinking Pie or Honey Pot?' *Global Environmental Politics* 2(4): 1–34.

Debaere, Peter, et al. 2014. 'Water markets as a response to scarcity.' *Water Policy* 16 (2014): 625–49.

Dellapenna, Joseph W. 2000. 'The Importance of Getting Names Right: the Myth of Markets for Water.' *William and Mary Environmental Law and Policy Review* 25: 317–77.

Demsetz, Harold. 1988. *Ownership, Control and the Firm, Volume I: The Organization of Economic Activity.* Oxford: Basil Blackwell.

———. 1997. 'Towards a Theory of Property Rights.' *Journal of Political Economy* 57: 347–59.
Diamond, Jared., 1997. *Guns, Germs, and Steel: The Fates of Human Societies.* New York: Norton.
Diehl, Paul F., and Nils Petter Gleditsch. 2001. *Environmental Conflict*. Boulder: Westview Press.
Dixit, Avinash, S. Skeath, and D. Reiley. 1999. *Games of Strategy.* New York: Norton.
Dixit, Avinash. 2003. *Lawlessness and Economics: Alternative Modes of Governance*. Princeton: Princeton University Press.
Downs, George W., and David Rocke. 1994. 'Conflict, Agency, and Gambling for Resurrection: The Principal-Agent Problem Goes to War.' *American Journal of Political Science* 38 (2): 362–80.
Doyle, Michael W. 1983. 'Kant, Liberal Legacies, and Foreign Affairs.' Parts 1 and 2. *Philosophy and Public Affairs* 12 (3): 205–35 and 12 (4): 323–53.
———. 1986. 'Liberalism and World Politics.' *American Political Science Review* 80 (4): 1151–70.
———. 1997. *Ways of War and Peace: Realism, Liberalism, and Socialism.* New York: Norton.
Easterly, William A. 2007.*White Man's Burden: Why the West's Efforts to Aid the Rest Have Done So Much Ill and So Little Good.* New York: Penguin.
———. 2014. *Tyranny of Experts.* New York: Basic Books.
*The Economist.* 2002. 'The Invisible Green Hand,' 4 July 2002. Available at http://www.economist.com/node/1200205 (accessed on 16 May 2015).
Eggertsson, Thráinn. 1990. *Economic Behavior and Institutions*. Cambridge: Cambridge University Press.
Eichengreen, Barry. 1996. *Globalizing Capital: A History of the International Monetary System.* Princeton: Princeton University Press.
Elmusa, Sharif S. 1997. *Water Conflict: Economics, Politics, Law, and Palestinian-Israeli Water Resources.* Washington: Institute for Palestinian Studies.
Esty, Daniel C., Jack A. Goldstone, Ted Robert Gurr, Barbara Harff, Marc Levy, Geoffrey D. Dabelko, Pamela Surko, and Alan N. Unger. 1998. *State Failure Task Force Report: Phase II Findings.* McLean, VA: Science Applications International.
The European Union Water Framework Directive. Available at http://ec.europa.eu/environment/water/water-framework/info/intro_en.htm (accessed on 16 May 2015).
Fearon, James D. 1995. 'Rationalist Explanations for War.' *International Organization* 49 (3): 379–414.
———. 1998. 'Bargaining, Enforcement, and International Cooperation.' *International Organization* 52 (2): 269–306.
Federation of American Scientists. The Arms Sales Monitoring Project Data. US Military Aid and Arms Sales to Turkey. Available at http://www.fas.org/asmp/profiles/turkey_weapons.htm (accessed 2 May 2015).
Finnemore, Martha. 1996. *National Interest in International Society.* Ithaca: Cornell University Press.
*Foreign Affairs.* 2015. 'Syria's President Speaks: A Conversation with Bashar al-Assad.' March April 2015
Frankel, Benjamin. 1996. 'Restating the Realist Case: An Introduction,' *Security Studies* 5 (3): xiv–xx.
Fromkin, David. 1989. *A Peace to End All Peace: The Fall of the Ottoman Empire and the Creation of the Modern Middle East.* New York: Avon Books.
Furubotn, Erik G., and Rudolf Richter. 1997. *Institutions and Economic Theory: The Contribution of the New Institutional Economics*. Ann Arbor: University of Michigan Press.
Gambetta, Diego. 1993. *The Sicilian Mafia: The Business of Private Protection*. Cambridge: Harvard University Press.
George, Alan. 1996. 'Syria and Iraq Threaten Anti-European Action.' *The Middle East* 255: 21.
Gilpin, Robert. 1981. *War and Change in World Politics*. Cambridge: Cambridge University Press.
———. 1996. 'No One Loves a Political Realist.' In Benjamin Frankel, ed., *Realism: Restatement and Renewal*. London: Frank Cass.

Giordano, Mark, Alena Drieschova, James A. Duncan, Yoshiko Sayama, Lucia De Stefano, and Aaron T. Wolf. 2014. 'A Review of the Evolution and State of Transboundary Freshwater Treaties.' *International Environmental Agreements: Politics, Law and Economics* 14 (3): 245–64.

Gizelis, Theodora-Ismene, and Amanda E. Wooden. 2010. 'Water Resources, Institutions, and Intrastate Conflict.' *Political Geography* 29 (8): 444–53.

Gleditsch, Nils Petter. 1997. *Conflict and the Environment*. Dordrecht: Kluwer Academic.

———. 1998. 'Armed Conflict and the Environment: A Critique of the Literature.' *Journal of Peace Research* 35 (3): 381–400.

———. 2012. 'Whither the Weather? Climate Change and Conflict.' *Journal of Peace Research* 49 (1): 3–9.

Gleditsch, Nils Petter, Kathryn Furlong, Håvard Hegre, Bethany Lacina, and Taylor Owen. 2006. 'Conflicts Over Shared Rivers: Resource Scarcity or Fuzzy Boundaries?' *Political Geography* 25(4): 361–82.

Gleick, Peter H. 1993a. 'Water and Conflict: Fresh Water Resources and International Security.' *International Security* 18 (1): 79–112.

———. 1993b. *Water in Crisis: A Guide to the World's Fresh Water Resources*. New York: Oxford University Press.

———. 1998. *The World's Water 1998–1999*. Washington: Island Press.

———. 2014. 'Water, Drought, Climate Change, and Conflict in Syria.' *Weather, Climate, and Society* 6 (3): 331–40.

———. 2015. *Impact of California's Ongoing Drought: Hydroelectricity Generation*. California: Pacific Institute.

Goemans, Hein E. 2000. *War and Punishment: The Causes of War Termination and the First World War.* Princeton: Princeton University Press.

Gowa, Joanne, and Edward D. Mansfield. 1993. 'Power Politics and International Trade.' *American Political Science Review* 87 (2): 408–20.

Green Cross International and AWIRU. 2000. *Water Wars: Enduring Myth or Impending Reality?* The Africa Dialogue Monograph Series No. 2. KwaZulu-Natal: Creda Communications.

Greenberg, Joel, 'Israel Drained Wetland, Reversing Pioneer' Feat, *New York Times*, 9 December 1993. Available at http://www.nytimes.com/1993/12/05/world/israel-restoring-drained-wetland-reversing-pioneers-feat.html (accessed on 16 May 2015).

Grieco, Joseph M. 1988. 'Anarchy and the Limits of Cooperation: A Realist Critique of the Newest Liberal Institutionalism.' *International Organization* 42 (3): 485–507.

———. 1993. 'Understanding the Problem of International Cooperation: The Limits of Neo-Liberal Institutionalism and the Future of Realist Theory.' In David A. Baldwin, ed., *Neorealism and Neoliberalism.* New York: Columbia University Press.

Gruen, George E. 2000. 'The Politics of Water and the Middle East Peace.' *American Foreign Policy Interests* 22 (2): 1–21.

Gunter, Michael M. 1997. 'The Foreign Policy of Kurds.' *Journal of South Asian and Middle Eastern Studies* 20 (3): 1–19.

Gurr, Ted R. 1985. 'On the Political Consequences of Scarcity and Economic Decline.' *International Studies Quarterly* 29 (1): 51–75.

Güner, Serdar. 1998. 'Signaling in the Turkish-Syrian Water Conflict.' *Conflict Management and Peace Science* 16 (2): 185–206.

Gürün, Kamuran. 1994. *Rowing against the Current: an Ambassador's Memoirs.* Istanbul: Milliyet Yayınları.

Haas, Ernest B. 1980. 'Why Collaborate? Issue Linkages and International Regimes.' *World Politics* 32 (3): 357–405.

Haas, Peter M. 1989. 'Do Regimes Matter? Epistemic Communities and Mediterranean Pollution Control.' *International Organization* 43 (3): 377–403.

———. 1992. 'Introduction: Epistemic Communities and International Policy Coordination.' *International Organization* 46 (1): 1–35.

Hanson, Victor. 2002. *Carnage and Culture: Landmark Battles in the Rise of Western Power.* New York: Anchor.
Hansen, Mogens H. 1991. *The Athenian Democracy in the Age of Demosthenes*. Cambridge: Blackwell.
Hardin, Garrett. 1968. 'The Tragedy of Commons.' *Science* 162 (3859): 1243–8.
Hauge, Wenche, and Tanja Ellingsen. 1998. 'Beyond Environmental Scarcity: Causal Pathways to Conflict.' *Journal of Peace Research* 35 (3): 299–317.
Hayek, Friedrich A. 1944. *Road to Serfdom.* Chicago: University of Chicago Press.
———. 1945. 'The Use of Knowledge in Society.' *American Economic Review* 35(4): 519–30.
———. 1967. 'Rules, Perception, and Intelligibility.' *Proceedings of the British Academy* (1962) 48, reprinted in *Studies in Philosophy, Politics, and Economics*. London: Routledge & Kegan Paul, pp.43–65.
Hems, Christine M. 1984. *Iraq: Eastern Flank of the Arab World.* Washington, D.C.: Brookings Institution.
Henry, Clement M., and Robert Springborg. 2002. *The Politics of Economic Development in the Middle East and North Africa.* Cambridge: Cambridge University Press.
Herz, John H. 1950. 'Idealist Internationalism and the Security Dilemma.' *World Politics* 2 (2): 157–80.
———. 1959. *International Politics in the Atomic Age*. New York: Columbia University Press.
Hillel, Daniel. 1994. *Rivers of Eden: The Struggle for Water and the Quest for Peace in the Middle East.* New York: Oxford University Press.
Hippocrates. *On Airs, Waters, and Places.* Available at http://classics.mit.edu/Hippocrates/airwatpl.mb.txt (accessed on 16 May 2015).
Hirschman, Albert. 1977. *Passions and Interests*. Princeton: Princeton University Press.
———. 1982. 'Rival Interpretations of Market Society: Civilizing, Destructive, or Feeble?' *Journal of Economic Literature* 20 (4): 1463–84.
Hiscox, Michael J. 2002. *International Trade and Political Conflict: Commerce, Coalitions, and Mobility.* Princeton: Princeton University Press.
Hobbes, Thomas. [1691] 1972. *Leviathan.* Baltimore: Penguin.
———. [1588–1679] 1983. *De Cive.* Oxford: Clarendon Press.
Holden, Paul and Mateen Thobani. 1996. 'Tradable Water Rights: a Property Rights Approach to Resolving Water Shortages and Promoting Investment.' *Policy Research Working Paper* 1727. World Bank, Latin America and the Caribbean Technical Department. Washington, DC: World Bank.
Homer-Dixon, Thomas F. 1991. 'On the Threshold: Environmental Changes as Causes of Acute Conflict.' *International Security* 16 (2): 76–116.
———. 1994. 'Environmental Scarcities and Violent Conflict: Evidence from Cases.' *International Security* 19 (1): 5–40.
———. 1999. *Environment, Scarcity, and Violence*. Princeton: Princeton University Press.
Homer-Dixon, Thomas F., Jeffrey H. Boutwell, and George W. Rathjens.1993. 'Environmental Scarcity and Violent Conflict.' *Scientific American* 268 (2): 38–45.
Horden, Pregrine, and Nicholas Purcell. 2002. *The Corrupting Sea: A Study of Mediterranean History.* Oxford: Blackwell.
*Human Rights Watch.* 2015. 'Iraq: Militias Escalate Abuses, Possibly War Crimes,' 15 February 2015. Available at http://www.hrw.org/news/2015/02/15/iraq-militias-escalate-abuses-possibly-war-crimes (accessed on 16 May 2015).
Hume, David. [1739–40] 1978. *A Treatise of Human Nature*, L. A. Selby-Bigge and P. H. Nidditch, eds, Oxford: Oxford University Press, 2nd edn.
Huth, Paul K., and Todd L. Allee. 2002. *The Democratic Peace and Territorial Conflict in the Twentieth Century.* Cambridge: Cambridge University Press.
International Freshwater Treaties Database. Available at http://www.transboundarywaters.orst.edu/database/interfreshtreatdata.html (accessed on 27 April 2015).

*International Organization Immigration*. 2009. 'Emergency Monitoring and Needs Assessments: Post-2006 Displacement in Iraq.' Available at https://www.iom.int/jahia/webdav/shared/shared/mainsite/activities/countries/docs/Iraq/IOM_Iraq_Review_of_Displacement_and_Return_in_Iraq_August_2010.pdf (accessed on 16 May 2015).

Isaac, Jad, and Leonardo Hosh. 1992. 'Roots of the Water Conflict in the Middle East.' Paper presented at the conference on The Middle East Water Crisis: Creative Perspectives and Solutions, 7–9 May 1992, University of Waterloo, Canada.

Jervis, Robert. 1976. *Perception and Misperception in International Politics*. Princeton: Princeton University Press.

———. 1978. 'Cooperation under the Security Dilemma.' *World Politics* 30 (2): 167–214.

Jervis, Robert and Jack Snyder. eds, 1991. *Dominoes and Bandwagons: Strategic Beliefs and Great Power Competition in the Eurasian Rimland*. Oxford: Oxford University Press.

*Jordan Times*. 22 March 2000.

Kahl, Colin. 2006. *States, Scarcity, and Civil Strife in the Developing World*. Princeton: Princeton University Press.

Karl, Terry Lynn. 1997. *The Paradox of Plenty: Oil Booms and Petro-States*. Berkeley: University of California Press.

Kecskemeti, Paul. 1958. *Strategic Surrender: The Politics of Victory and Defeat*. Stanford: California University Press.

*Keesing's Contemporary Archives*. August 1975.

*Keesing's Contemporary Archives*. June 1989.

*Keesing's Contemporary Archives*. October 1989.

*Keesing's Contemporary Archives*. November 1989.

*Keesing's Contemporary Archives*. January 1990.

*Keesing's Contemporary Archives*. September 1990.

*Keesing's Contemporary Archives*. November 1990.

*Keesing's Contemporary Archives*. April 1992.

*Keesing's Contemporary Archives*. August 1992.

*Keesing's Contemporary Archives*. December 1992.

*Keesing's Contemporary Archives*. April 1993.

*Keesing's Contemporary Archives*. September 1994

*Keesing's Contemporary Archives*. November 1994.

Kelley, Colin P., Shahrzad Mohtadi, Mark A. Krane, Richard Seager, and Yochanan Kushnir. 2015. 'Climate Change in the Fertile Crescent and Implications of the Recent Syrian Drought.' *Proceedings of the National Academy of Sciences of the United States of America* 112 (11): 3241–6

Kellogg-Briand Pact. 1928. Available as part of the Yale Law School, The Avalon Project, Documents in Law, History and Diplomacy online at http://avalon.law.yale.edu/20th_century/kbpact.asp (accessed on 7 December 2015).

Kennan, John, and Robert Wilson. 1993. 'Bargaining with Private Information.' *Journal of Economic Literature* 31 (1): 45–104.

Kennedy, Paul M. 1987. *The Rise and Fall of Great Powers: Economic Change and Military Conflict from 1500 to the Present*. New York: Random House.

Keohane, Robert. 1980. 'The Theory of Hegemonic Stability and Changes in International Economic Regimes, 1967–1977.' In Ole R. Holsti, Randolph M. Siverson, and Alexander George, eds, *Changes in the International System*. Boulder: Westview Press.

———. 1984. *After Hegemony: Cooperation and Discord in the World Political Economy*. Princeton: Princeton University Press.

———. 1986. 'Realism, Neorealism, and the Study of World Politics.' In Robert O. Keohane. ed., *Neorealism and Its Critics*. New York: Columbia University Press.

———. 1993. 'Institutional Theory and Realist Challenge.' In David A. Baldwin ed., *Neorealism and Neoliberalism: The Contemporary Debate*. New York: Columbia University Press.

———. 1997. 'Problematic Lucidity: Stephen Krasner's State Power and the Structure of International Trade.' *World Politics* 50 (1): 150–70.

Keohane, Robert, and Lisa Martin. 1995. 'The Promise of Institutionalist Theory.' *International Security* 20 (1): 39–51.

Keohane, Robert, and Elinor Ostrom, eds, 1995. *Local Commons and Global Interdependence: Heterogeneity and Cooperation in Two Domains.* Thousand Oaks: Sage.

Keynes, John M. 1920. *The Economic Consequences of the Peace.* New York: Harcourt, Brace, Jovanovich.

Kibaroglu, Aysegül. 2013. 'Transboundary Water Relations in the Euphrates and Tigris Region.' In Aysegül Kibaroglu, Adele J. Kirschner, Sigrid Mehring, Rüdiger Wolfrum, eds, *Water Law and Cooperation in the Euphrates-Tigris Region: A Comparative and Interdisciplinary Approach.* Leiden: Brill.

Kibaroglu, Aysegu, Annika Kramer, and Waltina Scheumann, eds, 2011. *Turkey's Water Policy: National Framework and International Cooperation.* New York: Springer.

Kienle, Eberhard. 1990. *Ba'ath Versus Ba'ath: The Conflict Between Syria and Iraq 1968–1989.* London: I.B.Tauris.

Kindleberger, Charles P. 1973. *The World in Depression, 1929–1939.* Berkeley: University of California Press.

Kirisçi, Kemal. 1997. 'Post Cold War Turkish Security and the Middle East,' paper presented at the *Conference on Israel and Turkey: Current Politics and Foreign Policy,* 14–15 January 1997, Bar-Ilan University, Israel.

Klare, Michael T. 2001. *Resource Wars: The New Landscape of Global Conflict.* New York: Metropolitan.

Kolars, John F. 'Hydro-imperative of Turkey's Search for Energy.' *Journal of Middle Eastern Studies* 40 (1):

Kolars, John F., and William A Mitchell. 1991. *The Euphrates River and Southeast Anatolia Development Project.* Carbondale: Southern Illinois University Press.

Koremenos, Barbara, Charles Lipson, and Duncan Snidal. 2001. 'The Rational Design of International Institutions.' *International Organization* 55 (4): 761–800.

Kramer, Annika and Alina Schellig. 2011. 'Meric River Basin: Transboundary Water Cooperation.' In Aysegul Kibaroglu, Annika Kramer, and Waltina Scheumann, eds, *Turkey's Water Policy: National Framework and International Cooperation.* New York: Springer.

Krasner, Stephen D. 1976. 'State Power and the Structure of International Trade.' *World Politics* 28 (3): 317–47.

———, ed., 1983. *International Regimes.* Ithaca: Cornell University Press.

———. 1983. 'Structural Causes and Regime Consequences: Regimes as Intervening Variables.' In Stephen D. Krasner, ed., *International Regimes.* Ithaca: Cornell University Press.

———. 1985. *Structural Conflict: The Third World against Global Liberalism.* Berkeley: University of California Press.

Krishna, Ray. 1992. 'International Watercourses: World Bank Experience and Policy.' Paper presented at the Conference on Water in the Middle East, 19–20 November 1992, School of Oriental and Asian Studies, London.

Kut, Gün. 1993. 'Burning Waters: the Hydropolitics of the Euphrates Tigris.' *New Perspectives on Turkey* 9 (2): 1–18.

Lake, David. 1992. 'Powerful Pacifists: Democratic States and War.' *American Political Science Review* 86 (1): 24–37.

Lansing, J. Stephen. 1991. *Priests and Programmers: Technologies of Power in the Engineered Landscape of Bali.* Princeton: Princeton University Press.

Layne, Christopher. 1994. 'Kant or Cant: The Myth of the Democratic Peace.' *International Security* 19 (2): 5–49.

Leeds, Brett A., and David Davis. 1997. 'Domestic Political Vulnerability and International Disputes.' *Journal of Conflict Resolution*, 41 (6): 814–34.

———. 1999. 'Beneath the Surface: Regime Type and International Interactions 1953–1978.' *Journal of Peace Research* 36: 5–21.
Legro, Jeffrey W., and Andrew Moravcsik. 1999. 'Is Anybody Still a Realist?' *International Security* 24 (2): 5–55.
Levy, Jack. 1989. 'Domestic Politics and War.' In Robert Rotberg and Theodore Rabb, eds, *The Origin and Prevention of Major Wars*. New York: Cambridge University Press.
Levy, Mark A. 1995. 'Is the Environment a National Security Issue?' *International Security* 20: 35–62.
Lowi, Miriam. 1993. *Water and Power: The Politics of Scarce Resource in the Jordan River Basin.* New York: Cambridge University Press.
———. 1995. 'Rivers of Conflict, Rivers of Peace.' *Journal of International Affairs* 49: 123–44.
Lynn-Jones, Sean M., and Steven E. Miller. 1995. 'Preface.' In Michael E. Brown, Sean M. Lynn-Jones, and Steven E. Miller, eds, *The Perils of Anarchy: Neorealism and International Security*. Cambridge: MIT Press.
Mack, Andrew, ed., 2005. *Human Security Report*. New York: Oxford University Press.
Mansfield, Edward D. 1994. *Power, Trade, and War.* Princeton: Princeton University Press.
Mansfield, Edward D., and Jack Snyder. 1995. 'Democratization and the Danger of War.' *International Security* 20 (1): 5–38.
———. 2002. 'Democratic Transitions, Institutional Strength, and War.' *International Organization* 56 (2): 297–337.
Maoz, Zeev, and Nasrin Abdolali. 1989. 'Polity Types and International Conflict.' *Journal of Conflict Resolution* 33 (1): 3–35.
Maoz, Zeev, and Bruce M. Russett. 1993. 'Normative and Structural Causes of Democratic Peace.' *American Political Science Review* 87 (3): 624–38.
MacFarquhar, Neil, and Nada Bakr, 'Isolating Syria, Arab League Imposes Broad Sanctions,' *New York Times*, 27 November 2011. Available at http://www.nytimes.com/2011/11/28/world/middleeast/arab-league-prepares-to-vote-on-syrian-sanctions.html (accessed on 16 May 2015).
Martin, Lisa. 1992. *Coercive Cooperation: Explaining Multilateral Economic Sanctions*. Princeton: Princeton University Press.
Mathews, R.C.O. 1986. 'The Economics of Institutions and the Sources of Growth.' *The Economic Journal* 96 (384): 903–10.
Mayer, Frederick W. 1992. 'Managing Domestic Differences in International Negotiations: The Strategic Use of Internal Side Payments.' *International Organization* 46 (4): 793–818.
McCaffrey, Stephen C., and Mpazi Sinjela. 1998. 'The 1997 United Nations Convention on International Watercourses.' *American Journal of International Law* 92 (1): 97–107.
McKeown, Timothy J. 1983. 'Hegemonic Stability Theory and 19th Century Tariff Levels in Europe.' *International Organization* 37 (1): 73–91.
Mearsheimer, John J. 1990. 'Back to the Future: Instability in Europe after the Cold War.' *International Security* 15 (1): 5–56.
———. 1994/95. 'The False Premise of International Institutions.' *International Security* 19 (3): 5–49.
———. 1995. 'A Realist Reply.' *International Security* 20 (1): 82–93.
Midlarsky, Manus I. 1995. 'Environmental Influences on Democracy: Aridity, Warfare, and a Reversal of the Causal Arrow.' *Journal of Conflict Resolution* 39 (2): 224–62.
*The Middle East.* 1993. Dam It. It's Our Water, December 1993, pp. 32–3.
*The Middle East.* June 1996.
*The Middle East.* July–August 1996.
*Middle East Economic Digest.* 28 July 1972.
*Middle East Economic Digest.* 30 May 1975.
Milliken, Jenifer, ed., 2003. *State Failure, Collapse, and Reconstruction.* Malden: Blackwell.
*Milliyet.* 6 June 1986.
———. 12 October 2012.

Ministry of Foreign Affairs. 1996. *Water Issues between Turkey, Syria, and Iraq*. Ankara: Foreign Ministry of Turkey.

———. Water Issues. Available at http://www.mfa.gov.tr/sub.en.mfa?7148b38a-0862-4a27-a006-2ca989a22629 (accessed 2 May 2015).

Montesquieu, Charles de. [1748] 1989. [Ann M. Kohler, Basia C. Miller, and Harold S. Stone, eds, *The Spirit of Laws*. New York: Cambridge University Press.

Morgenthau, Hans J. 1973. *Politics among Nations: The Struggle for Power and Peace*. New York: Alfred A. Knopf.

Naff, Thomas, and R. C. Matson. 1984. *Water in the Middle East: Conflict or Cooperation*. Boulder: Westview Press.

Nasrallah, Fida. 1990. 'Middle Eastern Waters: The Hydraulic Imperative.' *Middle East International*, 27 April 1990.

*The New Anatolian*. 13 May 2006.

Niou, Emerson M. S., Peter C. Ordeshook, and Gregory F. Rose. 1989. *The Balance of Power Stability in International Systems*. Cambridge: Cambridge University Press.

North, Douglass C. 1981. *The Structure and Change in Economic History*. New York: Norton.

North, Douglass C., John J. Wallis, and Steven B. Webb, eds, 2013. *In the Shadow of Violence: The Problem of Development for Limited Access Order Societies*. Cambridge: Cambridge University Press.

North, Douglass C., John J. Wallis, and Barry Weingast. 2009. *Violence and Social Order: A Conceptual Framework for Interpreting Recorded Human History*. Cambridge: Cambridge University Press.

Nozick, Robert. 1974. *Anarchy, State and Utopia*. New York: Basic Books.

Olson, Mancur. 1965. *The Logic of Collective Action: Public Goods and Theory of Groups*. Cambridge: Harvard University Press.

———. 1993. 'Dictatorship, Democracy, and Development.' *American Political Science Review* 87 (3): 569–76.

Olson, Robert. 1997. 'Turkey-Syria Relations since the Gulf War: Kurds and Water.' *Middle East Policy* 5 (2): 168–93.

Oneal, John R., and Bruce M. Russett. 1997. 'The Classical Liberals were Right: Democracy, Interdependence, and Conflict, 1950–1985.' *International Studies Quarterly* 41 (2): 267–94.

Ordeshook, Peter C. 1986. *Game Theory and Political Theory*. Cambridge: Cambridge University Press.

Ostrom, Elinor. 1990. *Governing the Commons: The Evolution of Institutions for Collective Action*. Cambridge: Cambridge University Press.

Ostrom, Elinor, Roy Gardner, and James Walker. 1992. 'Covenants with and without a Sword: Self-Governance is Possible.' *American Political Science Review* 86 (2): 404–17.

———. 1994. *Rules, Games, Common Pool Resources*. Ann Arbor: University of Michigan Press.

Ostrom, Elinor, Joanna Burger, Christopher B. Field, Richard B. Norgaard, and David Policansky. 1999. 'Revisiting the Commons: Local Lessons, Global Challenges.' *Science* 284 (5412): 278–89.

Owen, John M. 1992. 'How Liberalism Produces Democratic Peace.' *International Security* 19 (2): 87–125.

Oye, Kenneth. N., ed., 1986. *Cooperation under Anarchy*. Princeton: Princeton University Press.

Özis, Ziya. 1993. 'South East Anatolia Project in Turkey.' Paper presented at *The Internatinol Symposium on Water Resources in the Middle East: Policy and Institutional Aspects*, 24–27 October 1993, University of Illinois at Urbana-Champaign, Urbana-Illinois, USA.

Özdogan, Mutlu, Curtis E. Woodcock, Guido D. Salvucci, and Huseyin Demir. 2006. 'Changes in Summer Irrigated Crop Area and Water Use in Southeastern Turkey: Implications for Current and Future Water Resources.' *Water Resources Management* 20: 467–88.

Pearce, Fred., 2014. 'Mideast Water Wars: In Iraq, a Battle for Control of Water,' *Yale Environment 360*, 25 August 2014. Available at http://e360.yale.edu/feature/mideast_water_wars_in_iraq_a_battle_for_control_of_water/2796/ (accessed on 16 May 2015).

Perthes, Volker. 1995. *The Political Economy of Syria under Asad.* London: I.B.Tauris.
Posen, Barry R. 1984. *The Sources of Military Doctrine: France, Britain, and Germany between the World Wars*. Ithaca: Cornell University Press.
Powell, Robert. 1999. *In the Shadow of Power: States and Strategies in International Politics*. Princeton: Princeton University Press.
Przeworski, A. and F. Limongi. 1993. 'Political Regimes and Economic Growth.' *Journal of Economic Perspectives* 7 (3): 51–69
Putnam, Robert D. 1988. 'Diplomacy and Domestic Politics: The Logic of Two-Level Games.' *International Organization* 42 (3): 448–50.
———, ed., 1993. *Double-Edged Diplomacy: International Bargaining and Domestic Politics*. Berkeley: University of California Press.
Rabie, H. 1981. 'Some Technical Aspect of Egyptian Agriculture in Medieval Egypt.' In A. L. Udovitch, ed., *The Islamic Middle East, 700–1900: Studies in Economic and Social History.* Princeton: Princeton University Press.
Rabo, Annika. 1986. *Change on the Euphrates: Villagers, Townsman, and Employees in Northeast Syria.* Stockholm: University of Stockholm.
Raleigh, Clionadh, and Henrik Urdal. 2007. 'Climate Change, Environmental Degradation, and Armed Conflict.' *Political Geography* 26 (6): 674–94.
Rapoport, Anatol. 1964. *Strategy and Conscience.* New York: Schocken Books.
———. 1974. 'Prisoner's Dilemma: Recollections and Observations.' In Anatol Rapoport, ed., *Game Theory as a Theory of Conflict Resolution.* Dordrecht: Reidel.
Ray, James L. 1995. *Democracy and International Conflict: An Evolution of the Democratic Peace Proposition*. Columbia: University of South Caroline Press.
Reiss Hans, ed., 1991. *Kant: Political Writings*. New York: Cambridge University Press.
Reiter, Dan, and Allan C. Stam. 1992. 'Democracy, War Initiation, and Victory.' *American Political Science Review* 92 (2): 377–90.
———. 2002. *Democracies at War.* Princeton: Princeton University Press.
*Reuters.* 8 March 2015. 'EU Accuses Syrian Man of Buying IS Oil for Govt.' Available at http://www.reuters.com/article/2015/03/08/us-syria-crisis-eu-idUSKBN0M40EQ20150308 (accessed on 16 May 2015).
Ricardo, David. [1817] 1996. *On the Principles of Political Economy and Taxation*. Amherst: Prometheus Books.
Richards, Alan, and John Waterbury. 1996. *A Politic Economy of the Middle East.* Boulder: Westview Press.
Richardson, J. S. 1983. 'The Tabula Contrebiensis: Roman Law in Spain in the Early First Century BC.' *Journal of Roman Studies* 73: 33–41.
Robins, Philip. 1991. *Turkey and the Middle East.* London: Pinter.
Ross, Michael. 1999. 'The Political Economy of the Curse.' *World Politics* 51 (2): 297– 322.
Rostow, Walt W. 1960. *The Stages of Economic Growth: A Non–Communist Manifesto.* Cambridge: Cambridge University Press.
Rotberg, Robert I. 2002. 'The New Nature of Nation-State Failure.' *The Washington Quarterly* 25 (3): 85–96.
———, ed., 2003. *State Failure and State Weakness in a Time of Terror.* Washington: Brookings Institution Press, 2003.
———. 2004. *The Failure of Nation States: Causes, Consequences, and Reconstruction*. Princeton: Princeton University Press.
Rousseau, David, Christopher Gelpi, Dan Reiter, and Paul Huth. 1996. 'Assessing the Dyadic Nature of the Democratic Peace.' *American Political Science Review* 90 (3): 512–44.
Rousseau, J. J. 1984. *Discourse on Inequality.* New York: Penguin Books.
Rouyer, Alwyn R. 2000. *Turning Water into Politics: The Water Issue in the Palestinian Israeli Conflict*. London: Macmillan.
Russett, Bruce. 1993. *Grasping the Democratic Peace: Principles for Post–Cold War.* Princeton: Princeton University Press.

Russett, Bruce, and John Oneal. 2001. *Triangulating Peace: Democracy, Interdependence, and International Organizations*. New York: Norton.

*Sabah*, 'Bagdat ve Sam'a Arabulucu Ziyareti,' 1 September 2009. Available at http://www.sabah.com.tr/siyaset/2009/09/01/bagdat_ve_sama_arabulucu_ziyareti (accessed on 16 May 2015)

———, 'Turkiye'nin Suriye'ye Ihracatinda Eski Gunlere Donuldu,' 25 February 2015. Available at http://www.sabah.com.tr/ekonomi/2015/02/25/turkiyenin-suriyeye-ihracatinda-eski-gunlere-donuldu (accessed on 16 May 2015).

Salha, Samir. 1995. *Turkiye, Suriye ve Lübnan Iliskilerinde Asi Nehri Sorunu.* Ankara: Hacettepe Üniversitesi Dis Politika Enstitüsü.

Schelling, Thomas C. 1966. *Arms and Influence.* New Haven: Yale University Press.

Schultz, Kenneth A. 1998. 'Domestic Opposition and Signaling in International Crises.' *American Political Science Review* 92 (4): 829–44.

———. 1999. 'Do Democratic Institutions Constrain or Inform? Contrasting Two Institutional Perspectives on Democracy and War.' *International Organization* 53 (2): 233–66.

———. 2001. 'Democracy and Coercive Diplomacy.' London: Cambridge University Press.

Schweller, Randall L. 1994. 'Bandwagoning for Profit: Bringing the Revisionist State Back In.' *International Security* 19 (1): 72–107.

———. 1996. 'Neorealism's Status quo Bias: What Security Dilemma?' *Security Studies* 5 (3): 90–121.

———. 1997. 'New Realist Research on Alliances: Refining and Not Refuting, Waltz's Balancing Proposition.' *The American Political Science Review* 91 (4): 927–30.

———. 1998. *Deadly Imbalances: Tripolarity and Hitler's Strategy of World Conquest.* New York: Columbia University Press.

Seale, Patrick. 1988. *Asad of Syria: The Struggle for the Middle East.* Berkeley: University of California Press.

Sen, Amartya. 1999. *Democracy as Freedom.* New York: Anchor.

Shiva, Vandana. 2002. *Water Wars: Privatization, Pollution, and Profit.* Cambridge: South End Press.

Smith, Adam. 1761. *The Theory of Moral Sentiments.* London: A. Miller.

———. [1776] 1976. *An Inquiry into the Nature and Cause of the Wealth of Nations.* Oxford: Oxford University Press.

Snidal, Duncan. 1985. 'Limits of Hegemonic Stability Theory.' *International Organization* 39 (4): 579–614.

———. 1986. 'The Game Theory of International Politics.' In Kenneth N. Oye, ed., *Cooperation under Anarchy.* Princeton: Princeton University Press.

Snyder, Jack. 1991. *Myths of Empire: Domestic Politics and International Ambition.* Ithaca: Cornell University Press.

Spiro, David. 1994. 'The Insignificance of Liberal Peace.' *International Security* 19 (2): 56–86.

Stam, Alan C. 1996. *Win, Lose, or Draw: Domestic Politics and the Crucible of War.* Ann Arbor: University of Michigan Press.

Soysal, Ismail. 1991. 'Seventy Years of Turkish-Arab Relations and an Analysis of Turkish-Iraqi Relations (1920–1990),' *Studies on Turkish-Arab Relations,Special Issue on Turkey and the Gulf Crisis, Annual* 6. Istanbul: Foundation for the Study of Turkish-Arab Relations [TAIV].

Starr, Joyce R. 1991. 'Water Wars.' *Foreign Policy* 82: 17–36.

Strassler, Robert B., ed., 1996. *The Landmark of Thucydides: A Comprehensive Guide to the Peloponnesian War.* New York: Free Press.

T.C. GAP Regional Development Administration. *The Brief History of GAP.* Available at http://www.gap.gov.tr/site-icerik/gap_in_tarihcesi.aspx (accessed on 2 May 2015).

———. *GAP Action Plan.* Available at http://www.gap.gov.tr/dosya_ekleri/pdf/GAP_EYLEM_PLANI.pdf (accessed on 2 May 2015).

*T.C. Resmi Gazete.* 10 December 1987, no: 19660.

T.C. State Planning Organization. 1989. *GAP Master Plan Final Report*. Volume 4. Ankara.

T.C. Turkish Statistical Institute (TURKSTAT) Energy Statistics. Available at http://www.tuik.gov.tr (accessed on 2 May 2015).

Taliaferro, Jeffrey W. 2000/2001. 'Security Seeking under Anarchy: Defensive Realism Revisited.' *International Security* 25 (3): 128–61.

Taylor, Andrew. 2013. *State Failure*. New York: Palgrave Macmillan.

Theisen, Ole Magnus. 2008. 'Blood and Soil? Resource Scarcity and Internal Armed Conflict.' *Journal of Peace Research* 5(6), pp. 801–18.

———, Nils Petter Gleditsch, and Halvard Buhaug. 2013. 'Is Climate Change a Driver of Armed Conflict?' *Climatic Change* 117 (3): 613–25.

Themnér, Lotta and Peter Wallensteen. 2014. 'Armed Conflicts 1946–2013.' *Journal of Peace Research* 51 (4): 541–54.

Thompson, William R. 1988. *On Global War: Historical Structural Approaches to World Politics.* Columbia: University of South Caroline Press.

Tilly, Charles. 1975. 'Reflections on the History of European State-Making.' In Charles Tilly, ed., *The Formation of National States in Western Europe*. Princeton: Princeton University Press.

———. 1990. *Coercion, Capital, and European States, AD 990–1992*. Oxford: Blackwell.

Tir, Jaroslav, and Paul F. Diehl. 1998. Demographic Pressure and Interstate Conflict: Linking Population Growth and Density to Militarized Disputes and Wars. *Journal of Peace Research* 35 (3): 319–39.

Tir, Jaroslav, and Douglas Stinnett. 2012. 'Weathering Climate Change: Can Institutions Mitigate International Water Conflict?' *Journal of Peace Research* 49 (1): 211–25.

Tsipris, J. and M. Meron. 1998. 'Climatic and Hydrological Aspects of the Hula Restoration.' *Wetlands Ecology and Management* 6: 91–101

Turan, Ilter, and Gün Kut. 1997. 'Political and Ideological Constraints on Intra-basin Cooperation on Transboundary Waters.' *Natural Resource Forum* 3: 139–45.

*Turkish Daily News*. 6 May 1996.

*Turkish Probe*. 26 January 1993.

The UCDP/Prio Conflict Data. Available at http://www.pcr.uu.se/research/ucdp/datasets/ucdp_prio_armed_conflict_dataset/ (accessed on 20 March 2015).

Umbeck, John R. 1981. *A Theory of Property Rights*. Ames: Iowa State University Press.

United Nations Conference on Trade and Development (UNCTAD). 2004. *The Agreement on Reciprocal Promotion and Protection of Investment*. Available at http://investmentpolicyhub.unctad.org/Download/TreatyFile/2335 (accessed on 2 May 2015).

———. 2004. *The Agreement on Reciprocal Promotion and Protection of Investment*. Available at http://investmentpolicyhub.unctad.org/Download/TreatyFile/2702 (accessed on 2 May 2015).

United Nations Development Programme. 1994. *Human Development Report 1994*. New York: Oxford University Press.

United Nations Environment Programme. 2000. *Global Environmental Outlook 2000*. Available at http://www.unep.org/Geo2000 (accessed on 16 May 2015).

———. 2001. *The Dams and Development Project*. Available at http://www.unep.org/dams/About_DDP/ (accessed on 16 May 2015).

———. 2001. *The Mesopotamian Marshlands: Demise of an Ecosystem.* Available at http://www.grid.unep.ch/activities/sustainable/tigris/mesopotamia.pdf (accessed on 16 May 2015).

*UNEP News Release*, 5 August 2002. 'Sustainable Development Security Imperative: Says Top US Government Official.' Available at http://www.un.org/jsummit/html/media_info/pressreleases_factsheets/unep_press_release_508.pdf (accessed on 16 May 2015).

United Nations Economic and Social Commission for Western Asia. 2013. *Inventory of Shared Water Resources in Western Asia*. Available at http://www.escwa.un.org/information/pubaction.asp?PubID51362 (accessed on 16 May 2015).

United Nations Food and Agriculture Organization AQUASTAT. 2008. *Syrian Arab Republic*. Available at http://www.fao.org/nr/water/aquastat/countries_regions/syr/index.stm.

United Nations Food and Agriculture Organization. 2012. *Syrian Arab Republic Joint Rapid Food Security Needs Assessment.* Available at http://www.fao.org/giews/english/otherpub/JRFSNA_Syrian2012.pdf (accessed on 16 May 2015).

*UN-Inter Agency Information and Analysis Unit*, June 2012. 'Climate Change in Iraq.' Available at http://iq.one.un.org/documents/468/Climate%20change%20In%20Iraq%20Fact%20sheet%20-%20English.pdf (accessed on 16 May 2015).

United Nations Refuge Agency. *Stories from Syrian Refugees. Discovering the Human Faces of a Tragedy.* Available at http://data.unhcr.org/syrianrefugees/syria.php (accessed on 16 May 2015).

United Nations World Health Organization. 2000. 'Global Water Supply and Sanitation Assessment 2000 Report.' Available at http://www.who.int/water_sanitation_health/Globassessment/GlobalTOC.htm (accessed on 16 May 2015).

US Government. 1994. *Comprehensive Report of the Special Advisor to Director of Central Intelligence on Iraq's Weapons of Mass Destruction.* Available at https://www.cia.gov/cia/reports/iraq_wmd_2004/ (accessed on 16 May 2015).

———. 1996. *A National Security Strategy of Engagement and Enlargement.* Washington: The White House.

———. 2006. *The National Security Strategy of the United States of America.* Washington: The White House.

Van Evera, Stephen. 1984. 'The Cult of the Offensive and the Origins of the First World War.' *International Security* 9 (1): 58–108.

———. 1998. 'Offense, Defense, and the Causes of War.' *International Security* 22 (4): 5–43.

———. 1999. *Causes of War: Power and the Roots of Conflict.* Ithaca: Cornell University Press.

Varisco, Daniel Martin. 1991. *Medieval Agriculture and Islamic Science: The Almanac of a Yemeni Sultan.* Seattle: University of Washington Press.

Vasquez, John A. 1997. 'The Realist Paradigm and Degenerative versus Progressive Research Programs: An Appraisal of Neotraditional Research on Waltz's Balancing Proposition.' *The American Political Science Review* 91 (4): 899–912.

Villiers, Marc de. 1999. *Water Wars: Is the World's Water Running Out?* London: Weidenfeld & Nicolson.

Viries, Michiel S. de. 1990. 'Interdependence, Cooperation, and Conflict: An Empirical Analysis.' *Journal of Peace Research* 27 (4): 429–44.

Wagner, R. Harrison. 2000. 'Bargaining and War.' *American Journal of Political Science* 44 (3): 469–84.

Walt, Stephen M. 1987. *The Origin of Alliances.* Ithaca: Cornell University Press.

Waltz, Kenneth N. 1954. *Man, the State, and War: A Theoretical Analysis.* New York: Columbia University Press.

———. 1979. *Theory of International Politics.* New York: Random House.

———. 1989. 'The Origins of War in Neorealist Theory.' In Robert I. Rotberg and Theodore K. Rabb, eds, *The Origin and Prevention of Major Wars.* Cambridge: Cambridge University Press.

*Washington Post*, 4 April 2015. 'The Hidden Hand behind the Islamic State Militants? Saddam Hussein's'.

*Al-Watan al-Arabi.* May 1996.

Waterbury, John. 1979. *Hyrdopolitics of the Nile Valley.* New York: Syracuse University Press.

———. 2002. *The Nile Basin: National Determinants of Collective Action.* New Haven: Yale University Press.

Weber, Katja. 2000. *Hierarchy amidst Anarchy: Transaction Costs and Institutional Choice.* Albany: State University of New York.

Weingast, B. and J.W. Marshall.1988. 'The Industrial Organization of Congress; or, Why Legislatures, Like Firms, Are Not Organized as Markets.' *Journal of Political Economy* 96 (1): 132–63

Weiss, Edith B., and Harold K. Jacobsen. 1999. 'Getting Countries to Comply with International Agreements.' *Environment* 41: 16–23.

White, Jeffrey. 'Syrian Regime Military Operations Against ISIS,' 13 March 2013. *The Washington Institute for Near East Policy*. Available at http://www.washingtoninstitute.org/policy-analysis/view/syrian-regime-military-operations-against-isis (accessed on 16 May 2015).

Williamson, Oliver E. 1985. *The Economic Institutions of Capitalism: Firms, Markets, and Relational Contracting*. New York: Free Press.

———. 1986. *Economic Organization: Firms, Markets and Policy Control*. Brighton: Wheatsheaf.

Wittfogel, Karl. 1956. *Oriental Despotism: A Comparative Study of Total Power*. New Haven: Yale University Press.

Wolf, Aaron T. 1995. *Hydropolitics Along the Jordan River: Scarce Water and its Impact on the Arab Israeli Conflict*. Tokyo: United Nations University Press.

———. 1999. 'The Transboundary Freshwater Dispute Database Project.' *Water International* 24: 160–63.

World Commission on Dams. 2000. *Dams and Development: A Framework for Decision-Making*. Available at http://www.unep.org/dams/WCD/report/WCD_DAMS%20report.pdf (accessed on 16 May 2015).

World Health Organization. 2000. *Global Water Supply and Sanitation Assessment 2000 Report*. Available at http://www.who.int/water_sanitation_health/Globassessment/GlobalTOC.htm (accessed on 16 May 2015).

World Resources Institute. 2000. *Pilot Analysis of Global Ecosystems (PAGE): Freshwater Systems 2000*. Available at http://www.wri.org/wr2000/freshwater_page.html (accessed on 16 May 2015).

World Water Organization. http://worldwater.org/water-data/ (accessed on 16 May 2015).

Yesilnacar, M. Irfan, and Sinan Uyanik. 2005. 'Investigation of Water Quality of the World's Largest Irrigation Tunnel System: The Sanliurfa Tunnels in Turkey.' *Fresenius Environmental Bulletin* 14 (4): 300–06.

Yetim, Müşerref. 2006. 'A Bargaining Framework for Explaining International Water Rights Conflicts: The Case of the Euphrates and Tigris.' PhD. Thesis, University of Texas at Austin.

Young, Oran R. 1975. 'Strategic Interaction and Bargaining.' In Oran R. Young, ed., *Bargaining: Formal Theories of Negotiation.* Urbana: University of Illinois Press.

———. 1989. *International Cooperation: Building Regimes for Natural Resources and the Environment.* Ithaca: Cornell University Press.

Young, Oran R., George J. Demko, and Kilaoarti Ramakrishna, eds, 1996. *Global Environmental Change and International Governance.* Hanover: University Press of New England.

Zakaria, Fareed., 1998. *From Wealth to Power: The Unusual Origins of America's World Role.* Princeton: Princeton University Press.

Zartman, I. William. 1995. 'Introduction: Posing the Problem of State Collapse.' In I. William Zartman, ed., *Collapsed States: The Disintegration and Restoration of Legitimate Authority.* Boulder: Lynne Rienner.

# INDEX

Note: *n* attached to a page number denotes an endnote, with appropriate number; page numbers in **bold** refer to tables and in *italic* to figures.

www.ingramcontent.com/pod-product-compliance
Ingram Content Group UK Ltd.
Pitfield, Milton Keynes, MK11 3LW, UK
UKHW021908150926
475560UK00003B/250

9 781784 535520